The Essential Dear Dara

THE ESSENTIAL DEAR DARA

Writings on Local Characters and Memorable Places

DARA MOSKOWITZ GRUMDAHL

MINNESOTA
HISTORICAL
SOCIETY PRESS

mnhspress.org

The Minnesota Historical Society Press is a member of the Association of University Presses.

Manufactured in Canada.

10 9 8 7 6 5 4 3 2 1

∞ The paper used in this publication meets the minimum requirements of the American National Standard for Information Sciences—Permanence for Printed Library Materials, ANSI Z39.48–1984.

International Standard Book Number

ISBN: 978-1-68134-275-7 (paper)

ISBN: 978-1-68134-276-4 (e-book)

Library of Congress Control Number: 2023936006

Contents

· · · · · · · · · · · ·

Introduction

. . . .

Bleary with exhaustion, I will sometimes end one of my three- or four-hour mega-interviews by telling the person on the other end of the line: "Congratulations, you've had the full Dara experience. It's exhausting. It's unique! You'll never forget it. Hopefully no one else will either." They laugh. Usually.

Of course I don't always get hours for an interview, but for a longer article, I try. People usually have only half a dozen things they want to say. If I keep at them after they've shot their shot, circling back and circling back, I'll get past everything they usually say and find: a story.

Story. This little word drives me nuts. On the one hand, it's all I do, all I care about, what I've built my life around, and I truly believe it's what distinguishes humankind from all the other stardust. We are the commenters upon, critics or appreciators of, and storytellers of the universe. We say: "Hallelujah!" We say: "Never again!" We say everything there is to be said, and we're the only ones who do. On the other hand, not a few snake oil salespeople make such a smarmy fuss about the holy sanctity of "story." I play a game, popular among certain gimlet-eyed writers, of hunting out book-jacket blurbs that proclaim someone a "master storyteller" and then snickering. On the third and final hand, a mutant growing unnaturally from my torso and sprouted specifically for this metaphor, the word *story* sounds so very insignificant in common parlance that people blow past it. *What's the story here? Oh, if I buy two cans of paint I get a third free? Got it . . .*

I suspect everyone shares my vexed under- and overestimation of the concept of "story." The first thing I say to any potential source or subject is: "I'd like to talk to you for a story." I say what I say, but they hear what they hear. Usually, they hear something like: *I'd like to say nice things about you and so provide to you money or status or both.* But that's not what I mean.

What I mean is: I am going to do some combination of three things: I am going to make my readers laugh, cry, or think. This is my personal vaudeville creed and how I have kept a roof over my head since 1995. *Make 'em laugh, make 'em cry, make 'em think!* Most times I can pull off two of the three at the same time in one story; occasionally all three.

When I tell a source or a subject, "I'd like to talk to you for a story," what I really mean is: I'd like to build a piece of emotion-capturing nonfiction on the scaffolding of the true facts you're going to tell me.

I started writing in and about Minneapolis and St. Paul in the summer of 1992, weeks after I graduated from Carleton College. My launch pad was a $425-a-month apartment beside the exhaust pipe of Rudolph's Bar-B-Que (now long gone) at Franklin and Lyndale. My boyfriend and I toured the apartment in the pre-barbecue morning, and we were enchanted by the bright emerald climbing vines scampering over the windows, sunbeams sparkling through the rustling green. When we hauled in our concrete-block-and-board bookcases on moving day, we were instantly perplexed: Why is the air thick with a smog of pork?

I had a fifteen-dollar thrift shop bike and four jobs—two for money, one for free, one for almost-free. One money job was working at a phone bank for Bill Clinton, where I'd call people in the 218 area code of northern Minnesota and chat with them in their cow barns. Money job two? Waitressing and cocktailing at the dismal corporate Mexican behemoth Chi-Chi's in downtown Minneapolis, where I wore a purple polyester shirt printed with toucans.

My nonpaying jobs were what mattered to me. They were where I worked my big plans—to be the next Dorothy Parker, or Joseph Mitchell, or pick your pre–Vietnam War *New Yorker* modernist: maybe J. D. Salinger, if I could pull it off. These jobs included reading manuscripts for Graywolf, the publisher, and a grab bag of freelance journalism projects, including sending envelopes of news, 'zines, and ephemera to *Harper's* for their "notes" section and, most importantly, writing.

Shortly after settling in to my barbecue-scented apartment, I started writing for the alt-weekly *City Pages*. I wrote inch-long book reviews, each of which took me the better part of a day at first, and for which I got paid by getting to keep the books I was reviewing. Everyone liked my work so much that I was promoted to writing little essays quilted together from material I gathered on the spot at some event or scene. I'd write them on the eighty-dollar spindle-leg folding table I bought in college and which is currently in my dining room. This table is beneath my elbows as I type these lines today; there's a little hole in it from the time an apple resting on the table held a worm, which started chewing its way toward freedom. My own freedom came tiny story by tiny story, written on my little Mac Classic II with the paperback novel–sized screen. I'd save each story to a little hard disk, put the disk in a backpack, and bump along on a trail beside the train tracks in the trench through downtown to the *City Pages* office. There I'd hand over the disk, then wait to see if my editor could actually pull the story off the disk. (It was a creaky time for data.) I typically got paid ten or fifteen dollars per story; in a great while, thirty-five.

If I have one piece of advice for aspiring writers, it's this: Keep your expenses low. Super low. I will never forget bicycling with my first published piece, the entire unimaginably important inch of it, to the Uptown Kinko's, where I paid ten dollars for copies so I could pitch other publications and maybe get ten dollars in return.

This life of ten-dollar assignments was how I learned to write. I would send in stories to *City Pages* editor Monika Bauerlein, a true genius who is now CEO of *Mother Jones*. She would return them with notes like, *You don't have a transition here; you don't have a transition there*. I spent about two years bumping my head against transitions. I now believe I can run a graceful (enough) transition between Mother Teresa in paragraph one and dodo birds in paragraph two.

Speaking of dodo birds and other wonderful things that are no longer with us, *City Pages* seemed like the coolest place on earth in the mid-1990s. Writers I admired were lurking around being surly and insightful (Britt Robson), or bright as a spring wind (Josie Rawson), or tenacious and morally admirable (Beth Hawkins), or tapped into the wisdom of the universe (Bauerlein), or culture-wise and all-around brilliant (Terri Sutton). It was my own version of the Paris salons I'd read about. Everyone was such a good writer, and there we all were, writing.

City Pages had a problem, though. They had a lot of restaurant advertisers, and no one there wanted to do restaurant reviewing and food news. The big writers found it beneath them; they wanted to do "real news." They used to pass around a pseudonym, Sybil French, for whomever got the scut work of writing the food column of the week. I believed there was something about it being feminine-coded that made people want to avoid food writing, but that didn't bother me. I thought I could do what I had been doing—writing about people and culture—but simply around the topic of food, and they'd give me pages and pages to play with. So that's what I did.

My first restaurant review wasn't really a review and was hardly about a restaurant. It was published April 2, 1997, on a somehow surviving elderly ladies' lunch counter called Lucille's Kitchen, opened in 1929. "I'm someone who likes the emotional and social paradox and resonance of food," I wrote, before going on about what mayonnaise and Jell-O meant in 1929, and how they showed up at Lucille's in 1997.

Unfortunately, it turned out I was entering alternative journalism at its end. I became the last alt-weekly restaurant critic standing when the Twin Cities Reader was bought and folded into City Pages later in 1997. True story: A City Pages editor offered me the staff position of restaurant critic for the newer, bigger, double paper one morning in a flurry of money and locking things down for the new owner, then rescinded the offer in the afternoon when they gave it to the Reader's critic, Rick Nelson, instead. I was so distraught I didn't know what to do except take a nap. I woke up to an answering machine message offering me the job again. I called back, having practiced my speech that I'd take the job but I had one demand: a company credit card, so I wouldn't be floating company expenses all the time. I got my answer right away: no chance. In a negotiation strategy that will not be taught in business schools, I took the job anyway.

I couldn't tell you how many times the paper was bought and sold between 1997 and the day I left—I'd guess at least six times. I recall a pet-food mogul buying us as a fun project for his twenty-something kids, and the time Monika peered at her computer and said, "We're owned by a Dutch venture capital firm now!" New Times, a Phoenix-based group of libertarians, were the last and ab-solute worst. They installed machismo-drenched pretenders and removed both maternity leave and the opportunity to use vacation time for maternity leave. I was five months pregnant. "What do you expect me to do?" I asked a jerk in Phoenix. "If we do this for you," he explained, "we have to do it for everyone." So in the last days of 2007 I quit *City Pages* after fifteen years of writing for the alt-weekly—first as a freelancer (1992–97), then as a staff writer (1997–2007). I accepted a job offer from *Minnesota Monthly*.

While at *MnMo*, I also was editor in chief of and wrote for a magazine called *Real Food*. I left there in 2012 for a joint job be-tween *Delta Sky Magazine* (2012–20) and *Mpls.St.Paul Magazine*, which were published by the same company under one roof. I've also been contributing to *Experience Life* magazine since 2002 or so.

Throughout these twenty-five years, I've contributed to doz-ens of other outlets too, publishing some 250,000 words a year at times, particularly in the 1990s. I interviewed Bake-Off winners of yore and wrote a Pillsbury Bake-Off cookbook. I wrote for *Saveur*, *Bon Appétit*, *USA Today*, *Midwest Living*, *Wine & Spirits*, Microsoft Sidewalk, numerous bridal magazines, *Cooking Light*, and vari-ous publications throughout the Condé Nast empire, where I was part of the writing team at a start-up set of "digital magazines" with names like Epicurious, Phys, and Swoon. This Condé Nast part of my life led to years as a contributor at *Gourmet*, especially from 2001, when I won my first James Beard Award for my *City Pages* restaurant reviews, through 2009, when *Gourmet* was cruelly shuttered.

· · · · · · ·

Here's a secret for you: The reason I became a food writer at all was because very early in my professional, if low-paying, writing career, I had one of those life turning points. It was just before Christmas 1994, and my college sweetheart and I went grocery shopping in the old Rainbow Foods in Uptown. We were so broke. Our grocery budget was forty dollars. We filled the cart with commodities from the lowest shelf: rice, beans, and lentils. We reached the cheese case. *No way, no chance.* I remember staring into the open refrigerator case of bright orange blocks and marbled triangles and thinking: *I could shoplift cheese.* Also: *I could get arrested for shoplifting cheese.* And the necessary corollary: *What the blank am I doing with my life?* We left without cheese.

This whole can't-have-cheese-without-crime situation made my skin crawl; it made me nauseous; it put me on full fight-or-flight alert. This was the past I was trying to escape from. This was me, as a 'tween, standing at the end of the aisle at Grand Union supermarket while my mom stuffed food up her shirt. This was me as a young teenager stealing from Macy's Herald Square for a fence who paid crisp twenties for garbage bags of stolen clothes.

Shortly after my pivotal moment of not stealing cheese, I got a call. There was a new thing coming to town, Microsoft Sidewalk. The world's largest software company had an idea: replace the Yellow Pages with a parallel service, but on the internet. All the restaurants would have trusted thumbnail reviews from an editorial team. The offer: For each one we'll pay you fifty dollars and reimburse you for your meal. *Me, the girl who can't afford cheese but who is also living in a cloud of baby back ribs?* Count me in.

Years later the champagne brand Dom Pérignon would fly me first-class to Barcelona to spend thirty-six hours drinking bubbly with super-chef Ferran Adrià. Years later I'd be flown to Tuscany, Napa Valley, Mexico City. Years later I'd be chatting on the phone with Idris Elba, Julia Louis-Dreyfus, and Jennifer Hudson. Years later Netflix would pay for a makeup artist for my appearance on *Chef's Table.* Years later I'd have so much food that my cat would sit on the floor, indifferent, amid ten bakery boxes of croissants. Years later I'd be onstage with Andrew Zimmern and Anthony Bourdain, some species of food royalty with my six James Beard

Awards, my fifteen James Beard nominations, my bizarre status as a judge on various international judgy panels I'm not allowed to name. But maybe it all started at the Rainbow Foods open-top cheese refrigerator, communing with the fluorescent lights above and all my greatest fears.

Anthony Bourdain—my friend and ever-aching hole in my heart—famously said that restaurants are pirate ships, home to lawless swashbucklers. I'd add that they're also a magnet to the food insecure. I have talked to many people in food who started work as a twelve-year-old fruit picker, a fourteen-year-old burger flipper. This is always viewed as: *Wow, look at all that gumption, pulling themselves up by their bootstraps!* No. If you take away one thing from this book, let it be this: If a twelve-year-old has a real and dirty job, it is because that twelve-year-old needs money. Full stop.

After years of threats, the first time my dad actually kicked me out of the house I was thirteen. He drove me into the town center of Wellfleet, Massachusetts, and said, "Get out of the car. You're on your own." I ducked into the kitchen of the nearest restaurant and asked if they were hiring. The chef looked at me, told someone to show me how the dish pit worked, and six hours later made me a plate of chicken, which I ate on a tree stump near the kitchen back door. One of the greatest meals of my life, despite the fact that I was soaking wet.

People always ask me why I, a fourth-generation child of New York City, razzle-dazzle glamorous New York City, would move to Minnesota. I have never given the real answer, for a lot of reasons. Mainly, I have never given the real answer because I thought no one would believe me, for I spent a good chunk of my early childhood telling people things that no one believed. Because I figured my role in this community was as Champagne Barbie, bringing the fun and the wit, creating the illusion of a perfect life in my wine-and-cheese Barbie dream house, a living mascot for the good life. *People need dreams!* I told myself.

The real story? It took me decades to understand that I hid my real self and my real story for the most tawdry and obvious reasons: because I was ashamed of everything behind the pivot of the day I got that dishwashing job. You can't talk about that which you hide from yourself. How can the story hunter hide her own story from herself? It's easy; people do it every day. But because you are reading this book, you will get the real, secret-until-now story. (Also, you get the story because I've been in therapy with one Minnesota therapist or another since the late 1990s. Shout-out to Cindy, Richard, Charme, Nancy—we did it!)

The real story goes like this: I didn't grow up in the New York City you see on TV where everything is red carpets and limousines. The New York City I grew up in was florid domestic violence, where you shriek into the phone at 911 because your dad is kicking your mom as she's curled up on the floor and your brother is beside you screaming too. The New York City I grew up in is the one where, when the cops arrive, they ask you, the oldest child, what you want to do, because Mom's smoking in the kitchen disassociated and Dad's telling the cops Mom's insane, and you kind of agree, so you cling to your father's leg and beg the cops: "Don't take Daddy away. He's right; she's crazy." So when Dad, controller of money, leaves town, Mom spends her time trying to convince you that it's you who are crazy. "Why are you on the side of a man who keeps condoms for his whores?" she asks bitterly. "Why are you on the side of a man who forced me to have an abortion, then ran off with his secretary and left us to starve?"

Even as I type this in my current secure life, my heart is racing. But that's how a 1970s childhood could pass. One time my dad had the power to our house in Queens shut off and left the country, so we ran an extension cord through the yard from a neighbor's, and my family just lived around the end of that cord. One time my dad was beating my brother, who then climbed out on the snow-covered roof with a forty-foot drop to the street, and my dad locked the window on him, and then pummeled us both when I let my brother back inside. As Maria Bamford once told me, the 1970s were the golden age for hitting children. It's taken me a long time to understand that to my parents—who had their heads put through walls and were regularly whipped—smashing a kid into, but not through, a wall or hitting them as they crouched in a ball or kicking them as they tried to hide in a closet, that was *less* violence, that was *restraint*. I've spent many years thinking about forgiveness, healing, truth, all that good stuff. I think part of why I've been successful in writing is because my wrestling and delving peeks out in the breaks between the words, like light seen through loosely woven fabric held up to the window. What's the difference between humans and all the other stardust? The artifacts of that moral wrestling, among many other things.

My father was a Wall Street star, brilliant, holder of a PhD in economics. If you watched Louis Rukeyser's *Wall Street Week* or read *Barron's* in the 1980s, you'd know him: bearded guy pontificating on markets and interest-rate movements, more right than not. He predicted the 1987 market correction, which made him a lot of friends and a lot of money. He was also physically abused by his own father, the angriest plumber in New York City, a man so explosive he was blackballed by his union, a man who put his children's heads through walls. As they say, hurt people hurt people, and the easiest people to hurt are tiny and live in your house.

So I spent a lot of time as a tiny person hiding in closets and monitoring the household from the stair landing. I learned that if you get hit, don't cry because that will just make them madder. And when you're outside the house, be perfect, be absolutely perfect, be funny and brilliant and get all the gold stars because perfect girls are safe. Or so I thought.

As I tell my own kids, the parent-child relationship is like a seesaw. One day you're born, and the parent has all the power and the kid has none, up in the air on the far side of the seesaw. With each passing day, the balance of power shifts, the seesaw gets more even, until one day the kid gets to eighteen, or often some younger age, and their feet reach the ground and they can walk away from that seesaw. Then the kid has all the power. Because if the kid walks away and never looks back, the parent has failed.

For me, the day my feet unexpectedly touched ground was the day I walked in the back door of that kitchen after my dad kicked me out of the car and told me I was on my own. I met the chef, an old-school lesbian named Ana Annunziata. She stood, just my own tiny height, on calves like veined barbells—fearless, pugnacious, my savior. She happened to have worked previously as a social worker. When my dad tracked me down and came to reclaim me at the end of that day—hoping to have scared me into submission, unaware that I had used the day to find a new place to live with some college kids who worked at the restaurant—Ana stood with him in the dark and empty dining room and barked up at him in a rat-a-tat-tat of orders. I watched, terrified, through the circle windows of the swinging doors; I didn't hear any of it. Years later, my chef filled me in. My father had a lot to lose, she told him. She knew the system, in and out. She knew kids like me by sight. If he laid a hand on me again, she'd call child protection, she'd call every newspaper in New York. Welcome to a new world where he was no longer in charge. I turned fourteen a few weeks later, and I was saved. Or so I thought.

I've always been smart. In junior high I was the only girl on the math team; you know the kind, one of the nerd boys but with lavender eyeglasses. I tested into New York City's elite math and science high school, Stuyvesant. My first two years of high school I was nuts. Truly nuts. I was a furious binge drinker, the Drew Barrymore kind, literally passing out in Lower East Side gutters. I was a mad club kid, doing the drugs you should never do, the ones strangers hand you in the dark. I made money shoplifting for a fence. I lived wherever someone gave me a key—for a while with my boyfriend Tony Ward, who went on to be Madonna's boyfriend; for a bit with my boyfriend the house music DJ, who also hosted in his apartment Moby, found beside the bed much of the time wearing headphones and squinting at the recording equipment. I was a very fun, very troubled semi-homeless apartment/couch surfer, living out of a backpack and moving in with "boyfriends" twice my age.

I also spent a lot of time thinking about *The Brothers Karamazov* and whether I was morally obligated for the good of my family to murder my father while I was still a juvenile. The whole idea made me want to throw up, which made me feel like a failure.

During two summers as a teenager in the 1980s, I followed my chef, Ana, to her new restaurant in Provincetown, at the tip of Cape Cod in Massachusetts, a restaurant called Ana Ana Ana's. I held down the fort of the kitchen while Ana brought meals to AIDS patients and donated meals to AIDS charity fundraisers and

AIDS killed everyone and the world didn't care. Back in New York, I marched with ACT UP and concluded that Ronald Reagan's America didn't care if everyone I loved died, or if schoolkids suffered malnutrition because ketchup was a vegetable. I was a high school freshman who got home via the Fourteenth Street subway the afternoon in 1984 when Bernhard Goetz waited on a Fourteenth Street subway platform before shooting four teenagers. If your father doesn't kill you, your fellow straphangers will? I read a lot of Albert Camus and agreed with him that the only philosophical question was whether to commit suicide. I resolved to kill myself on my sixteenth birthday. I planned to walk into the sea—big, big Virginia Woolf fan here—but after sitting on the sand for a while— pink ribbon clouds above, sailboats bobbing at anchor—I couldn't do it. I stood up from that beach and looked at the buoys and the clouds and the little boats, and I had another thought: *Plan B. I'll stop all this nonsense and do the only other thing worth doing besides cocaine while dancing on a nightclub catwalk. I'll be a writer.*

And that is the secret story behind all the stories collected here, and many more. It took me decades to be able to string together that bit of nonfiction about myself. It took me decades of healing in Minnesota to understand that the trauma I endured as a kid is what makes me empathetic today, what allows the tendrils of my empathy to reach out and find the tendrils of empathy in others. Needless to say, I'm glad I didn't walk into the sea, although I can see now it would be a better story if I walked in and was, say, saved by a talking seagull or hauled out of the surf by a one-legged scuba guy just back from the war.

A one-legged scuba guy! I came up with that just now. And he appeared in your mind!

I love writing. I cannot fully express to you how much I love writing. It is joy incarnate to me: sitting around, putting one word after another, beads on a string, symbols on a treasure map, and suddenly you're not just in a chair, you're in someone's head, making pictures—pictures of one-legged scuba guys or libertarians at the gas station.

Writing is a form of telepathy. I put the symbols in a line, and you follow along with your eyes, and what's in my mind appears in your mind. This telepathy is so strong it can continue after death, even. "They fuck you up, your mom and dad," wrote the poet Philip Larkin, who died when I was in high school but just reappeared in all our minds.

My love of writing started when I was very young, and I've been at it ever since. I was the main contributor and titular editor of the P.S. 94 Queens kindergarten haiku anthology. I was a writer on my high school newspaper, an editor of a *Village Voice*–style high school magazine, a writer on the Carleton College newspaper, an editor of a *Village Voice*–style Carleton magazine called *Currency* (with staff writer Jonathan Capehart!).

I ended up in Minnesota at Carleton in order to get as far away from New York City as I could, psychically and physically, and Minnesota is farther from New York than California is, if you catch my drift. Minnesota, too, because I was a huge Hüsker Dü fan, a Babes in Toyland fan, a ride or die F. Scott Fitzgerald fan. I do remember thinking: *I'm going to the part of America where the people are good.*

I ended up at Carleton largely out of the blessings of a generous universe, thanks to luck, and because I am smart. Because I am smart, I had incredible writing samples and a National Merit scholarship. Because I am smart, by the time I decided to drop out of high school and road-trip through the country with Ana's chef at the time, it turned out I had received so many credits in extra literature and humanities classes that my guidance counselor simply added up my courses and congratulated me on my early graduation.

A lot of teachers and friends thought I needed to get out of New York, mostly for sixteen-year-old-doing-cocaine reasons. Chef Ana encouraged me to go to college for writing, not to cooking school. She told me she wouldn't write a reference to cooking school and would in fact deny she'd ever heard of me. So go to college already! She saved my life so many times. Then she died of cancer when I was just out of college. She died before I even knew she was sick. One great regret I have in life is that I never said thank you. Thank you, my fierce protector.

The last words I ever spoke with my dad were via a curly-cord landline in my barbecue-fogged Minneapolis apartment. He called to demand I stop pursuing my dreams of being a writer. He told me I would end up as a heroin-addicted prostitute on the street, and he would never speak to me again. As he described the groveling I would do and the diseases I would acquire, I remember my hands turning to ice; I remember looking out the window at my Minneapolis alley and my mind turning to a blank, trembling thing, unreachable with complete dissociation. He told me he disowned me, and then he hung up. I never spoke with him again. Twelve years later he died. None of his children or siblings went to his funeral.

Sometimes I think my desire to be a writer was a subconscious urge to get into the places my father's attention was: the *Wall Street Journal*, the *New York Times*, the *New York Post*. Sometimes I think I wanted to be a writer because my mom is a serial liar, one of those people who lies about everything. Maybe all those lies made me obsessed with getting to, and controlling, what I perceived to be "the truth." Sometimes I think I wanted to be a writer because I could go into the page, following my words, and live in the only safe space, writing. Any which way, or all those ways together: Writing saved my life. Where I write is Minnesota. Ergo: Minnesota saved my life.

Minnesotans, especially Minnesotans who grew up here, always want to say that Minnesota is boring, that it's provincial, that, in myriad ways, it's less than. They're wrong. As far as I can tell, Minnesota is the place that puts you back together when you're almost irreparably damaged but not quite. To me, Minnesota is the healing place.

Upon hearing that I was working on this book, a friend said, "Of course! Your whole career has been a love letter to Minneapolis." I nearly curled up and died. It sounds so saccharine. A love letter is just flattery and wooing, right? Love letters are just the good stuff, right? Aren't love letters where you write: *What eyes, what hair, let's go to a movie!*

Don't get me wrong. I do love Minneapolis, and St. Paul. And Ely, Pipestone, Grand Marais, and even you too, Edina. But what I've been doing in this state for twenty-five years is not the same as writing a love letter.

Though it is love, a knottier type of love. Let me explain. Two famous social science experiments help outline what to me is an epic difference. New York psychologist Arthur Aron conducted an experiment about how to make people fall in love. First, find a partner and ask and answer thirty-six key questions about each other. Then, stare into each other's eyes for four minutes. Odds are good you'll fall in love. The other experiment that explains my career was devised by Timothy Wilson, a Virginia psychologist. He left people in an empty room without their phones or anything else to distract them and said, "Be alone with your thoughts for fifteen minutes, or you can leave if you give yourself an electric shock." Two-thirds of the men and a quarter of the women mildly electrocuted themselves to avoid being alone with their thoughts.

I have stared deeply, unblinkingly, at Minneapolis and St. Paul (and Grand Marais, Stillwater, and yes, you too, Edina) for much longer than four minutes (maybe twenty-five years, actually). I have asked many more than thirty-six questions (maybe hundreds of thousands, actually). And I have sat alone with my thoughts, year after year after year.

I have stood on the banks of the frozen Mississippi River beneath the Franklin Avenue bridge and watched deer on stick-thin legs pick their way across the ice, beneath the arcing bows of concrete, and I have thought: *That's all of us in winter: fragile in this dangerous beauty. Also, please don't fall in.* I have sat at one table at Meritage, the French restaurant in St. Paul, and talked to the famous chef Lidia Bastianich about the excellence of chef Russell Klein's chicken thighs and thought: *Cooking, feeding, admiring— this is human.* I have sat at another table at Meritage and thought: *My God, is that Pharrell in that booth? I should do something.* I have stared at a CNN anchor standing on a tower of apple boxes across from George Floyd Square, on the day of George Floyd's funeral, and I have thought: *God hold us and keep us. God help us all.*

Is there a kind of love where you look at each other and you see that your beloved has a lot of great unremarked-upon noble characteristics, but also a lot of flaws and is, in different moods, indifferent, suffering, generous, and blithe? Is there a kind of love during which, contemplating all your beloved's good and bad points, you find you love them more deeply, and that love has made you regard your own flaws and sufferings with more sympathy, and so your love for them turns into love for yourself, and then for the humans around you? If that's the kind of love that could go in a love letter, then actually, yes: You are holding in your hands a very fat, page-numbered love letter.

It was mind-breakingly difficult deciding what to put in this anthology/love letter. Should it be my favorite stories, or the ones I think readers will find most helpful in the year 2023? When my editor told me I'd best write explanatory notes for everything I picked for this book, I panicked: *Explaining? Ugh!* Generally in writing, when you're explaining, you're failing. But in going through this towering pile of stories, I see a thing I never expected. I see a smart, damaged kid welcomed into these Twin Cities and healed by years and years of conversation with you and for you. So that's what I picked for you: the stories that show the evolution, the empathy, the conversation of our twenty-five years together.

Look at us, me and you! What a journey we've been on! We've met so many people together, we've been to so many places together, we've had so many meals together, and we've endured so many changes together. We've had a life together! And you've supported me every step of the way. Thank you.

When I thought about what I'd want to know if I were a longtime reader of Dara, I thought: *I'd want to know the story behind all these stories, who exactly was out there, gazing, gazing, asking question after question, year after year.* Now you know. You now have had the full Dara experience. Hopefully you'll never forget it. I know I never will.

SECTION 1

People

I entered the 1990s a kid in college, and after graduating in 1992, I spent the better part of the decade writing about people for *City Pages*. In 1997 I became the alt-weekly's restaurant critic. I realize that, for a lot of people, I'll always be a restaurant critic. For me, it evokes a joke by comedian Mitch Hedberg: "I don't have a girlfriend," he quipped. "But I do know a woman who'd be mad at me for saying that." Similarly, I have never written primarily as a restaurant critic, but I do know there's a population who'd be shocked to hear that.

The truth is, my success in restaurant criticism stems from the fact that I've always approached food writing as people writing. Well, people writing with a little extra seasoning. I wrote my way into this form of prose in the early 1990s, following the scent of my own personal vision of what a writing career might be, filing hundreds of thousands of words for anyone who would have me.

One question I've always wanted to pursue is: What would happen if I just wrote about everybody? In Edgar Lee Masters's poetry collection *Spoon River Anthology*, he tells the story of nearly every person interred in a graveyard in the town of Spoon River. I've always felt called to do something like that, at scale. I am convinced the world would have many fewer problems if we did that—just wrote about everybody. Naive? I'll defend a certain amount of naivete to the death.

We have a US Poet Laureate; could we have a Nonfiction Profile Laureate too? I've been doing something like that, as the self-appointed Joseph Mitchell of the Twin Cities—telling the stories of people, be they famous or obscure, to help all of us to understand the place where we live.

People! I love the people-ness of people. And other people are all we have. For twenty-odd years, I've been helping people see other people, in the way people see: through stories.

SuperAmerica Man

· · · · · · · · · · · ·

City Pages, January 4, 1995

Back in the mid-1990s, when I was cranking out stories as a freelancer for *City Pages*, my friend Pat told me about something amusing going on at the SuperAmerica. So I went and stood in the parking lot and scribbled as fast as I could in a spiral memo pad. Today, as I look back on this story of an otherwise anonymous cashier at an otherwise generic Minneapolis gas station, I become melancholy. I don't think anyone would want a piece like this today, about a person without any power bobbing on the waves of society. I pine, at least a little, for the idealistic mayhem of 1990s *City Pages*, where we had so many pages to fill that some really weird stuff, by nobodies about nobodies, slipped through.

Imagine this. You're tooling through the relatively quiet Wedge neighborhood [of Minneapolis] on a summer's night. You're a little thirsty and low on gas. The SuperAmerica at the corner of Lyndale and Twenty-Second glows like a jewel in the night. You pull up to get gas, unhook the nozzle, and are fitting it in your tank when the PA system sputters to life.

"Welcome to SuperAmerica," it barks. "As of this nocturnal business hour all petroleum products or byproducts are prepay with the exception of authorized emergency vehicles. Please hang up the hose in the pump and pay in advance. Thank you for your patience and patronage."

The gawky phrase echoes off the low brick buildings like a dada poem in the night. You blink. You enter the glowing convenience store and find yourself in a festive mood. You pick up a six-pack of tasty 3.2 and a frosty Bomb Pop. You slide your merchandise across the counter and mumble something about pump four, five dollars of unleaded.

"Have you got some form of ID, please? It's nothing personal, merely professional. I'm sure you understand. It is the law," says the clerk.

Odd. You fish out your license and hand it over. He looks at it while you examine his bright American-flag tie. "In your maturity you exhibit a very youthful disposition," he says. He returns your license and rings up your beer, gas, "and one frozen novelty."

You've just entered the world of the SuperAmerica guy. His real name is Dan Daehlin, and he's famous throughout the city for his strangely poetic bureaucratese, his American-flag ties, and his unique take on customer service. He calls his torturous turns of phrase "spontaneous occupational speech therapy," and he creates them to engage and amuse customers.

"Most of the time I can make sure the customer leaves the store smiling, having had a joyful experience," he says. And we do. In bars across Minneapolis arguments rage as to whether he calls matches incendiary devices or inflammatory devices. Whether he calls ice cream bars *frozen novelties* or *frozen novelty treats*. Whether he has one or multiple American-flag ties. (Answers: incendiary, novelty, multiple.) People travel blocks out of their way to visit his SuperAmerica, in a neighborhood amply saturated with SuperAmericas, just for the chance to hear some odd phrase of his.

Dan seems huge behind the counter, at least seven feet on the raised floor. He has bright brown eyes, pink midwestern skin, and a deep, confident voice. He is most easily identifiable, though, by his American-flag ties. He wears them as evidence of another part of his life, that of a fiercely committed Libertarian.

He attributes his Libertarian consciousness to Ayn Rand, whom he was introduced to while studying at Concordia College in Moorhead. He stoutly defends all Libertarian principles: the right to absolute control of private property, including one's sexual habits, abolition of all government except the police or the military—even "government schools" and the post office—and, basically, the right of all people, corporations, and states to do whatever they want that isn't criminally harmful to others, tax-free.

Dan left Concordia after his political "rebirth" to work as a Libertarian fundraiser in Fairbanks, Alaska, for several years and since then has attended the Libertarian national convention every year. At one convention, in a fit of freedom of expression and right to private property, he even burned one of his ties. "I was out partying with some guys, and I just up and burned my flag," he says.

In fact, though, he much prefers the Statue of Liberty to Old Glory. "The flag is a limited symbol. The specific, sovereign autonomous republic of America. The Statue of Liberty represents an international or global, cosmic or universal idea." Dan is well occupied with ideas: He's a voracious reader and likes to pepper his speech with quotes from Jefferson and Churchill. He says his mother calls him "a walking book of statistics." If you're lucky, if you ask what date it is while writing a check, he'll reply: "The twenty-second; the thirty-first anniversary of the assassination of John F. Kennedy," or "the eighteenth; the sixteenth anniversary of the massacre at Jonestown."

Not everyone appreciates Dan's knowledge or humor, though. After two and a half years at SuperAmerica he has received no promotions and one demotion. He says he's perceived as "a loose cannon by my superiors and regarded as kind of rocking the boat." He doesn't see himself as advancing in his job: "Even though I endear myself to the public in a very charismatic or ingratiating demeanor I may be shooting myself in the foot as far as making any headway" at SuperAmerica. In fact, a few weeks ago at a meeting between SuperAmerica management and a neighborhood group concerned about noise pollution, some Scrooges fingered Dan publicly as a noise polluter.

"I was told by my manager that some anonymous individuals at that meeting specifically designated me, by name, in front of my boss—not only my boss, but my boss's boss—as a kind of a talk radio personality doing my own original shtick on the PA system. Because I'm doing my own thing, I'm kind of causing friction and jeopardizing my position here."

Which has given Dan some ideas. Many of his devoted customers have suggested over the years that he go into some other line of work: stand-up comedy, radio, or television. Dan's been studying

Rush Limbaugh, trying to pick up some of his talk tricks of the trade, and hopes one day to marry his two talents—Libertarianism and spontaneous occupational speech therapy—into a career, somewhere over the airwaves.

If he does make that transition, let's all hope he can do for vaster audiences what he's done for Minneapolitan convenience store shoppers—treat them to a unique, intelligent, and human experience where there was once merely a corporate one.

The Fanciest Cat

· · · · · · · · · · · ·

City Pages, October 9, 1996

At *City Pages*, as well as everywhere I've ever written, *The New Yorker*'s "Talk of the Town" section loomed large. That's the bit in the front of that magazine where the most important writers in the world—say, Ian Frazier—get into important rooms—say Itzhak Perlman's dressing room. That's what we wanted to write at *City Pages*; that's what we wanted to give to our readers. Unfortunately, we didn't have the most important writers or access to the most important rooms, but we did have me—and a regional arena full of fancy cats.

You'll know them by the glittering pom-pom-tipped wands that bulge from their pockets. By the bright feathers clutched in their hands. By the telltale wisps of fur clinging to their shoes. They're the Twin City Cat Fanciers, and they recently met up for a local feline beauty pageant.

"There are seven ancient mutations that account for nearly every sort of cat you might recognize," explained judge Patty Jacobberger. "Brown mackerel tabbies are the prototype cat. *Felis lybica*." The other mutated cats are the fancy ones—long haired, blue-eyed, solid colored, or unusually colored, like smoke cameo calico or blue. These ancient mutations lined the aisles of the Aldrich Arena ice hockey rink, in Maplewood. Burmese mewed, with lapis lazuli eyes and fur like golden smoke; Persians stared, as flopsy and fluffy as chiffon dusters; Devon Rex—the Chihuahuas of the feline kingdom—wrinkled and bug-eyed, tore around their cages, batting their paws between the bars.

Jacobberger slipped cats in and out of their cages, placing them on the judging platform, ruffling their fur, examining their faces, dancing her poufy wand before their faces to capture their attention. Whenever she finished with a cat, its owner rushed up to rescue it from its judging cage, cuddling it, kissing it, and murmuring into its ears. Girls at the sidelines, like ball boys at Wimbledon, sprang for the newly emptied cages, Windexing and toweling them out. No little boys wiped out cages. Kim, one of Jacobberger's young cage monitors, explained: "Guys like dogs because they can control them, but cats they can't control." Amy, Kim's cage-cleaning partner, clarified: "Girls are right."

Right or not, there's something especially girlie about cat-fanciers' accoutrements. Barbeedoll Cattery owner Bill Barbee is a large man, and macho enough, but sitting in a row of cat's cages he looks like a refugee in a war between Dolly Parton and Vanna White. Gold lamé abounds, looped and draped in astonishing curtain poufs; diamond-crusted medallions, bows, gauze, sequins, and fringe spill all over, camouflaging the plain wire cages and concealing cut-crystal kibble bowls. Barbee stands watch over Cybil, who lives in an elaborate upholstery of bubble gum–pink satin trimmed with seed pearls. A series of framed color portraits of Cybil rest atop her cage, and a pink feather boa curls among them, coyly revealing business cards. A cattery indeed.

Cybil is a nine-month-old dilute calico—a foggy dream of creamy ivory, shell pink, and abalone gray. Cybil looks exactly like a cloud, an angel—or a cartoon character whose face was squashed dead-flat by a falling anvil. Persians' heads are supposed to be utterly round, and their noses are not supposed to break the plane of their faces. Cybil's face is so smushed that it's made her a Grand Champion as a nine-month-old virgin. Which is good for Bill Barbee, because cat-fancy cash is all in the kittens. According to Twin City Cat Fancier president Linda Berg, the offspring of top cats sell for $2,500 to $3,500. And cats, frankly, breed like rabbits.

Cybil is a top show cat, a cat fancier's wet dream. "When I die I want to come back as a top-quality show cat," joked Jacobberger to Cybil. "As a Persian. And I want to be a calico. Or a dilute calico. I'll be carried everywhere. My feet will never touch the ground." She turned to face the cat, whose liquid eyes look uncannily like pleading. "And awl the judges will wuv me."

But all is not cream and mackerel snacks for Cybil. She hardly ever leaves her cage. She never goes outside—her feet have literally never touched God's brown earth. Barbee says she stays in her cage in a private room in her house and doesn't mix with the rest of the household, to guard against infection. (When Barbee mates Cybil, her intended will be isolated for three months in a separate room, again to guard against infection.)

When Cybil's not in isolation, she's washed, conditioned, blow-dried, trimmed, powdered, styled, eye-droppered, nose moistur-ized, and restrained. She wears a lace ruff to prevent her from licking her own fur, which would result in little unbrushed-looking curls. (Other cat fanciers put coffee filters around their cats' heads.) If Cybil isn't sleeping or being groomed, she's flying around, winning awards, lounging in hotels. Judge Evelyn Prather's highest praise for a cat that won an early round? "It must be a joy to take this kitty and go with her into motels and just be with her."

Just being Cybil—so cute, so docile, and such a perfect example of ancient mutations—she conquered all. Cybil racked up more points than any other adult cat, and winged home to Memphis to await her precisely picked prince charming—the fanciest cat at the cat fancy.

Dogs of War

· · · · · · · · · · · · ·

City Pages, October 16, 1996

I have thought about this story just about every day of my life since reporting it. The super–blue blood, preppy, Waspy women and completely tricked-out, leather-draped leather-men hugging—it was my dream of a perfect world. No one in tribes; everyone full of love. Except it was also supremely weird. Which I like!

Ancient Europeans guarded against demons by erecting gargoyles, the theory being that the gargoyles would out-scare the demons. That same premise led Herr Ludwig Dobermann to develop, through crossbreeding, the Doberman Pinscher, the fiercest-looking, pointiest-eared, demon-eyed dog there could be. And they do look scary—very scary. Somehow, however, nine hundred of them in a ballroom look a lot less scary. Maybe it was the chandeliers, or maybe it was the way they don't bark at each other? Maybe it was because the dogs were more on display than on the attack last week as part of the Seventy-First Annual National Show of the Doberman Pinscher Society of America at the Bloomington Radisson South.

Bizarre scenes played out constantly: Elevator doors swooshed open to reveal five Dobermans stepping out like perfectly choreographed dancers. Dogs bound by wire-thin choke collars that looked as if they could slice off their heads like cake, at a single misstep. Handlers in three-piece double-breasted wool sprinted around a rubber-floored ring, a leash in one hand, fresh liver glistening in the other. Folk in head-to-toe shiny black leather who looked very S&M hugged dumpy fellows in Doberman sweatshirts and Dockers. Women in bright-colored, gold-buttoned power suits swimming with gold jewelry demanded: "When are black bitches?" "Did you see Joan's new bitch?"

The air is full of language that sounds problematic. "The DPCA must prevent the breeders of 'white' Dobermans from further contaminating our gene pool . . . the danger lies in the colored littermates. The prospect of having to cull 'whites' from our litters has been unheard of in the history of our breed. When the novelty has worn off, DPCA members will be left to clean up the yet unpredictable genetic problems . . . " warns a pamphlet, directed at albino Doberman owners who might be tempted to crossbreed and create new species. Between the shades of eugenics and the sleek, sinister dogs, the hotel brims with danger.

But Peggy Adamson says it's all an illusion. "Dobermans have gotten a very bad reputation over the years from the movies and television, because when they want to show a dog that is what they call a 'killer dog,' that will strike terror in everybody, they always use a big black Doberman showing his teeth." With that Peggy bares her own teeth—which are small, and perfect, and peek out between the coral lipstick that is particular to women of a certain age and certain class who have held court at country clubs since World War II. Which is when Peggy fell in love with the dogs.

"My husband was a Marine captain, and I watched some of the first platoons of Dobermans being trained to go overseas to the Pacific. They used them to search out land mines, and search caves and forests. The amount of things they were able to teach them was just amazing." Soon Peggy and her husband drove from California to Ohio to get a purebred red Doberman, Dictator, who won the club show in 1943. Peggy's been professionally judging, and in love with, Dobermans ever since. However, whether this fondness is despite or due to their reputation is unclear.

"Macy's used them in the store in New York," Peggy says enthusiastically, her face lighting up with the mischief of the idea. "At night they let Dobermans loose in the building, so nobody dared come in. Then a movie came out called *They Only Kill Their Masters* [in which a Doberman is unjustly accused of murder]. Unfortunately they showed a black Doberman showing his teeth, and that's how this reputation of fierceness got established and why, even today, in the movies or TV when they want to show a dog that will strike fear in everybody, they always use a black Doberman. And this is so crazy, but it's also very useful." She whispers conspiratorially: "The Doberman people don't feel too badly about it because we can't afford to have nice, sweet, wonderful dogs, and even my postman, who has never been inside my house and can only hear my Dobermans when he comes up, is terrified. In fact, I don't even lock my door at night." Peggy raises her voice again. "In the Marine Corps they called them Devil Dogs."

This military history is treasured by Doberman lovers. They say they still crop ears—cutting off the lower part of the ear that would otherwise become long and floppy—and train them to stand upright in order to maintain the dogs' "working" history. However, during wartimes the dogs' ears were almost entirely trimmed off, to prevent the enemy from grabbing them, so today's very long croppings appear to be as much for fashion as anything. Near the judging arena, sculptor Susan Bahary Wilner sells reproductions of a statue commissioned by the Pentagon to honor World War II's "Devil Dogs." A life-sized bronze Doberman rests on a black marble base inscribed: "25 Marine war dogs gave their lives liberating Guam in 1944. They served as sentries, messengers, scouts. They explored caves, detected mines and booby traps. Semper fidelis." Like the Washington Vietnam memorial, the names of the lost dogs are engraved in stone. Some—Blitz, Duke, Ludwig, Max—are testament to the dogs' ferocity. Others—Bunkie, Missy, Tubby, Koko—show their sweeter side.

Lester Cannon has been showing Dobermans for nearly twenty years. "The Doberman is a dog that's going to be continuously under your foot," he says. "They're like an appendage. They attach themselves to you. If you go into the shower, and you forget to close the bathroom door, you've got a Doberman in the shower." Other owners say the dog is so attuned to people they understand fashion, whimpering at the sight of lipstick, realizing that their owner is about to go out, and also grasp the concept of loopholes, taking a "no sitting on the couch" directive as not including sitting on the couch with two feet on the floor.

Peggy says that the dogs were intended to be smart and intimate from the beginning. "The whole idea of the Doberman breed was to have a companion and protector in the family. It was the idea of the Germans to have a dog that would be with the children and friendly, but would protect them if anyone tried to come into the home." Or if they encountered anyone who didn't want to pay their taxes.

Good old Ludwig Dobermann—the nineteenth-century German tax collector and animal shelter keeper who developed the dogs to protect him on his rounds—would no doubt be delighted to see the success with which the Doberman satisfies Americans' craving for loyalty, style, and menace. He might be puzzled, however, by the sight of these once-working animals sitting elegantly on carpets in a cocktail lounge. And heaven knows if he'd understand the vast amount of cultural priority and personal fantasy that these shiny beasts unknowingly convey.

(Second) Oldest Living Aquatennial Queen Tells All

· · · · · · · · · · · · ·

Microsoft Sidewalk, August 6, 1997

> I'm so happy I made a printout of this article back in 1997. I didn't even remember writing it until I found it in a box of papers in the basement. This is classic Dara. I could talk to people all day and forever about how they remember life fifty years ago.

Pageant queens, like aerosol cheese, used-car salesmen, and Dan Quayle, are among the easiest targets for cynics. The very phrase conjures up images of strained smiles pulled back from Vaseline-coated teeth, bathing suits held in place with glue, and easy lies about dreaming of world peace. But it wasn't always like that. There was a time when a pageant crown was simply a miraculous moment given to an ordinary person, such as young Vivian Hofstad, Aquatennial Queen of 1942.

It was the height of World War II. Gas and food were rationed. Six days a week Vivian took the streetcars from her parents' modest north Minneapolis home to her job in the mail-order department of the Lake Street Sears. She came home and helped her mother with their Victory garden (to take pressure off food for the troops) and helped her father cover up all the windows and doors during blackout drills to prepare for potential German air attacks. Meanwhile, city fathers feared that the Aquatennial might seem frivolous in light of the war, so they wrote for permission to President Roosevelt. He said go ahead; it would be good for morale.

In those days Aquatennial queen contestants were nominated by their hometowns or companies, and Vivian's manager asked her to go. She said no as she had the year before—until she learned it meant a free shopping trip to Dayton's Oval Room. "I always loved fine clothes," remembers Vivian, now Vivian Semple, a sweet silver-haired grandmother. "Though I didn't have much opportunity to get any, so this was a fairy-tale moment for me." The fairy tale continued through Aquatennial week. Every day, crowds of neighborhood kids appeared in front of Vivian's house awaiting the arrival of the Sears-provided chauffeur and his shiny convertible. (Little did those kids know that the Buick made a daily detour for an unauthorized pickup: The chauffeur "was really taken by Miss Robbinsdale," remembers Vivian. "He thought she was about the cutest thing around.")

The judging was swift and informal. Judges simply chose by observing the week's Aquatennial festivities and crowned the queen just before the parade. Vivian was flabbergasted when she won. "I just stood around there kind of awed. I really was in a state of shock. . . . I put on the coronation gown, which was very lovely white organza, and rode a float that was called, I think, 'Up in the Clouds,' down Nicollet Avenue in the Torchlight Parade. It was blue and white, and I was seated in something that looked like a cloud, and the other girls were in great big swans."

Some 300,000 people watched that parade. Vivian and her family returned home that night to find their block abuzz, their house surrounded by neighbors, and inside a surprise of twenty-one long-stemmed roses. "My mother was running all over the neighborhood borrowing vases. It was a neighborhood fairy tale."

This daughter of Norwegian immigrants who had never been west of Lake Minnetonka found herself the very next week on the West Coast USO circuit, hobnobbing with Bob Hope and Bing Crosby. She spent the rest of her year helping to sell war bonds and attending charity events. Yet, even as the most eligible bachelorette in Minneapolis, she could hardly find a date. "All the boys of the right age were off in the war, and everyone left had flat feet or something—and who wants that?"

The Birth of BeBe Zahara Benet

Mpls.St.Paul Magazine, September 2021

During the two summers when I worked for my beloved chef Ana in Provincetown, I spent too many dark, wee hours drinking too many fuzzy navels at a lesbian dance club called the Pied Piper and hanging out with drag queens. I can't even remember the social security–card name of the wonderful person I was often sidekick to. I knew her as Baby, and she called her garden apartment Patsy Cline's Mountainside Retreat. I'd sit on her couch while she told me everything there was to know about life. Anyway, I love the smell of Aqua Net on old wigs, and I love drag queens. To me, drag queens have always had the most accurate critiques of the clichés of patriarchy. As RuPaul said, "You're born naked, and the rest is drag." Why do women today wear dresses like manly man Henry VII used to wear? Ask a drag queen! It's all arbitrary; it's all drag. I could talk to drag queens every day all day, and once in a great while I get to.

BeBe Zahara Benet is one of the biggest drag stars to come out of Minneapolis. But behind it all, Marshall Kudi Ngwa is a Minnesota homebody on a trajectory he never saw coming.

It was a cold November night in Minneapolis when Africa's most important drag queen was born, whole and entire, right on Hennepin Avenue.

The year? 2000. The place? Where else? The sprawling complex then and still called the Gay 90's. Once just a dinner-nightclub, it too was born on Hennepin Avenue, swallowing its neighbor, and then another neighbor, then another, in Minneapolis's gay-after-dark district, becoming the biggest gay bar between the coasts, with half a dozen venues attached by jerry-rigged hallways.

Fresh out of Cameroon, skinny as a sapling, eighteen-year-old Marshall Kudi Ngwa stepped into this new-to-him but long-to-Minneapolis world. He climbed the staircase to the upstairs show lounge beside his friend Cathy and took a chair.

"I'd never heard of drag in my life!" says Kudi, who is now better known as BeBe Zahara Benet, international star of stage and screen. "But it was in me; *it was in me*." With that, he puts his fingers together and places them at his heart, then draws them out, as if tracing the path of the radiant sunbeams that then emerged.

Like Athena from the head of Zeus, enter BeBe! Hourglass figure, hair regal as a lion's mane and four times bigger, the glamour of Diana Ross riveted like rhinestones onto the fierceness of Grace Jones. A star was born.

· · · · · · ·

I meet Marshall Kudi Ngwa on the rooftop deck of his apartment building just steps from the Stone Arch Bridge. It's a late-summer day, and across the river, downtown Minneapolis looks like a rocky cliff face, the various buildings made one by the bright sun's glare, the heavy humid air, and the ever-present smoke this year.

We have a lot to talk about, including the documentary of his life, *Being BeBe*, which will have its Minneapolis premiere in November, following up its world premiere at the Tribeca Festival in June of 2021 and, later that month, a triumphant run at the Provincetown Film Festival (where it was crowned with the audience award for best documentary). I also want to learn about his role anchoring the new performance spot Roxy's Cabaret, opening in the former Ichiban on Nicollet Mall, and his growing presence as an interior designer and event planner through his company, The Lavish Lab.

Did you know BeBe has been choosing chandeliers and layering animal prints in select local living rooms? "If a Minnetonka girl wants to live out loud, it is not always easy to find support in her community," says Kudi with a nod. "So she finds me. BeBe understands a Minnetonka girl only has one life too, and she wants to seize it!"

"Minnetonka girls" are one of the lesser-known parts of Kudi's life he's now willing to talk about.

You see, BeBe Zahara Benet/Marshall Kudi Ngwa is known for using bold elements—African music, fabrics, patterns—onstage. In fact, BeBe's fans in the seats yell *Cameroon!*—not like it's a home country but like they're yelling *Amen!* Or maybe: *Free Bird!* At first Kudi thought this was bizarre, like yelling *Canada* at Justin Bieber, but now he slightly enjoys it, receiving his *Cameroons* as an expression of faintly odd but nonetheless well-meant love.

Despite Kudi's country of origin and BeBe's global stage, the character BeBe Zahara Benet is Minnesota born and bred, as Minnesotan a character as Viktor the Viking (of the NFL), Nick Carraway (of *The Great Gatsby*), or Charlie Brown. BeBe Zahara Benet is just like them: more real in our imaginations and revelatory of the human experience than many real people, commercial but artistic, made in Minnesota in various significant ways but also made elsewhere in other various significant ways.

Kudi often brings up Tyler Perry's character Madea as the way to think about his character BeBe Zahara Benet. Neither Madea nor BeBe is small and personal; they are global in every sense: globally famous and marketable, globally relevant as illuminations of the human condition. "I say BeBe is a global girl. Not everyone is one thing from one place anymore, and BeBe certainly isn't." Also, Tyler Perry uses "he" pronouns; so does Marshall Kudi Ngwa, though he doesn't object when people use "she" or "they," which can seem more natural, especially when you're talking about what BeBe Zahara Benet is up to.

Whatever pronoun is used, one thing Kudi does not like is the tendency among some writers to see drag as the inevitable outward manifestation of born inner sexuality—what Kudi does is art and work, and no less work than that done by a doctor or lawyer. He wants his drag performance acknowledged as the combination of his relentless work and well-honed talent, which he intentionally fuses into moneymaking art. Every wig takes hours and days and money. Every dress requires the same. Every lip-synced song involves dozens or hundreds of hours of preparation and lots of talent. And then there are BeBe's original songs—those take even more. (BeBe is taking a swing at a breakout pop hit. The biggest original song, "Jungle Kitty," has a million plays on YouTube, though for my money last year's original "Banjo" is the banger.) All of BeBe takes work, time, talent. Makeup, photo planning, photo styling. Hours and connections and talent.

And magic. As BeBe says in one scene in the TLC TV series *Dragnificent!*: "We queens, we always have tricks—under our sleeves and under our skirts!"

One trick BeBe is ready to reveal is that there's a serious Minnesota homebody behind one of the most riveting beauties on Instagram. Here's what Kudi does when BeBe's not onstage: He cooks, he sews, he plays with nieces and nephews, he rehearses, he meditates.

BeBe is ready to show this homebody and Minnesota-made side now, particularly in light of the collective trauma and international infamy Minneapolis earned following the murder of George Floyd. BeBe Zahara Benet/Marshall Kudi Ngwa wants the world to know that his is a face of Minneapolis too.

The day we talk, Kudi is on the eve of a departure for a UK tour (London loves BeBe). As he looks over the Mississippi toward the haze-fused dreamscape of Minneapolis, he explains how critical this city is to both how BeBe was born and where he's going.

Looking back on that fateful night in 2000, please keep in mind that Kudi had not come here to be fabulous. He was here to live in Minnetonka with family and take classes at MCTC so that he might one day bring the stable glory that only a child with a solid middle-class career can bring to a West African family. He was not the first in his family to move here and join the small but church- and profession-oriented community of Cameroon expats in the Twin Cities. MINCAM, an organization of Minnesotans from Cameroon, puts the current local Cameroonian population at five thousand. Marshall Kudi Ngwa most certainly did not come here to become one of the biggest drag stars to ever come out of Minnesota.

Yet, in this television age, BeBe Zahara Benet has certainly become just that. BeBe's international reputation rests primarily on having won the first season of *RuPaul's Drag Race*. It was the hardest season, because BeBe had to invent the whole genre as she went! To the RuPaul generation, BeBe Zahara Benet is Marilyn Monroe, or maybe actually Jean Harlow, the star who made the shape in the sky the other stars must match. BeBe is also revered for returning as one of RuPaul's All Stars and for going on as one of the leads in the 2020 TLC series *Dragnificent!*—a makeover show like *Queer Eye* but with a big Oprah-style meaning-and-spirit anchor. In one memorable scene from *Dragnificent!*, BeBe, wearing a giant turban with a peacock feather arching regally over one ear, officiates a wedding ceremony, and you instantly feel the foundation of the church in her life. (Through her company, The Lavish Lab, BeBe taps her church roots to officiate weddings in real life too.)

Church choir and choir solos were where young Marshall Kudi Ngwa first seized the microphone. "Growing up in Yaoundé, we did not know drag. But it was in me," says Kudi as he thinks about his childhood. Drag was in him at his parents' house, where he'd dabble in his mom's makeup. It was in him as he watched the popular Cameroonian band Zangalewa toy with Monty Python–style burlesque comic characters onstage. If he had even thought about men dressing as women back then, which he didn't, he says he'd have taken it as a fairly ordinary part of Cameroonian life, because it was part of Elizabethan theater and Greek theater, and why make a scandal out of what was obviously a well-wrought path of human endeavor?

And yet there was the news this very summer out of Cameroon of the government arresting and sentencing two men to five years in prison for sitting at a restaurant dressed as women. The crime charged? "Attempted homosexuality." "No, my parents did not send me to Minnesota to keep me safe," Kudi tells me on his Minneapolis rooftop. "They sent me for the West African dream— every West African parent wants their child to become a lawyer, a doctor. I am the proof a child can be as successful as a lawyer but not be a lawyer."

Sent to Minnesota to go to church and be a lawyer or a doctor, Marshall Kudi Ngwa got a job at the Galleria and enrolled at

MCTC. That's where he met his friend Cathy, who said, "You have to see a drag show at the 90's."

· · · · · · ·

Kudi seems to look off through his thick-framed Buddy Holly glasses into a rich memory as he recalls that night in 2000. "The curtains parted, and Roxy Marquis, may she rest in peace, entered. The most beautiful woman, glamorous, *glamorous*—gorgeous. My face, if you could have seen it, was the face that saw a ghost. At that moment I felt validated for all the thoughts I had as a child—what I was doing in Cameroon was never valid, never important. The puzzle all came together in one night. *Oh my God, this is it!* Performance, illusion, fantasy—all of this made sense to me, coming together in one art form. That's where the birth of BeBe really happened. And why Minneapolis will always be a very, very special part of me."

He woke up the day after this revelatory night and went to his job helping brides trying on wedding gowns and others shopping for prom dresses at the Jessica McClintock store at the Galleria. Simultaneously, he began learning from the show lounge stars of the 90's, who inspired him to become an international phenomenon. (Of course I ask the obvious question about his clientele at the Galleria, and Kudi says that Edina mothers of the bride at the Galleria are indeed fiercer than Hollywood agents—and good training for anyone heading into showbiz. "I call them my Minnetonka girls, and they have always been some of my biggest supporters. And if you think Minnetonka girls don't understand the importance of illusion? Think again.")

In the early 2000s, drag beauty pageants were an important step for Kudi on the road to building up a reputation, gaining name recognition, and scoring a spot on a drag tour. It just so happened that one of BeBe's backup dancers for a Texas pageant had a sister, Emily Branham, who was a budding filmmaker and who was fascinated by the drag world. Branham was so charmed and intrigued by BeBe at that pageant fifteen years ago, she began filming this character over the years and, in the process, ended up capturing facets of young BeBe well before the *Drag Race* triumph.

Being BeBe, the product of that fifteen years of filming, is touching in a surprisingly Norman Rockwell and the-value-of-family sort of way, showing Kudi with his Cameroonian family and BeBe with her Minnesota and NYC drag family, both worlds supporting and loving one soul. It's a very Minnesota story full of local stars, like Kudi's best friend, Brady, who brilliantly does BeBe's hair and performs himself under the stage name Ana Stasia (on Instagram as @_Anadu_) and Rae Ann Annala of Hopkins, the tape measure–toting old-school seamstress and designer who made a lot of those *Drag Race*–winning outfits. As BeBe tells me: "She makes my costumes a 10; I make them a 20!" (Please know that somewhere in Minneapolis is a warehouse holding the collection of BeBe Zahara Benet gowns, shoes, and wigs—think of it as the Fort Knox of local drag.) You'll also see Kudi's sisters and brother, who also live in Minnesota and with whom Kudi spends a lot of his downtime these days, cooking Cameroonian foods for big Minnetonka family dinners.

The film is largely arranged around Cameroon's anti-gay sentiments and Kudi's counterexample. In it, Kudi mentions that it will be very hard for many Cameroonians to live out loud and be themselves because of anti-homosexual norms, laws, and traditions. But you also see one of Kudi's sisters as she prays over him on the eve of a (brief) move to New York: "Lord, we call upon you. . . . This is a new beginning for him. . . . Fulfill his dreams, amen." I tear up.

After the trauma of the murder of George Floyd, it's been hard at times to remember the side of Minneapolis where an African immigrant working as a bridal consultant at the Galleria has a super-supportive family, Black and white, born and chosen, who will love him and work to help him become one of the biggest drag performers in America—and almost certainly the biggest out of Africa. This film shows a good, real, and little-seen side of our beloved hometown.

Releasing this documentary is only one of the big moves Kudi is making this fall. He's also about to anchor a new creative home in downtown Minneapolis. Roxy's Cabaret is a brand-new venue scheduled to open by Halloween in the former Ichiban space on the southernmost end of Nicollet Mall. The historic Japanese steak house is being transformed. The blue roof will be replaced by two enclosed rooftop lounges, with a third that can be opened when weather permits. The ground floor will be split between the Nicollet Diner (which is moving from a few blocks over and will continue to be open twenty-four hours) and a 125-seat state-of-the-art drag theater. Local drag legend Nina DiAngelo is managing the spot. DiAngelo was a mentor to BeBe and is now another of her besties—so Roxy's will be BeBe's new home.

"Monica [West], BeBe, and me—when we were the Ladies of LaFemme at the [Gay] 90's, it was a big deal. Everyone said it was the best drag show between the coasts," explains DiAngelo, born Jamie Olsen, whom I talk to on the phone while he supervises construction at Roxy's. "When we left [in 2015], it was a big deal. It wasn't an amicable split. We had issues with how we were treated. Look, the 90's is why I am where I am. It's an institution, and we're not going to be in competition with them. We're going to be something else, more Vegas-like, really high production values. When BeBe said we would be her home base, that was it. I knew we would be big, national, tourist destination, all that."

Whether BeBe will appear at Roxy's quarterly or weekly when she's in town, or whether Roxy's will be to BeBe something like the Paisley Park dance club was to Prince, just a place she might pop into whenever she has the time and feels like it, remains to be seen. But the tradition of great entertainers being associated with venues is not uncommon—like Eartha Kitt reliably at the Carlyle or Dizzy Gillespie popping up routinely at the Blue Note. If all of BeBe's friends are doing something fun with a nice dressing room and great lighting right near her house, why wouldn't drag fans make a point of hanging out there just in case?

Speaking of an expanding Minnesota presence, lately Kudi has been thinking he'd like to get married and have two kids. So if you know anyone . . .

"I could film a *Dating Game for BeBe* here in Minnesota. You know that would be a hit!" Kudi tells me, lifting his black wool porkpie hat briefly off his head to make way for a laugh that needs that much room.

As our time runs out, Kudi suggests that the two of us could throw the most fabulous party, and of course I say we must. A black and white ball; a red ball, like he's thrown in LA; a masquerade ball? Everyone invited. We'd celebrate BeBe's twentieth birthday. We'd celebrate the Minneapolis we all want, the one that's so beyond fabulous because everyone is invited.

"After everything we've been through, I just want people to see how beautiful Minneapolis is in so many ways—I want to bring back *the special* of Minneapolis," says Kudi as we leave our interview. When emphasizing "the special," he uses one hand to circle and pluck a bit of air in front of him, as if pulling a bit of magic out of a crystal ball.

"If you see Minneapolis the way I see Minneapolis, then you see something special. It just needs a little BeBe *zhuzh*," he says, using the all-purpose word that means sparkle, vision, and glamorous transformation. "This city allowed me to be me. This is where I was born. Now I am going to do what I can to allow Minneapolis to be the best Minneapolis it can be. Inside, Minneapolis still has its spark, and it can be born again here too."

The Miniature Dogs of Lucy Francis

Mpls.St.Paul Magazine, February 2020

I was born to write this story. I just love eccentric people, and Minnesota does too. We have our famous eccentrics—Prince, Bob Dylan, Jesse Ventura, Maria Bamford, Judy Garland, Thorstein Veblen—and our lesser-known eccentrics, like Lucy Francis, conjurer of miniature whippets. I truly believe Minnesota is the place where people who march to a different drummer find space to be themselves.

In the magazine world, we talk about "intros," "outros," and "dektros." Intro—that's obvious, it's an introduction. An outro is the opposite, and I've had many thoughts in my life about whether an outro is best when it raises new questions or when it ties up the story with a nice, neat bow that has a kissing relationship to the intro. A dektro is when a headline deck—that is, subtitle—has to do a lot of exposition. This piece has one of my career-favorite outros.

Good girl! The internationally renowned master of the two-inch-tall dog would like to give you a treat.

Ever seen five dogs lying flat on the palm of one hand? I have, on the Instagram of local artist Lucy Francis.

Francis holds open her hand, and on the plane of her palm rest five perfectly formed whippet hounds. Snouts tucked and snouts lifted, tails curled and tails curious—five whippets straight from some Italian count's villa, where they were resting on their pillows. Then, suddenly, an alien ray gun shrank them small enough to carry through the world in a coat pocket! Five whippets, one hand.

I immediately found artist Lucy Francis's website. I coldly

calculated the artist's tab for five such dogs ($300 a head, minimum) and calculated that this handful of whippets cost as much as my first car. Ever started driving one chill but bright winter morning to see an artist about tiny dogs? I have, to Hastings, to visit Lucy Francis, likely the world's foremost creator of miniature, mostly bespoke, handmade, lifelike dogs.

Lucy Francis lives on a hill, in a low house with board-and-batten siding, near the Vermillion and Mississippi Rivers. When I arrive, I stir up quite a ruckus, led by Fred, a nine-pound rescue with the barky charm of a toy fox terrier, with his sidekick Bob, a cairn terrier given to fluffy commotions, following suit. The slight but firm Lucy Francis scoops her tiny guardians back from the thigh-high wire barrier that prevents them from roving. Taken in whole, the situation feels like a nursery rhyme: *There was a little woman who lived upon a hill, with two tiny dogs and—*

How wrong I was. Lucy Francis lives with at least twenty tiny dogs, and they're much tinier than a nursery rhyme can well convey. They're plum-sized dogs, gumball-sized dogs, stick-of-butter-sized dogs. The first thing she does is show me the Plexiglas case where she houses her back catalog. There's Eddie, the dog from *Frasier*, smaller than half a cork and posed on his famed armchair. There's a collie with flicked-out ears and a curiously tilted snout— the telltale expression of a dog that hears a beloved person in the distance, perhaps approaching the driveway.

An astonishing little puff of a two-inch dog sparkles at us from a little vignette carpeted with moss. "Mabel," says Francis, seeing some unfinished flaw I cannot. "Alaskan Eskimo dog. She's getting there."

I mention how grateful I am to be let into Francis's workshop, peering into a two-foot-long stage set with a ten-inch couch. There, two other dogs in progress stand, awaiting their final photo shoot.

"Oh, this isn't my workshop," Francis corrects me. "This is just where I keep things and photograph things." She stoops down to open a metal chest. "I like to work out there"—she gestures toward the open-plan living room and kitchen—"with the TV and the coffee—and the dogs!"

With that, Francis lifts from the chest a ten-inch-high stack of specialty magazines: *Fido Friendly*, *Dollhouse Miniatures*, *FDQ* (that's *Fashion Doll Quarterly*, a big glossy title not unlike *Women's Wear Daily*, but featuring models who can't age), Spain's *Miniaturas*, the UK's *Mini-ologie*, *Teddy Bear Times & Friends*, and many more. All feature spreads devoted to Francis's work, which also appears in the Kentucky Gateway Museum Center. Pieces sell through the Spielzeug Welten Museum Basel, Europe's premier toy museum, in Basel, Switzerland.

"Oh yeah, they put my youngest through college," says Francis of the Spielzeug Welten. (Get ahead of the Swiss: LucyFrancis Miniatures.com.) Francis also served as the official miniaturist of the Rin Tin Tin museum in Crockett, Texas, before it closed.

Francis flips through her pictures of famous people with their miniature dogs. Some of the celebrities who own Francis's dogs, she says, include Shirley MacLaine, Andrew W.K., John Prine, Martha Stewart, and a member of the royal family in Qatar, whom Francis says she's not at liberty to name. (It is likely Ahmed Al Thani, a legend for his big spending at the world's premier miniatures show, the Kensington Dollshouse Festival.)

To date, Francis has sent teeny-tiny figurines to seventeen countries, including much of Europe, South Africa, and Japan. "My dogs have been lots of places I'll never go!" she says.

As I flip through the glossy spreads, I become dissatisfied, because photography really doesn't do justice to these miniature canines. Shot in close-up, they look merely to be photographs of dogs; pictured with a human, they lose their astonishing detail and seem mere figurines. The only way to really appreciate the life and energy in these sculptures is to get up close and turn them around and around in your hands. The muscles, the fur, the ears, the *life*—they look ready to run, shake hands, roll over!

While Francis makes me a cup of tea, she recounts how she learned to fabricate these models. The basic craft seems straightforward. She studies a photograph of a real dog and, when appropriate, consults breed pictures.

Next, she crafts a wire armature—the equivalent of a skeleton. This, Francis says, is the key moment: The success of the model relies on the ratios of snout to skull, leg to body, body to head. If she's making a reclining dog, she will still start with a standing-up armature, only bending it once she's many steps along in the process.

She wraps this wire blank in successive layers of natural fibers (alpaca yarn is a favorite). Using these fibers, Francis builds up the equivalent of muscle, fat, and sinew. To this base of wire and fiber, she adds layers and layers of additional fibers. Some of these may be commercial products; others are actual dog fur, clipped by owners who have commissioned pet look-alikes or memorial pieces.

Inventing and getting a hang of this process, Francis says, took eight years.

Francis made her first dog as a present topper for a fellow dog person. At that point, she was a stay-at-home mom with four kids, living in Welch, a rural town southeast of St. Paul. In 2001 Francis turned the creation of tiny dogs into a public-facing business.

Francis shows me certain markers of her progress. Dog #7 had fur that looked too large for its body. Dog #16 didn't look *real*—a mere doll. Later dogs appear so perfectly muscled and furred, so curious in their expressions and alive in their eyes, that you wonder if they go places when your head is turned.

Francis leads me on a tour of her tiny work space. Pins serve as her primary tools, along with tweezers. She uses special clamping tweezers to get muscle definition in her tiny dogs' legs.

"Eight years is as long as it takes to get through medical school," I observe.

"You're not the first to say that about medical school." She nods. Some dogs, she adds, are reasonably quick work, taking just a few weeks. Other dogs demand months. "But I'm not at it night and day," Francis says. "I live my life."

. . . .

Francis's life, in thumbnail, is this: Born in 1953 in Lilydale, she grew up with a mother who worked as a seamstress and a father who worked as a welder at American Hoist and Derrick. For fun, he bred German shorthaired pointers.

Francis remembers caring about nothing but dogs as a little kid: "As soon as I learned to talk, I begged for a dog. And everything after has just been a crazy dog thing—I just love dogs." Francis remembers getting a Barbie doll as a kid, along with Barbie's poodle, and thinking, "This is great and all, but it could be better."

Nearly twenty-five years on, Francis says, her biggest projects tend to be memorial pieces for pets nearing their final dog years. Francis fills her days corresponding with pre-grieving dog lovers. They send digital photos, tufts of fur, and memories.

"They want to connect with someone who cares about their dog," says Francis—not just someone collecting a check. "That's what I like about it. I'd always rather do something meaningful. A lot of my dogs end up on urns."

I notice a shoebox filled with individually labeled bags of dog hair. "Merlin, middle of back & sides," read one. Or: "Maggie, butt & feathering."

Francis says she stopped doing the big juried miniatures show in Chicago, named after its founder, Tom Bishop, because she'd rather devote herself to commission work. Though that has its pitfalls too. "One time I made a Weimaraner for this lady in Germany, and that's a hard dog to make. She got it; she loved it. Well, a couple weeks later, she wrote me. His brother"—that is, the deceased dog's littermate—"ate him." The client's next request? "Can you make another one?"

Telling the story, Francis lowers her hazel eyes, in the way of someone talking about the common tragedies we all must endure. "This is not the first time that happened. Dogs!"

As Francis leads me through her work, I can't help but notice that she really sparks to life when she's talking about dogs. The particulars of grooming cairn terriers. Or what Mabel, the Alaskan white puff of a dog she's working on now, is *really, really* like. And there's always the mischief of Bob and Fred underfoot.

"You seem to think of yourself more as a dog person than a fine artist?" I ask.

"Oh, absolutely," she says, nodding her head so her high ponytail whips in echoing emphasis. "Just dog crazy. I remember my mom saying, when I was a kid, 'Are you ever going to talk about anything except dogs?'" Francis mimics her response, as a teen with a rolled-eye expression. "Well, *yeah*—but what else is there?"

As the years progressed, Francis's mom never came to terms with her daughter's growing renown. "She would say, 'Are you still making those little dogs?' I'm like, *Mom. I was on TV for them, twice.*"

Francis doesn't even like people to think of her little dogs as a craft. Twenty years ago, TV producers invited Francis to appear on Martha Stewart's show. Their idea: Stewart would hand Francis an eye or something, let her work for a moment, and then they'd show the finished craft to the camera. Francis considered this proposal preposterous: to mislead viewers about how long her work takes. And the finishing touches are absolutely minute—hardly camera friendly. Francis told Martha Stewart no.

If these dogs are not fine art and not really a craft, what are they?

"A dog thing," Francis says firmly.

I gently suggest that the Smithsonian is chock-full of miniatures, particularly miniatures of loved ones who've passed on, and that Francis is carrying on a noble artistic tradition. Francis knows all this. She works with the TV on, mainly, and arts documentaries may be her favorite background noise.

Suddenly, an interruption. *Squirrel!* As the critter approaches the recycling bin out the window, Bob and Fred storm across the kitchen. It's their lunchtime, Francis suggests, which renders them particularly excitable.

I make my goodbyes, and walking outside, I notice big eyes in the windows of the little house. Bob and Fred are tracking my departure.

My mind turns back to that half-imagined nursery rhyme:
There was a little woman, on a little hill,
making little dogs, by her windowsill.
Bark a happy bark;
she's making more dogs still!

Con Artistry

Mpls.St.Paul Magazine, March 2014

In college I went to Amsterdam for a semester abroad and then extended my time there by getting an informal internship with the Rembrandt Research Project. I lived in the top-floor quasi attic of the family home of Ernst van de Wetering, and I trailed him while he authenticated, or de-authenticated, the wide world of real and fake Rembrandts. I've been fascinated by fake art ever since—Is it fake? It's still art, right? Imagine my delight when I found the Fort Knox of so-called fake art right here in my own backyard.

The real story of how the world's most notorious art collection wound up in Minnesota.

In late 1976 Mark Forgy returned to Minnesota with all the earthly possessions of Elmyr de Hory, the greatest art forger of the twentieth century. Now a museum's-worth of fakes resides in his modest home near New Prague. But is it a time bomb poised to destroy the twentieth-century art market, or treasure?

Early in 1976, Mark Forgy was a gorgeous, tawny, blue-eyed hippie from Hopkins, Minnesota, sitting in the back seat of a car racing through the distant roads of Ibiza, cradling the frail and dying body of Elmyr de Hory—the greatest art forger of the twentieth century.

De Hory had come to international attention as a master draftsman who could manufacture his own Modiglianis, Matisses, Picassos (and more) at will; he had been exposed as the single hand behind the hundred-million-dollar art-fraud perpetrated against Algur Hurtle Meadows, a Dallas oil baron who had thought he was swindling desperate dealers out of masterpieces torn, possibly illegally, from war-wracked Europe. He wasn't. When the collection for which Meadows had so ruthlessly bargained was appraised, experts agreed that the swindler had been swindled. That's how the world learned of de Hory, Hungarian aristocrat and master forger.

The master forger part was true, as was the Hungarian part. Aristocrat, not so much. A gay Jew born in Hungary in 1906, de Hory had trained with the renowned French painter Fernand Léger and came up in the same School of Paris art scene that gave birth to Picasso, Modigliani, and Matisse. But he was born a generation behind those greats and spent what would have been the critical years of his career evading Nazis. War-ravaged Europe was the set on which he designed his signature con: He pretended to be an aristocrat down on his luck and forced to part with his precious art. He sold drawings, mainly "Picassos," which he'd toss off three at a time in the mornings. (I spoke to a handful of curators and critics who said there are without question dozens, or hundreds, if not *thousands* of de Horys living cherished lives as Picassos, so many that ever finding them would be impossible—because they would be compared to other Picassos that were de Horys.)

Eventually de Hory moved from drawings to the big money of oil paintings, mainly Modiglianis and Matisses but also paintings in the style of Raoul Dufy, André Derain, Maurice de Vlaminck, and Kees van Dongen, among others. He was good. Van Dongen himself authenticated one of de Hory's van Dongen pieces, telling the dealer that he remembered the model well and that he and the model had often left off painting for lovemaking. De Hory spent the better part of the 1950s and 1960s enlarging the bodies of work of the world's most collectible artists. If you do it well enough, he found, and sell at a discount, whoever buys will have as much invested in defending the work's "realness" as you ever did, and so the con grows out like ripples from a stone, turning others into con men for your cause.

But during that 1976 car ride with Mark Forgy, de Hory was dying from a self-inflicted cocktail of cognac and pills. And in the back of that car, Forgy heard the death rattle of the seventy-year-old he had come to love like a father.

Sitting in an Uptown café thirty-odd years later, Forgy comes to tears remembering the awful end. It was the only time he ever saw de Hory unshaven. When they finally reached the hospital, the nuns who ran it pronounced de Hory dead, leaving Forgy with three problems: how to get a stateless suicide buried on a small, Catholic island, what to do with the massive collection of de Hory paintings he had just inherited as sole heir, and what to do with the rest of his life.

Forgy and de Hory's friends managed to piggyback de Hory's burial on that of a recently deceased good Catholic, leaving de Hory to enter the cemetery the same way he entered so many museums: under someone else's good name. Forgy then waited around while he was cleared of murder charges by all the suicide letters Elmyr (pronounced *el-meer*) had sent out, and used the time to deploy the carpentry skills he had learned in Minnesota to fashion shipping containers for everything de Hory had left behind, including nearly three hundred drawings and paintings. He sent them to his parents' house in Hopkins and returned home with de Hory's dog, Moody. Back in Hopkins, he grieved, and he built a shed for the containers.

That's how the greatest collection of forged art came to reside in Minnesota. It has been here through Twins World Series victories, Halloween blizzards, and the entire life of the Metrodome. And it is still here, as it ever was, poised to make Forgy very rich— or lay waste to the market for twentieth-century art.

Southwest of the Twin Cities, the Minnesota River twists and ambles through green and rolling hills. It is fertile land, legendarily fertile. The Jolly Green Giant marketing campaign was born here, in the town of Le Sueur, and the green-ness and fertile-ness is mass merchandised on all Green Giant packaging. In the dips between many of those legendarily green hills are lakes. Mark Forgy lives on one of those lakes with his wife, Alice Doll.

Forgy and Doll were married ten years ago, discovering one another in a late-life romance that has them grabbing for each other like teenagers. From the street, the couple's red wooden house looks like any generic Minnesota postwar cabin, small and modest with a carport and a red-painted cardinal bird feeder. From the street, you'd think this little house on a lake holds nothing more valuable than wood grain TV trays and Fleet Farm floor mats. But open the door. Open the door and it's like stepping through a wormhole into the Louvre.

The walls are tiled with masterpieces. Modigliani, Modigliani, Modigliani. Cézanne, Cézanne, Cézanne. If you know art, it gives you vertigo. Matisse, Matisse, Matisse. Derain. Dufy. Of course all the art is by Elmyr de Hory, who, once he was found out in 1966, became a full-fledged counterculture hero living the high life in Ibiza with Forgy at his side.

He threw parties. His good friend Ursula Andress, the Bond girl, attended most of them. He dined with Douglas Fairbanks Jr. and Marlene Dietrich. He had tea with Sir Noël Coward. Kirk Douglas wrote in his autobiography that he still has two de Horys—a "van Gogh" and a "Monet"—and adores them. Forgy recalls scrambling with de Hory down steep cliffs to swim in the Mediterranean with Brigitte Bardot during one particular after-party.

Like so many others, filmmaker Orson Welles was drawn to the story of de Hory. So drawn that he decided to make a documentary called *F for Fake*. It wasn't the only movie made about the witty, super-talented queen who'd been shafted by the twentieth century and responded by sticking it to oil billionaires and shady, snobby art gallery types. De Hory relished the attention. "I don't feel bad for Modigliani; I feel good for me," he shrugged to the cameras.

All that was a far distance from the Hopkins of Forgy's childhood. His father was a tool and die maker who worked for Honeywell. His mother was an interior decorator for Sears. Forgy grew up watching the Vietnam War with an ever-increasing sense of dread. Forgy's father had fought in World War II in New Guinea and believed when your country called, you went. His youngest son had different ideas.

"In 1967, 1968, I was a full-fledged member of the hippie generation," Forgy says. "It was a different world. You could go to Seven Corners and there was someone every few feet saying: hash, hash, acid, acid, whatever you want. It all seemed like a fine idea to me. I had pictures of Che Guevara and Ho Chi Minh on my wall. We are not just products of our mother and father. We are products of our times, and my times were say yes to drugs and no to war."

Forgy hadn't been much of a student, and in 1968, with the assassinations of Martin Luther King Jr. and Robert F. Kennedy, something in Forgy gelled. He started saving the money he earned at a night janitor's job at Honeywell. "By 1969 I had made up my mind. I was going to Europe," he says. "We had sleeping bags. Everywhere you went you were invited into people's homes. You'd just be standing at a street crossing in Denmark and a woman would look at you and say, 'Do you need a place to spend the night?'"

Forgy befriended a young British man also named Mark who was also backpacking around Europe, and they ended up on a ferry to Ibiza, the island in the Spanish Mediterranean. "Mark and I were weaving in and out of the portside bars when I ran into Elmyr," Forgy says. De Hory, who was in his sixties, offered Forgy his guest room, as he had offered it to many young men before.

"Elmyr could cruise through the cafes and bars on a spring or summer evening, sit down with many friends, and meet whomever he liked," author Clifford Irving writes in *Fake!*, his biography of de Hory. "Unfortunately the relationships that developed out of these encounters were rarely satisfactory. For one thing, although de Hory liked young men who were, as he put it, 'undemanding,' he himself made more demands than were to most people's liking, and in his house he tended to treat his companions—unless they bore a title before their name or had money—more as servants than as guests. For another, his taste often ran to types who in any other kind of community would have been labeled as juvenile delinquents, and for this he paid the price. He was even more of a natural victim in his personal life than in his profession."

The strategy of guest rooms for travelers never worked for de Hory until the boy from Hopkins came along. Forgy says he made it clear he wasn't interested in a romantic relationship, and de Hory was willing to settle for companionship and help. He hired Forgy to be his personal assistant, to run to the bodegas for champagne, to be there for every meal, to be decorative and charming and go with him to the doctor or the courthouse as required.

In film footage of de Hory from the early 1970s, Forgy is omnipresent—floppy-haired, fine-boned, lanky, ice-blue-eyed, like a waif Shaun Cassidy come to life in tawny porcelain. In one scene of *F for Fake*, de Hory stands with a bouquet of pink and white flowers and bends to kiss Forgy. A few seconds later, Forgy, looking perhaps stoned or perhaps just camera-frozen, explains how he got to Ibiza: "Several months ago I read an article about Elmyr de Hory and I was so impressed that I decided to come from Minnesota to Ibiza in the hope of meeting Elmyr, and now I've become his bodyguard."

That was a lie.

"A complete fabrication," Forgy says. "He gave me money when I needed it, and I was thrust into this world beyond the looking glass I never would have been able to discover without him, so I stayed. I don't know why I ever said it. Except that Welles said, 'This guy who keeps hanging around, we need him to say something. This is what I want you to say.' If Oscar Welles tells you to say something, you say it." De Hory did what he could to be the Henry Higgins to Forgy's Eliza Doolittle. De Hory enrolled Forgy in French classes, taught him European table manners, and even scoured the island for a proper American Christmas turkey so the young American could have a proper American Christmas. (The turkey didn't fit in their oven, remembers Forgy.)

"My family was completely disengaged," Forgy says. "I remember my mother did call once, and Elmyr picked up the phone and scolded her for not taking more of an interest in me. My dad was a workaholic and probably an alcoholic. He was never comfortable with the parenting role, so I fell into that role with Elmyr, who was everything a father should be: caring, nurturing, interested in educating me. We were very much alike. We were both trusting people, too trusting. I think in his whole life I was the one person he could always count on."

When de Hory had kidney stones, Forgy flew with him to Barcelona and stayed at his side. "Elmyr hated being alone," Forgy says. "His need for constant companionship was the portal which allowed me into his life." When de Hory faced extradition to France as part of a fraud trial involving his former art dealers, Forgy sat beside him in court hearing after court hearing. "Everything he ever said, I swallowed hook, line, and sinker," Forgy says. Except maybe the part when de Hory said he didn't know the forgeries were sold as real.

Fraud in painting is actually difficult to prove. It is not illegal to paint in the style of Picasso or Rembrandt or Raphael. It is not illegal to sculpt a *David* in the style of Michelangelo. In fact, imitating great art is a key way of learning art technique. Michelangelo himself is said to have carved a cupid in the style of the ancient Romans and to have buried it to age it before presenting it to Lorenzo de' Medici as proof that, *Hell yeah, I can sculpt!* Whether by Michelangelo or de Hory or you yourself, making work in the style of someone else is never illegal. What is illegal is to sell art as something it's not. That's fraud. (A curious case has been unspooling in America for several decades, in which a mentally ill but very gifted copyist named Mark Landis creates paintings and tries to donate them to museums as historical masterpieces, but because he never tries to get money, he has never gone to jail.)

De Hory committed fraud, but he started small. The big fraud came when another young man he had let live with him, Fernand Legros, began to act as his dealer. Legros took a younger lover, Réal Lessard, and the two abused de Hory, giving him $2,000 and $5,000 checks for the paintings they were selling for hundreds of thousands of dollars, all the while threatening to get de Hory imprisoned on charges of homosexuality or convicted of fraud if he didn't make more pictures. Legros was eventually arrested, and part of what made de Hory sympathetic to the international art world was his role as the gifted, exploited victim to Legros. De Hory didn't even own the house he lived in on Ibiza; Legros did.

After the arrest, de Hory and Forgy were thrown out of the house, and the two moved to a villa in the countryside without a phone. Forgy headed out one morning to find a phone, to discover whether there was any news about the latest extradition hearing. "I was told he would be extradited. I was in shock. I came back and I told him. At that point I did know he was going to take the overdose." De Hory, then seventy, went to his room to commit suicide with cognac and sleeping pills, and Forgy suddenly found himself helpless. "Do I intercede?" he asks, years later. "I knew what his wishes were. He did not want to go to France to prison. That was his greatest fear. And it was only a matter of hours until the Spanish police came to drag him off in chains."

De Hory believed that his longtime abuser Legros had a plan to have him killed when he got to a French jail, at which point Legros would blame de Hory for the fraud and walk away. He couldn't face that, and he had been making plans to avoid such a fate. In retrospect, says Forgy, he should have realized that de Hory had planned to commit suicide. "We had gone to a notary to make me the sole heir."

After Forgy told him the news, de Hory went to his room to ingest cognac and pills. Forgy felt helpless. "I knew what his wishes were. He couldn't tolerate the total humiliation. He said that again and again. He was older and wiser. I didn't know what to do."

Forgy drove to a friend's house. The friend convinced him that they must save de Hory. They rushed back. "He was lying in his bed. He was on his stomach. I went up to him. I shook him a little. I said, 'Elmyr, Elmyr.' He looked at me. His eyes were completely vacant. I took him to the car. I cradled him in my arms. I heard the death rattle. When we got to the clinic, a nun said she was sorry— it was too late. I spent time with him. A curtain came down on my life that I couldn't lift for thirty years."

Forgy's hair is silver now, but he is still recognizable as the same beautiful boy on-screen in the movies about the great forger. "I went as a twenty-year-old who was going to have adventures on the beach. I came back as a shell-shocked twenty-seven-year-old with Elmyr's dog and life's work. I think my father welcomed the dog more than me," laughs Forgy, ruefully. "Even today I don't know if I have ever fully recovered."

What are forged paintings or drawings? Are they merely evidence of a crime, like forged checks? Or are they something more? "People like the story of the rogue who thumbs his nose at the art world and gets away with it," says Colette Loll, founder and director of Art Fraud Insights, a company that helps detect fraudulent paintings. "But what does it do economically and legally to the heirs of the estate?"

If there are only five hundred paintings by Modigliani, who

died at thirty-five, and de Hory adds fifty, that drives the supply up and the price down. Ditto if there are five hundred excellent paintings by Modigliani but de Hory adds fifty trite ones that diminish Modigliani's reputation.

"One mission of museums is to display original art to the public," Loll says. "When you show something as authentic which isn't authentic, it is a violation of that trust." If de Hory inserted a thousand illegitimate works of art into the art market, as he was thought to have done, how many artists, heirs, and public institutions has he damaged? "Hundreds of years ago it was commonly assumed that students in workshops would copy the master's work, and if it was good enough the master would sign it," Loll says. "Nowadays authenticity means something different. Is there a palpable link to the moment and person and time? I need to be able to create a line, and that connection equals value. If I can't prove that Warhol had a hand in making a silkscreen, is it authentic?"

That's a good question, especially because artists' work can now be reproduced without them. The silkscreens Andy Warhol used to make silkscreen prints, the molds used to cast Rodin sculptures, and the negatives used to make Ansel Adams photographs are all still in use. What's the difference between a de Hory Matisse from the 1960s and a brand-new, legally authentic Rodin issued by Rodin's estate a hundred years after Rodin's death?

"Well, what's the difference between a Prada purse and a knock-off?" Loll counters. "I have an Elmyr in my kitchen. It brings me joy. It's a beautiful picture. But I know what it is. If I bought it as something else and found out it wasn't, I might feel differently. There's something called neuroaesthetics. What people believe changes their experience of an object. If you are told something is a great work by a real master, you enjoy it. If you're then told it's actually a fake, then you don't like it anymore. Elmyr was very sweet to Mark Forgy. But to others, he was a con man. He swindled them out of millions of dollars. Even today plenty of people buy Elmyr Modiglianis planning to pass them off as Modiglianis. It's ongoing fraud."

That's why, in France, a perfectly beautiful Chagall forgery is about to be burned. The British businessman who bought it in

1992 for 100,000 pounds says he is fond of it and would like to hang it on his wall. But the committee that authenticates Chagalls, headed by two of Chagall's granddaughters, has decided it's a fake and must be destroyed. If Mark Forgy's art collection of Elmyr de Horys was currently in France there's every likelihood they would be burned in front of a magistrate, because forgeries have the possibility of destroying art markets, and in this case they have the possibility of destroying dozens of art markets.

Art critic Blake Gopnik has no problem with forgeries. "What I argue is that they're not by the forger at all; they're by the artist," says Gopnik, who writes for the *Daily Beast*. "The crucial thing about them is not the manual skill of making the art—that's a very small part of any artwork. It's the idea—the idea and the way of moving your hand. Artists make discoveries. They discover an idea plus a technique. Forgers are just people who have this weird ability to channel the ideas of other people through their manual skill. In Rembrandt's day only he could figure out how to move his hand and use paint to convey his ideas, but once he discovered what he discovered, no matter how profound, others could create those Rembrandtian objects. Today everyone knows how gravity works and are free to use that themselves. You're not damaging Isaac Newton when you use his idea of gravity."

Similarly, you're not damaging Matisse if you use the color and line discoveries of Matisse. "Rembrandt produced works the way Armani produces works. It is about training up a bunch of people who can make Rembrandtian objects," Gopnik says. "A good forger doesn't deserve much more thought than a good employee of Armani. And it's not as if people don't love copies. We live in the midst of millions of perfect copies. They're called posters. The market, the art market, is what hates forgeries."

The art market hates forgeries because they interrupt the idea of what the market wants art to be: a precious object that goes up in value. But there's another way to value art, and that's in the marketplace of ideas. To the extent that Mark Forgy's house of de Horys on the lake gets us to consider the discoveries Matisse made, argues Gopnik, a de Hory is as valuable as a Matisse. And

Forgy's house on a Minnesota lake isn't a fake Louvre; it's its own sort of Louvre.

The scandal of de Hory has always resided in the basic assumption that a Modigliani painted by Modigliani is inherently better and more valuable than a fake. But what if that's not true? In the book *Forged: Why Fakes Are the Great Art of Our Age*, Jonathon Keats points out that over thousands of years, art has done many things: inspired devotion to the baby Jesus, connected the present to the ideals of classical myths, and showed new and valuable ways of seeing the world. At the same time, forgers have always been there, forging whatever at the moment is most popular.

De Hory made larger than life most of the biggest concerns of the twentieth century: identity, originality, authenticity, identity politics, and man in the face of history. And he did it in a way that causes tension, anxiety, and self-examination in the art market and resists commodification to this day. "Think of all of those paintings as props in this larger act of deception," Keats says. "It is work which is becoming more problematic years after his death. There's something very deep with de Hory at the level of how we appreciate art, how we engage with art, how something becomes authentic, and de Hory brings these issues to the very nature of truth, and the more you consider it the more it seems to expand out to everything we do. Straight artists have a way of entering museums and becoming too safe and challenging nobody. With a forger's art nobody is in control, not even the forger, and when work is not even in the artist's control that has the potential to become interesting. And this hoard that Forgy has is important. It will end up somewhere. It may be dispersed, it may end up in a museum collection, it may end up in ten museum collections, but wherever it goes it will remain something that has to be contended with."

Contended with the way Marcel Duchamp's purchased and signed urinal, titled *Fountain*, had to be contended with; the way Andy Warhol's supermarket-bought, gallery-displayed Brillo boxes had to be contended with; the way Robert Rauschenberg's act of erasing a Willem de Kooning had to be contended with; the way Sherrie Levine's photograph of one of Walker Evans's photographs had to be contended with. Today originality, the artist's hand, and appropriation are core concepts, ones that Forgy and de Hory enlarge.

"Forgery and appropriation are different," says Erik Doeringer, an emerging artist whose work deals with appropriation. "Forgery attempts to pass itself off as something it's not, and appropriation asks questions about art. But forgers end up asking questions appropriation can't, such as: How much are they actually faking being a forger? What is real and what is boasting? Some forgers who have been caught say, 'My work is in tons of museums.' You don't know how much truth there is to that and how much they're exaggerating to make themselves look more masterful."

Marcel Duchamp and Andy Warhol questioned their own art. Sherrie Levine dragged in Walker Evans. De Hory drags in dozens of towering artists, plus every institution and private collector that has their work. On top of that, says Doeringer, there's something very contemporary about de Hory. When we look at an artist like Cindy Sherman who creates characters, dresses as them, and photographs herself, we see someone playing with identity; de Hory, whose birth name was probably Hoffman, fully invented an identity and moved in.

"One reason why stories about forgery are popular with the general public," Doeringer says, "is that it ties in with this perception that the art world is bogus, or that anyone can make these things, that experts are fools, that a little guy can go against a rich robber baron and win. There's also this element of an endless hoax, which seems contemporary."

Bad-boy British artist Damien Hirst, thought to be the richest contemporary artist of our day, suffers frequent accusations of plagiarism. He's accused of not being, for instance, the first person to present an embalmed crucified sheep as art. Plagiarism, of course, is the mirror image of forgery: In forgery, you present your work as someone else's; in plagiarism, you present someone else's work as yours. In the age of the internet, in which any two or three words in a Google search are likely to reveal that someone, somewhere, has already crucified a sheep, why continue to live in thrall to 1950s ideas of forgery and plagiarism?

"The MIA did a show on fakes maybe thirty years ago, and it was fascinating," says Eike Schmidt, a curator at the Minneapolis Institute of Art. "There was one piece that was supposed to be an Aztec sculpture. It was very old Hollywood really, but if it had been authentic someone could have gone to jail because it would have been illegally removed from Mexico. At that point, perhaps you're relieved to find you have a fake. And of course there have been cases of art that was thought to be fake which was destroyed, and then someone realized no, it was real all along. Oops."

Schmidt says he's not comfortable with the fashion for burning fake art. "You can learn so much about art, so much about the human mind, so much about humanity by considering a forgery," he says. "There's the issue of imitation, the issue of intention—you really would have to put someone on the psychiatrist's couch to know if their ultimate intention was financial gain, showing you're better than others, bucking the system, making art, or what."

The Italian baroque painter Artemisia Gentileschi, born in 1593, was considered one of the greatest artists of her time, but after her death she wasn't fashionable and her works were typically assigned to other artists and often given new signatures to fetch higher prices; she disappeared. When she came back into fashion in the twentieth century, art historians made careers of reassembling her body of work.

There are hundreds of valuable artists about whom almost nothing is known—the Master of Frankfurt, for instance, is one of the most important painters of the northern Renaissance. The Master of the Housebook was the most important German engraver before Dürer. By consensus their names were not important at the time, so we don't know them. What is valuable in art is an act of consensus, says Elizabeth Armstrong, curator of contemporary art at the MIA. Consensus between the art market, the lawyers, and the public. "The vast majority of art in the world is authentic but not at all valuable. So no one is forging it. Value, monetary value, is only and always will be a function of what the market will bear. The market is people, so you can never tell what the market will do."

If the de Horys are not worth anything today, who knows what the world will make of them in four hundred years. De Hory could be the next Artemisia Gentileschi. Or the world could go in a different direction and decide that all early twentieth-century paintings are more or less a similar class of objects, in the same way that we think of medieval French tapestries. Maybe a de Hory will by consensus become interchangeable with a Matisse. Or maybe it won't.

Mark Forgy may be sitting in a museum of treasure, trash, crime, memories, or objects that estate sale–goers will buy, take home, and bring to *Antiques Roadshow* for the next five hundred years, giving headaches to Modigliani, Dufy, and Matisse scholars for the next thousand. No one knows. Without the consensus of society to give them a value, the paintings throb with all the anxiety, uncertainty, beauty, and mystery with which de Hory imbued them, and they make Forgy's house feel like a butterfly cage, alive and bright and unnerving.

Whatever they are, Forgy would like to sell a few of them to fund new adventures in travel with his wife. But as the owner of the greatest collection of real de Horys, Forgy has a new problem: fake de Horys. One of Legros and de Hory's scams, back in the day, was to make a painting, photograph it, have the photograph printed on glossy paper, and then take a glossy color plate out of an art book on, say, Matisse and replace it with de Hory's own new color plate for instant provenance. In the 1990s a man named Ken Talbot republished Clifford Irving's book *Fake!* with dozens of new color plates of brand-new de Horys, using the old dealer's ruse against him at industrial scale. So now Forgy spends his days patrolling the internet to warn people of the fake fakes.

"I was never Elmyr's bodyguard," sighs Forgy, tilting his head in the characteristic way that moves his floppy hair away from his beautiful eyes. "But now you could say I'm his body-of-work guard." The irony of the great faker being faked is not lost on Forgy, nor is the fact that somewhere, probably in China, there's a painter who is likely paraphrasing de Hory's own words. He or she likely doesn't feel bad for de Hory; he or she feels good for himself or herself.

Forgy feels what he always felt: bad for de Hory, mystified by de Hory, but above all grateful for de Hory, grateful for the sensitive genius who bucked the system till it bucked him. At home, Forgy makes coffee and watches the birds flit past the windows of his private Fort Knox of fakes, for which he traded his innocence. They are worth exactly as much as they were when he fled Minnesota in 1969, which is precisely nothing. Or a whole hell of a lot.

Primeval Connection

. . . .

Mpls.St.Paul Magazine, January 2022

I was an art history major at Carleton College, to my great surprise. (I went in expecting English, but found the English classes I encountered to be too much about theory.) Art history is also where I got my first-ever paper returned to me to do over. Professor Alison Kettering wrote something like: "You told me what you *think*, not what you *see*." Then she stood in the slide room as I verbally groped along in my analysis of a slide of a painting of Gabriel, the angel who told Mary she was carrying the son of God, in sunbeam/Godbeam–lit Renaissance glory. "No, that's not what you see; it's what you think," she said. Again and again. Finally I blurted out something like: "I see lighter yellow and darker yellow and it creates the impression of light." Today, I credit my entire food and wine criticism career to that moment. I always ask myself: *What do you see, what do you hear, what do you taste, how does it make you feel, how does all of that change over time?* Ask yourself these questions and bring back an enlightening answer to put inside a piece of nonfiction, and you've unlocked the secrets of all art—and food—criticism. What do you see? When I wrote about artist Kristen Lowe, I saw so much.

Kristen Lowe's new show of recent work at the Hillstrom Museum in St. Peter only further affirms she is one of the most important working artists in Minnesota. So how come she's not a household name?

Good luck to you if you want to draw a bald eagle. Not just because of the ordinary reasons—the difficulty in capturing the jet and ivory feathers, the glinting eye—but more because of how many banal patriotic eagle renderings surround us. Bald eagles are in your wallet; they're jangling in your coat pockets on your quarters that you roll unthinkingly into soda machines; they're gilded on state capitols; they're on postage stamps and truck flaps. This omnipresence renders them all but unseeable, like a single raindrop in rain—and it's likely why the first time I saw a Kristen Lowe eagle, I felt like I had the breath knocked right out of my chest.

The work is called *E Pluribus Unum*. An eagle—wing feathers and tail feathers all splayed in descent, like fingers spread wide, like a landing parachute—caught in the moment it settles into its nest of sticks and litter and night-black enormity. This gargantuan nest is both bigger than you can see up close and more detailed than you can take in at a distance, just like a real one, rendered in minute detail of a thousand bits of grass and stick. Above it, the eagle's face is intent upon the interior of the nest, absorbed in something only it can see. Babies? A delicious carcass? Regal, villainous, wild—that's a real eagle, I thought at once. It is all the things a real thing is: vulnerable; deadly; above all, complex. To emphasize the real of the eagle versus the symbolic omnipresence of eagles, Lowe has run a horizon line of antique postage stamps through the nest. Bright and dull simultaneously, as old stamps always are, they contrast with the ultra-black of Lowe's charcoal work. The flat and rah-rah stamps are small against this living ferocity. It's a work that asks urgent questions, such as, *This is our real country, isn't it? Fierce and vulnerable and inextricable from everything we've collected?*

For me, another question urgently followed: Who made this masterpiece?

Kristen Lowe. The creator of other alive-seeming charcoal works, some conveying deep unease through vulnerable sheep in cathedral-like shearing halls, others bursting with joyful busy foxes darting through foliage-rich river bottoms or shrieking ospreys crashing into spray or clashing, battling bucks. Each charcoal drawing is as full of passion and action as a still from a climactic cinematic scene.

How is it that I, a reasonably aware city type, don't know Kristen Lowe's name already? Her work is as distinctive, as moving, as recognizable as a Warhol or a Koons. So why don't all Minnesotans know her name? I dug in.

Girl with a No. 2 Pencil

Kristen Lowe is pure Minneapolis, born and bred, it turns out. She grew up near Fifty-Fourth and Penn, living with her mom, a secretary at Norwest Bank, and brother in one of the little postwar duplexes that dot the neighborhood to this day. She taught herself to draw largely with a No. 2 pencil and paper from a shelf at the local Tom Thumb and trips on her bike to the Hennepin County Library near Southdale. "I'd sit with the big Käthe Kollwitz book," says Lowe today. "I couldn't believe her drawings. They made me cry, they were so much about the human condition. The Leonardo da Vinci books, Rembrandt. Every single line seemed to represent something about the inner life of the artist and the inner life of what they were drawing. Hours, years, I looked at those books."

She also had a little spiral-bound drawing pad and would go down to what everyone in that part of town calls "the crick," Minnehaha Creek, where it winds through the city in a steep green ravine. "My family didn't have much money, and I was down there all the time. It felt like I was in heaven—the crick. I used to catch crawfish. I remember bringing one to school for show-and-tell. I was pretty secret about my drawing then. I felt like if I told anyone about my creative abilities, they'd say, 'Come make posters for sports.'" Still, her secret passion called. "I'd have my pencil, my pad, and I spent so much time down at the crick drawing grass. I drew so much grass, its pattern and rhythm."

At her grandparents' farm in Blooming Prairie, Lowe became an expert fire starter, turning pencil-sized sticks into charcoal. "My mom was a smoker, so you could always sneak matches. If you got about a pail's worth of sticks, leaned them into sort of a tipi shape, you could make a lot of charcoal. My brother and I would draw on the inside of snow forts we made. It's a natural human instinct, I think. When I learned that ancient people drew with charcoal in caves, it made absolute sense to me. I did too!"

In fifth grade or so, Lowe made her first notable animal work, a lion's head and mane that she entered into a contest. "I spent every ounce of skill I had on that and sent it off. I won an art class! My first. I remember it like it was yesterday. The teacher said, 'Remember, don't just draw the outline of the tree. These are cross-contour lines.' It was one of those moments: How could I have never seen that?"

Soon enough, she was a teenager with a decent grasp of cross-contour lines, taking the bus to MCAD with her best drawings stuffed into a stiff cardboard portfolio. "Leaving it there, I wanted to cry. I was so scared. When I got in [to the Minneapolis College of Art and Design], it felt like a miracle. I didn't do that well in high school, Southwest, but they wanted me anyway."

Lowe studied with the acclaimed teacher and artist Judith Roode. "She had each of us pick one thing, one kind of pencil or one kind of charcoal, and learn to play it as loud and as soft as you could, like an instrument. To this day, I believe it to be true: You are a musician; you learn one instrument. If you're using compressed charcoal, learn to make the softest mark you can with it and the largest mark you can. That's how you get the biggest vocabulary with that instrument."

Once compressed charcoal entered Lowe's life, it never left. "No drawing tool has as much of a vocabulary as charcoal," she says. She has a drawing kit she takes into sheep meadows and such that's not much more than those schoolroom-familiar slabs of pink pearl erasers, those other sorts of pencil-top erasers that come in packs of twenty-five for fifty cents, chamois, and charcoal. "I love everything about compressed charcoal," says Lowe today. "It's been around since the beginning of time. It's this thing of the earth, and we are the earth. It's the most fundamental, primeval connection between you and a mark."

And that's how you get from the Tom Thumb near Penn and Fifty-Fourth to the Louvre.

A Star Is Born

Lowe's early career was meteoric. She was invited to the Louvre to make a film about three works in its permanent collection using only images and sounds, not words. At one point during a break in shooting, she lay on the floor of the closed museum at night and couldn't believe her luck, the ornate ceiling stretching in every direction as limitless as hope. Her short documentary was so well received it would be shown at the Metropolitan Museum of Art in New York City and become part of the education collection at the Louvre.

Lowe's career took flight. She was written about, and her work was shown in Boston, in San Francisco; she received Minnesota State Arts Board grants; she was featured four times in columns by the *Star Tribune*'s art critic Mary Abbe; she starred in a segment of a public television documentary series (TPT's *Minnesota Original*); she sold out runs of work at her gallery (the Thomson Gallery in Minneapolis's Warehouse District). Lowe was the green-eyed blond who was the toast of the downtown Wyman Building art crawls. She fell in love, married, and had a baby girl, Francesca. Her husband took over the New French Café from founders Sam and Sylvia Kaplan, and Lowe jumped in to work as a host and help out. And then everything that happens to strand and vanish mid-career women artists like Lowe happened.

The transformation of the Warehouse District from art galleries to bars and sports caught the New French and ended it. And when Bob Thomson died, the Thomson gallery closed too. Even Lowe's San Francisco gallery shifted focus, and she decided to pull out of there. Art moved from front burner to back; child supporting took first priority. She and her husband divorced after the restaurant failed, and Lowe put all her energy into teaching to keep a roof over her and her daughter's heads. She's now a tenured professor at Gustavus in St. Peter. She shows her work at Form + Content in the North Loop, the artist's cooperative tucked deep into a building near Demi.

I met her there to see a portion of the work that will be on display at the Hillstrom from November to January. "Artists are either glorified or damned and ignored. There's no middle ground," she told me as we stood in the quiet gallery. I thought, *Especially artists who are women.*

For Women, Talent Isn't Enough

Rosa Bonheur (1822–1899) was one of the greatest painters of the nineteenth century, famed for her sensitive portrayals of animals.

She has been an influence on Lowe, who created a mother-and-lamb tribute to Bonheur, which will be on display at the Hillstrom. In her time, Bonheur was received by queens and presidents; she was given special dispensation from the French police to wear pants, then illegal for women, as she sketched. She was long called the greatest woman painter of all time but had her first retrospective museum show, the career overview that cements an artist's work, in 1997—nearly a hundred years after her death.

Judy Chicago, born 1939, has been the most visible and famed woman artist of her generation for fifty years, and she has her first retrospective show on view in San Francisco right now, at the de Young. Critic Dodie Bellamy kicked off her review of Chicago's show with a shameful litany of all the American women artists who labored ignored by the curatorial establishment and art world, gaining their first major shows in old age or posthumously. "Take any modern female artist with a long career and google her name plus 'long-overdue.' It will make you giddy," concludes Bellamy.

Earlier this year, researchers at Monash University in Australia found that 96.1 percent of all artwork sold at auction worldwide between 2000 and 2017 was attributed to male artists. An Artnet analysis in 2019 found that, between 2008 and mid-2019, Picasso alone brought in more money than all the top six thousand women artists in the world added together, including multimillion-dollar sellers like Yayoi Kusama. In that period, women accounted for 2 percent of art sales. In 1971 Linda Nochlin wrote a groundbreaking essay for *ARTnews* describing the art world's paradox: "Why have there been no great women artists?" she asked, considering the dynamic of male buyers and gallerists not showing or buying work by women, and then concluding there was no market enthusiasm—which the art community takes as proof of respect and regard.

It's not just the eternal "woman problem" that Kristen Lowe is up against. As she points out, "Since all the galleries in the Warehouse District closed, I think a lot of people in Minnesota got out of the habit of buying art here. Now they mainly buy art on vacation."

Lowe is hoping a few of her pieces at the Hillstrom sell because she wants to put money into a scholarship fund for art majors at

Gustavus. Teaching is now a great love of hers, and she remembers being a poor kid who thought art school was out of reach, burning sticks for charcoal and walking to the Tom Thumb for paper.

"It's a guy's game, that secondary market," she says as we stand together in the white gallery of Form + Content, surrounded by her recent charcoal scenes nested in bright carved wooden rounds. She explains that these were inspired by a trip to Pompeii, a site of beauty inextricable from catastrophe, which feels like the right perspective on our current world. The bright carvings are the enveloping catastrophe; the charcoal animals in the center are the beauty. Lowe tells me about where in the Minnesota river bottom a particular bit of flora was captured and shows me a bird's nest she found twenty-five years ago that she has been drawing ever since.

When, two hours into our talk, someone else finally enters this lonely gallery, Lowe tucks her nest back into its crumpled plastic Target bag. "I'm hoping, for me, the next ten years are gung ho," she tells me, finding a promotional postcard about her show. "I mean, you're here. That's got to mean something?"

Go to the Hillstrom

Do this: Drive down Highway 169 to the Hillstrom before Lowe's show closes January 25. If along the way you see sheep out the window, consider that those might be the exact sheep Lowe has drawn—dragging her bench easel into the fields, watching the sun change the trees hour by hour.

When you get to the gallery, pick an animal. Try to decide why you're drawn to an eagle or buck or lamb. Why does it tug your heart? Is drawing a language we forget that we know?

Consider what Lowe sees when she teaches drawing: "Drawing uses the thread between your hand and your heart," she says. "I've had students who start to cry when they first get it. Their hand and heart are talking, for maybe the first time."

Does it matter if for half the population—the women—that speech between their hands and hearts is not valued? Or has 4 percent, or even 2 percent, the value of the other half's speech?

It's hard not to notice that Lowe's magnificent *E Pluribus Unum*, her most expensive piece, costs $6,500, a pittance in an art world where it's nothing to spend five figures to inject a decaying Damien Hirst shark with formaldehyde, a necessary task for any owner of such a dead shark, to aid in preservation. Many of Lowe's other pieces cost as little as a couple of nice dinner tickets with a wine upcharge.

Lowe regards the art market with equanimity. "To me, it's like we're talking about the sky," she says. "The sky is the most democratic thing there is. No matter where you are, what your socio-economic status, you have the sky. For me, that's what drawing has always been. Wherever you are, you have the sky, and drawing."

And the sky is full of eagles, to see and speak uniquely.

Called Out

· · · · · · · · · · · · ·

Mpls.St.Paul Magazine, July 2015

One of the through lines in my work is writing about women in life-immersing battles that no one is aware of, except themselves. You can see this in so many of my profiles: the chef Ann Kim on her battle to bring her whole self into the public arena (see page 149), the writer Kate DiCamillo on her battle to keep a shy and childlike heart open in our cruel world (see page 108), and of course in this story of three women who want the church they grew up in to accept them as full, valuable souls. We talk a lot in the magazine world about the difference between a "topic" and a "story." A topic is something like: the Catholic church. A story is more like: three women, faith-bound, fighting the fight of their lives, that will inevitably lead to eternal damnation—or sainthood. I think about the women in this story all the time. I'd never heard the phrase "bloom where you are planted" before, yet it's all I've ever done.

The Vatican is doling out its harshest punishment to some of Minnesota's most devoted Catholics.

On May 17, Josie Petermeier took to the altar to be ordained as a Catholic priest. As ceremonies go, it was uneventful. Her small congregation gathered where it always does, in a modest Craftsman-style Methodist church below the Witch's Hat Tower in Prospect Park, to watch Petermeier receive the sacrament of Holy Orders from a bishop who flew in from Indiana.

As Petermeier took part in a tradition said to trace an unbroken line to the original apostles, she promised to carry out the work of Christ on earth. At that moment, she was excommunicated from the church. By order of the pope, she no longer can be buried in sacred ground. She cannot go to confession or receive the Eucharist.

Petermeier, sixty-three, is a former nun, a mom, a theology major, and a longtime Boy Scout leader. She has clear blue-gray eyes, sleet-white hair, and a welcoming habit of waiting for those she meets to speak first, in the way of someone who has spent many years helping children. She doesn't look like a danger to anyone. But the second she accepted the Holy Orders, she automatically received the most terrible punishment the church has— excommunication. She is from now on excluded from worship with Catholics in good standing. It's a punishment so extreme that it was deemed too harsh for the dozens of Minnesota priests who have been credibly accused by their own archdiocese of sexually abusing children. It's also deemed too harsh of a punishment for murderers.

"Murder is a grave sin," explains Susan Mulheron, the chancellor of canonical affairs for the Archdiocese of Saint Paul & Minneapolis, "and a person can confess that and be in communion with God. But there are certain actions that are recognized by the church as causing a detriment to the communion and unity of the church. A delict is a crime that goes beyond one person's action and affects the whole body of the church." Which is why murderers and pedophiles are not excommunicated, but Petermeier is.

At her ordination, Petermeier was joined at the altar by two other ordained Minnesota women who are also excommunicated. Together, they are pioneering their own version of what it means to be a "good Catholic" as they lead the women-friendly, gay-friendly, everything-friendly Compassion of Christ Catholic Community in Prospect Park. Their congregation is small, twenty folks on a good day. But the influence of these women is quietly growing.

The Scout Leader

Josie Petermeier grew up in the town of Remsen, in northwestern Iowa, in the 1950s. She was the eldest child on her family's farm, entrusted to drive the tractor, milk the cows, and lead "Granny," the old milk cow, on a tether to mow the ditches. "I got to the point I could ride a cow," she remembers, "but riding a cow is the lumpiest thing."

Even today Petermeier bears a farmhand's strength about her; she looks as if she could hurl a hay bale five yards anytime she wants. It's no wonder she volunteered to go to a special school to learn how to repair boilers when she was a nun.

Petermeier grew up a German Catholic, and she remembers the majority of the town being so German Catholic that the parochial school was four times the size of the local public school. On Sundays at church, Petermeier would watch the altar servers and long to join them, even though she knew she never could. Outside in the Iowa summers, she'd read about the lives of the saints and dream.

"I remember laying in the grass and looking at the blue sky and thinking it was Mary's cloak because it was the right color blue," she recalls. Before dinner during Lent, everyone in the family would kneel and say a rosary. A favorite aunt was a Franciscan nun. Petermeier didn't realize it at the time, but her faith was pulling her in another direction. "It was my chore to clean out the cream separator every day," she says. "I'd put the dust cover over my shoulders to use as vestment, take out this big circular filter to use as my host, and say Mass. I did this all the time." Only years later did Petermeier recognize this as what Catholics term "a call" or a vocation, a sign from God that you are to dedicate your life in service to the church.

At eighteen, Petermeier entered the convent and became a nun with the Holy Spirit Missionary Sisters in Epworth, Iowa, thinking that perhaps mission work would be the right path for her to follow Christ's directive to serve. She was a nun for nine years and attended three of her biological sisters' weddings in her trim blue habit. Over those years, however, Petermeier began to believe that her life had gone in the wrong direction, that if she stayed with the Holy Spirit sisters she would become nothing more than a facilities manager with a specialty in boiler repair. So she left.

She went to Creighton University in Nebraska to study theology, hoping that would put her on a clearer path. There, she was offered a job in education, and while doing that, she began to wonder if all those years as a nun had left her retirement account in a dire situation, so she decided to take a class in electronics in Minnesota, where she met her husband. Together the couple raised two boys, the youngest becoming an altar server.

Through it all, she maintained involvement in the Catholic Church and eventually concluded that her truest mission must be to help boys become Boy Scouts. She took special pride in working with boys one-on-one to help them become Eagle Scouts. "For years I thought: This is my ministry. Helping boys," she says.

As time passed, however, that familiar feeling of "Is that all there is?" rose in her again. Petermeier began longing to return to her path serving Christ. Her husband spotted an item about the female-led Compassion of Christ Catholic Community in a newspaper. They went to a service preached by Linda Wilcox. "I cried through most of it," Petermeier remembers. "It was like something in me cracked open. All of what I had ever wanted as a kid—to be a priest—was right there in front of me."

Petermeier was ordained as a deacon at Compassion a year ago, and she completed her Clinical Pastoral Education at University of Minnesota hospitals, praying with patients who request a Catholic presence. "I feel closest to the idea of anointing the sick," she says. "Being with people, praying with them, being able to serve people and listen to their stories. If you offer your heart and your hands to God and can be an instrument to help, that is very profound. Plus, if you have that sense of calling, you have to do it or it just niggles at you: Why are you doing any less than everything you can?"

The Choirgirl

Monique Venne, a Burnsville resident for thirty-three years, has soft reddish hair, fine porcelain skin, and a bookish aspect. She's a fan of the Weather Channel, and her hobbies include wildflower identification. She's been known to design a spring day around a state park outing when the native wood lilies are in bloom. She's a Minnesota State Fair ribbon-winning beader and embroiderer, and she chairs the beadwork section of the Needlework Guild of Minnesota. Like Petermeier, she's also been excommunicated.

Venne, fifty-eight, is retired from a career in meteorology, including a stint in the weather-watching headquarters of Northwest Airlines. And yes, it was part of her job to declare when weather reached "act of God" status, a fact she cops to with amusement.

Venne grew up in a family of French Catholics who came to the United States via Québec before she was born. She was the daughter of an air force pilot, and the family moved around, spending stretches of time in Massachusetts, New York, and Florida. Wherever she went, her greatest comfort was church. She was a choirgirl as a child, and after that a lifelong member of the choir. A pious child, Venne kept a Hummel nativity scene on her dresser alongside a little altar of Mary, as well as an ever-filled small font of holy water, which she replenished from the font at church. She never missed a church service. When the altar boys missed Mass, the priest would let Venne sit in the front pew—though she could never stand at the altar—and say the responses the altar boy would have said. She then clapped her hands when the bells were to be rung, as girls weren't allowed to ring bells.

Venne says she felt the call to serve Christ repeatedly as a child. "At home I liked to play Mass. I did this all the time," she remembers. "I'd take some bread and some grape Kool-Aid, get one of my mom's big pressed-glass wine goblets, mash the bread down to look like a host. I wore a bathrobe as a chasuble, and I'd say a Mass to my little sister."

Throughout her career Venne spent her evenings, when she wasn't beading, in Bible study. And after a lifetime volunteering at churches, she eventually decided her true calling must not have been the priesthood but to write Bible-study material for other Catholics. In 1998 she enrolled in a master's of divinity program at United Theological Seminary in New Brighton to pursue prayer writing. As Venne studied, she became more cognizant of what the Bible really did—and didn't—say about women priests and bishops. Then, in 2005, Venne says, she received a call from Christ that she could not ignore.

It happened on Holy Thursday at St. Edward's in Bloomington.

After the evening's service, Venne was sitting in the chapel, and the idea of women priests and bishops was weighing on her. "I said to myself, 'I know, God, it is not men who create priests, it is you. And then I felt a pressure on my head. It felt kind of odd, and I shook my head because I thought it was just something self-invented. But the feeling wouldn't go away, so I concentrated on it to figure out what it was, and I could feel hands on top of my head, and the words came to me: 'You are a priest forever, according to the order of Melchizedek.' Slowly," Venne recalls, "the pressure went away, and I was just filled with awe."

Melchizedek was the first priest, or at least the first mention of the concept of a priesthood in the Bible, in Hebrews 7:17. In Hebrew the word "melek" means king, while "tsedek" means righteousness. Theologians debate whether Melchizedek was an actual human being or a concept, but for Venne there was no debate.

"That was when I realized I had to live out my life as a priest," Venne says. "I didn't want to be excommunicated. But eventually I kept thinking: In baptism we are baptized into Christ. If we actually cannot act as Christ, why are you baptizing us? Because that's what every Christian is called to do, by virtue of baptism. To act as Christ."

Venne was ordained in 2011. She bakes the Eucharist they use at Compassion of Christ. It's gluten-free and unleavened, made with honey. She says it doesn't take long; she's done it so often she can throw a host together in less than thirty minutes. While it bakes she looks out at the wildflower garden she planted and prays.

The Grandma

The last of this gang of excommunicated rogues is Linda Wilcox, a sixty-eight-year-old grandmother of two whose eyes twinkle and whose cheeks dimple when she smiles.

Wilcox was such a rule follower as a child that her brother and sister mockingly called her "The Saint" or "Linda the Good." She grew up in Detroit before her family moved to Maplewood. She remembers being so desperate to find a sin to bring to confession that she once rifled through the garbage can in pursuit of a Campbell's soup can her mother had prepared during Lent—and she felt victorious and guilty at the same time for pointing out the vegetable soup her mother had served at lunch contained beef broth.

"I grew up in a *Father Knows Best* sort of household," Wilcox says. "Whether it was politics or religion, my father knew everything, and we listened. I wish I could do it all over again. I'd question. Everything."

Instead, Wilcox spent her forty-year career not asking questions but answering them, in the Saint Paul Public Library. "I always told myself the library was a sort of ministry," she says with a laugh. "Getting people what they needed, getting them the information, giving them service. Of course there was no God talk, but I thought it was a fabulous service. I loved finding answers for people. So it was ironic it took me, what, forty years to find my own answers."

Wilcox earned her master's degree in theology from St. Catherine's while she was still working, simply because she loved learning about the church. "In four years I never missed a single class. I. Just. Loved. It!" she says brightly. It was at a conference after she had graduated that Wilcox discovered the things that would have her defying two popes (so far). "I was just going to go to a Mass at the conference—I thought there would be good music. And then I saw. A woman. Behind the altar."

When Wilcox wants to punctuate something, she makes her words into happy little staccato pops. "I had never seen a woman behind the altar. Ne-ver. Ne-ver. Never! It was like I was cracked over the head. I mean, I was stunned. Absolutely cracked open wide. From that moment I was different. I remember where I was sitting, what she had on. Afterward, and this is crazy, I saw her in her street clothes and all I could think is: She looks just like me. The idea that I had to do this took hold. It would not let me go. I really struggled with the idea of excommunication. But finally I realized: I wanted to help make a path for the women who will come after me."

Wilcox was ordained in 2009, and she has since baptized her granddaughter. She says being an ordained priest is the greatest joy of her life. The Catholic Church calls it the worst thing a Catholic can do. "I love the church," she says, smiling. "I cherish the rituals of faith; sometimes just the smells and bells can be very meaning-ful. The music. It feels like home. I feel like I'm the shunned daugh-ter. But I'm welcome in the margins with all those other folks who are shunned, and we're having a good time."

Medieval Attitudes

The collision course between the pope and these Minnesota women started in either the thirteenth century or 1976, depending on how you look at it.

The thirteenth century was an important time in the Catho-lic Church. That's when the Fourth Lateran Council created the present understanding of ordination (there's no actual ordination recounted in the Bible) and decreed that priests, monks, bishops, and similar ordained officeholders must be celibate.

In the centuries immediately following Christ's time on earth, women had been powerful, according to a shelfful of scholarship written about female priests and bishops during the early Chris-tian church. History books offer pictures of a striking tile mosaic from about AD 820, showing Theodora, the female bishop of the Basilica of St. Praxedes in Rome at the time. A third- or fourth-century Christian female priest's grave was found on the island of Thera. Evidence of women's presence and leadership in the early Christian church is sprinkled throughout the Bible: There's Pris-cilla, who was entrusted with converting Gentiles; Lydia, who led a synagogue before becoming the first Christian convert in Eu-rope and thereafter leading a church; Chloe, the head of a house church; and Junia, the female apostle.

"The idea that only men were apostles, and therefore we have to follow Christ in letting only men be apostles, is a medieval idea," Venne says. "We know Jesus's disciples included women who traveled with him through Galilee; it's in Luke 8. But more im-portantly, it was women who were faithful to Jesus after his male disciples fled once he was arrested.

"Women accompanied him to the cross, to the tomb, and were getting ready to embalm his body when they discovered the tomb was empty. In all four gospels it is said that Mary Magdalene was the one Jesus appeared to as the risen Christ. Magdalene and the other women were commissioned to tell the rest of the disciples that Jesus had risen," Venne says. "The most important news, the core of our Christian faith, was entrusted to the women. But women can't bring the good news? As ordained priests? It's just crazy."

Venne is hardly the first to argue this. Catholic women in the United States and Europe have been pursuing women's ordination since the 1800s, when they were also pursuing women's right to vote and campaigning against slavery and racism. A number of modern churches—Methodist, Free Will Baptist, Unitarian—were founded with the ordination of women as part of their early principles. By the 1960s many religions, including Reform Jews, Anglicans, and Lutherans, were ordaining women.

In 1976 Pope Paul VI asked a pontifical biblical commission, made up mainly of cardinals, to look into the question: Could the Roman Catholic Church ordain women as priests? After about six months of deliberation, the committee returned with a thoroughly ambiguous report. On the one hand, it wrote, there's tradition, and on the other hand, there's really nothing consequential about the topic in the Bible one way or the other, leaving the decision to the present church. The church issued a statement saying that women's ordination was off the table because there would be no "'natural resemblance' which must exist between Christ and his minister if the role of Christ were not taken by a man."

Not everyone agreed.

Enough Already

Women's ordination has never been only a women's issue. In fact, last March in Milwaukee, Jesuit priest William Brennan posthumously released a video—seven months after he was buried in hallowed ground—affirming his support of women's ordination. In life, he had been sanctioned for leading a liturgy in public with a woman, and the church had retaliated by stripping him of his ability to act as a priest and forbidding him from attending public church services; they even forbade him to leave Milwaukee without permission from his supervisors.

Catholics who secretly support women's ordination call themselves "in the Catacombs" or "in Catacomb" or just "Catacomb," alluding to the Christians who hid from persecution in the tunnels beneath Rome. These supporters hide for fear of persecution. They worry about being excommunicated, fired, and stripped of pensions (if they work for the Catholic Church or an associated school) or otherwise sanctioned. Petermeier, Venne, and Wilcox estimate that there are three or four dozen active Catacomb members, including active male priests, in Minnesota right now. (I called some who declined to speak with me.)

By 2002 Bishop Rómulo Antonio Braschi had had enough of the secrecy and fear. He met with seven women on a boat in the Danube River and ordained all of them as priests. These women, in turn, ordained other women, who ordained others as members of Roman Catholic Womenpriests, the same organization that Petermeier, Venne, and Wilcox are now part of. Bishop Braschi has since met the same fate as the succession of women priests he ordained—excommunication.

Today, the greatest concentrations of women who consider themselves ordained Roman Catholic priests are in California. Minnesota has the most female priests per capita in churches in Red Wing, Winona, St. Cloud, Minneapolis, and St. Paul. There are more than seventy living in the United States, most in the public and a few in the Catacombs, having taken orders secretly.

A Commitment to Catholicism

I have to confess, hanging out with ordained Catholic women priests is incredibly dull. Petermeier, Venne, and Wilcox study the Bible and work on prayers. They feed the hungry. (I packed food with them one night to send to Haiti. Nothing noteworthy happened. A lot of food was provided.) They worship and they sing.

They sit with grieving parish members in support. Wilcox even sews mourning quilts from the deceased's favorite items of clothing to give comfort to mourners while praying.

When pressed about why they didn't leave the Catholic Church and become Anglican priests, the women have a matter-of-fact answer: Why didn't Rosa Parks just take a cab instead of going to jail for refusing to move to the back of the bus? Why didn't the four students leave the Woolworth's lunch counter in 1960, when surely a more pleasant lunch could be found nearby?

"You grow where you're planted," Wilcox explains in her quiet Afton house, where she cares for her elderly mother. "Why should I be pushed out because of the sin of sexism?"

It was only in 1989 that the Vatican decided once and for all that, in the words of Pope John Paul II, "Harboring racist thoughts and entertaining racist attitudes is a sin." Prior to that, decisions like refusing to ordain African Americans were accepted. In 1886, Augustus Tolton, America's first black priest, traveled to Rome to be ordained since no American seminary would do it. The excommunicated women of Minnesota imagine that a future pope will say the same thing about sexism that present popes say about racism.

It's also important to note that excommunication is not always binding. Joan of Arc was excommunicated, then burned at the stake, and finally made a saint. Likewise, the Carmelite nuns who supported Spain's St. Teresa of Ávila were excommunicated, then brought back into the church. St. Mary of the Cross MacKillop was also excommunicated before her ultimate sainthood. Excommunication today is not always excommunication tomorrow.

Prayers for Change

Anne E. Patrick is a Catholic theologian and author of *Conscience and Calling: Ethical Reflections on Catholic Women's Church Vocations*; she's the William H. Laird Professor of Religion and Liberal Arts, emerita, at Carleton College, and she has been following the movement to ordain women for more than forty years. She says that even though the quiet, devout Minnesota women priests of Compassion of Christ Catholic Community seem to be laboring in obscurity, the eyes of the world are upon them.

"It's too early to tell whether these people are going to be thought of as St. Catherine of Siena," she says, "or Martin Luther." (St. Catherine of Siena being a legendary church reformer, Luther being a Catholic priest who became so disenchanted that he was excommunicated after speaking out and went on to found Lutheranism.)

According to Patrick, a 2005 survey of American Catholics revealed that 54 percent would welcome ordained married women as priests, and 61 percent thought celibate women should be ordained as priests, while 29 percent would strongly oppose a change. That's a recipe either for change or for schism, Patrick says. "These women are practicing 'prophetic obedience,' the idea that they are obedient to God, not to human authority. That idea has, for a long time, held a lot of power in the church," says Patrick. "What gives me hope is actually when Pope Francis says he refuses to talk about it.

"The writer Kathleen Hall Jamieson was once asked, 'Does papal teaching ever change?' She said, 'Yes, but only after there's a period of papal silence on a question.' This silence now, it might be fifty years, it might be two hundred years, but I think they're very important, these women. These women are putting their lives on the line—not that they're going to be killed, but they're making great personal sacrifices to implement a vision of what Catholic life should be like."

On the other hand, says Mulheron, the chancellor of canonical affairs, ordained women are not heroes. "When I talk about the constant universal and unbroken tradition of the church, handed down since Jesus Christ himself, it's a male tradition. A public challenge of that creates confusion. The excommunication is for the effect this confusion has on the whole community." In other words, people who go to these Minnesota women for the Eucharist are not really getting a Eucharist, the children being baptized are not really baptized, the people being married are not really married.

What fate awaits this tiny Minneapolis congregation on the hill, led by an excommunicated grandma, an excommunicated scout-master, and an excommunicated ribbon-winning beader? Will the church make them all saints in five hundred years? We might not know in our lifetimes, but we do know one thing.

Every time these excommunicated women priests get together, they pray for cardinals and bishops worldwide. They pray for Pope Francis. And they pray for Archbishop John Nienstedt of the St. Paul and Minneapolis archdiocese and its churches that are in bankruptcy. The women pray that these people might find peace and find wisdom in Galatians 3:28: "There is neither Jew nor Greek, there is neither slave nor free man, there is neither male nor female; for you are all one in Christ Jesus."

How to Interview Anyone

There's an unfortunate truism in our go-go world, which is that most people do not engage in conversation; they only wait for the other person to pause so they can take their turn to speak. In my career I have interviewed some big celebrities—Idris Elba, Julia Louis-Dreyfus, Martin Amis, Fran Lebowitz, Jennifer Hudson, Sharon Salzberg, to name a few. I have also interviewed countless people no one else has interviewed for public consumption; I'm thinking here of chefs and business owners, mainly.

Big names are hard to interview because they usually have a couple dozen talking points they want to stick to. If you let them do that, the reader will be bored, and in the end the stars themselves will not be well served by the final story. I've had PR people on one line and a distracted star on the other and found myself announcing: "You're not giving me anything I can use. Let's call this a failure and wrap it up!" That move can spark better answers.

National Book Award winner Pete Hautman sent me a follow-up email after I pestered/interviewed him for three hours: "Your interview technique must be brilliant because I'm pretty sure I said a lot of shit that my internal editor usually deletes." I don't know about brilliant, but I do know that, like the Royal Canadian Mounted Police of yore, I always get my man. My man, in this case, being *the story*.

First-timers are even more difficult to interview, because they may tell you things that are inappropriate to use in the piece—about a child's health, about their own finances or marriage, for instance—or they might trash-talk a rival and then deny they said it. You have to be careful and creep back and forth in the conversation, occasionally asking, "Is that something you want said, publicly, in a story?"

Interviewing is an art. An art in which you create and then harvest conversation to use as the raw material for a nonfiction *story*. A story that makes your readers laugh, cry, or think.

Following are some of my tips on how to do interviewing well.

1) Listen.

If you can't fully be present and focus the whole of your attention on another person, you'll never get a good interview. Listen to what they're saying; listen to what's behind what they're saying. Say out loud what you think they're saying, and get them to agree (or disagree). Listening is training all your senses on the person talking to you, so that they can actually *feel you listening* with their own senses. Listening: It sounds so easy, so obvious. It is not. I bet some significant percentage of people never do it, ever. Especially not with strangers.

2) Know as much as you can before you go into the interview.

When I interviewed Jennifer Hudson, I read probably twenty stories and listened to a hundred bits of random radio interviews, podcast clips, and the like. I was able to say to her, "You said this one time; you said another thing another time." She knew I cared enough about her to put in the effort and do the research. When people feel like you care enough to learn things about them, they're more likely to respond with kindness, which in an interview takes the form of being disclosing and intimate. On the other hand, if I don't know anything about an interview subject, I'm very comfortable saying, "I feel foolish because I don't know anything about you, but I should." That's the second-best approach, and if someone's words are not available online or in print because they have never done an interview before, it might be all you can say. And in that case, you've still completed your mission: knowing as much as you can.

3) Create common feeling.

When I'm interviewing someone, especially on the phone, I push my personality through and emphasize whatever things about me I suspect would create commonality with my subject. *I was a thirteen-year-old dishwasher. I am a single mom going crazy with COVID and kids at home. I am famous too. I am misunderstood too, all the time in this wild world*. All true. I contain multitudes. You do too. So say whatever it takes! This is easier to do over the phone; in person, the fashion part can make it harder to say, "I'm just like you."

4) Never be afraid to say: "I don't understand."

Never be afraid to say: "I don't know what this word means." Or, "Can you explain? I feel like I'm lost." If interview subjects confuse and therefore rope-a-dope you with jargon or shorthand, you've failed. If you are carrying basic misapprehensions about someone into an interview—like where their money comes from or how they spend their days—and then you come out with the misapprehensions intact, you've failed. It can help to jot down what you think you know about someone and see if it's supported by any available evidence. When I interviewed pop star Ricky Martin, I realized I had assumed he had retired, and then in talking to him I felt myself assuming he had nannies and outsourced a lot of the mess of parenting. Getting him to tell me facts about his life instead of relying on my ill-informed assumptions gave me one of the most illuminating interviews of my career. (Ricky Martin changes diapers, in case you were wondering.)

5) Your job as an interviewer isn't to show how smart you are; it's to come out with clarity.

I cannot tell you how many published Q&As I have seen where the interviewer seems to be trying to impress the subject with the interviewer's great knowledge. You're not there to impress a famous person; you're there to bring home a story for your readers. Where's the line between preparing for an interview and showing off your preparation for an interview? There's the art.

These two tips are especially for journalists:

6) Time is everything.
If I have unlimited time, I like to find out where people were born, about their childhoods, all that good stuff. It leads to so much insight. When given no time, I might start off with something crazy—like, "Is your cat in the limousine with you right now?"—just to get them talking. If you have only ten minutes, only ask questions they don't have canned answers for. If you waste your time with "How are you?" small talk, you're doomed. "Oh I'm fine, a bit tired, you know, it's raining, but this hotel is great. Super talking to you." *Click.* I usually scratch out a wish list of things I want out of an interview beforehand, keep one eye on the clock, and then feel no fear about being pushy: *Your team tells me you have only a couple minutes, so I need you to answer X.*

7) Compose your story in the moment, from the answers you get in the moment.
Composing on the fly is really hard and comes with instinct and practice, but ideally, you are seeing a story take shape in your mind as you talk. Be sure to ask the follow-up questions you need in order to make a totally original, insightful, make-'em-laugh, make-'em-cry, make-'em-think story in the limited time you have. No pressure!

If I've followed all these tips, when I get done with an interview I sometimes feel like a wrung-out dishrag. Interviewing is hard work; when done right, it's whole body and soul work. It's very difficult to be that present, that on-the-hunt for clues, and that creative as you build a story in real time. But it's worth it.

The King of HmongTown

Mpls.St.Paul Magazine, October 2018

I had never heard of the Hmong people before I started writing about their food some twenty-odd years ago. I remember reading the fantastic book *Harvesting Pa Chay's Wheat: The Hmong and America's Secret War in Laos* and just goggling at all the history I never knew. Since then, as St. Paul has become the worldwide capital of the Hmong diaspora, I've gotten to know Hmong cooks, farmers, and bakers, who share feisty eye rolls and big laughs with me, and somehow remind me of New Yorkers: tough and kind. I probably spent fifteen years writing little stories about HmongTown, hanging around, letting my reputation as a decent friend spread, and just generally being me—which coincidentally laid the groundwork to get this story. I'll never forget how intense and quiet it was in that room as I finally learned what I'd always wanted to know.

Since 2005, St. Paul's HmongTown Marketplace has become one of the best Asian markets in the United States. You wouldn't believe what it took for Toua Xiong to build it.

Ask me to name the person who has most changed the Twin Cities in the last decade, and my answer would be someone you've likely never heard of. Toua Xiong, the wiry, freckled incarnation of sheer willpower who's behind HmongTown Marketplace, the market of two hundred or three hundred Hmong vendors that crouches behind the state capitol in St. Paul.

I say two hundred or three hundred because the market is bigger in the summer, when the farmers' market expands to include outdoor stalls, and some 20,000 visitors stream through weekly.

It's smaller in winter, when the market contracts to merely fill the collection of squat outbuildings constructed over a century to form what was once Shaw/Stewart Lumber Co. I think most people look at HmongTown and imagine it was an inevitable occurrence. After all, some 100,000 Hmong people live in and around the Twin Cities, and a few years after the market opened a copycat called Hmong Village popped up on the east side of town. But I have been writing about Twin Cities food and culture for a long time, and I can tell you that, like any Thanksgiving table laden with treats, it didn't just happen. It came about from work and a vision.

Over the years, Xiong has told me different details about HmongTown's founding, and I've always wanted to gather them up and set them down. In honor of this, the season of Thanksgiving, when Native Americans shared their treasure trove of food with immigrants—and in defiance of recent politics, when immigrants have become so besieged—I visited Xiong at HmongTown. And that's one of the first things I learned about the place: Xiong wants to be done calling it the HmongTown Marketplace. He wants it to be known as HmongTown—like Chinatown. Not just a bazaar but a community unto itself.

To find Xiong's office, you make your way to one of the least trafficked corners of the market, back near the medicinal tea parlor and the insurance agency. There, beside one of the look-alike stalls stuffed to the brim with three-dollar rhinestone earrings and embroidered Hmong ceremonial toddler dresses, you climb a staircase lined with a threadbare carpet that's the same dingy brown the lumberyard bosses picked out decades ago, presumably because it was the color of sawdust.

At the top of the stairs lies Xiong's attic office, which has an interior window overlooking the different stalls in the west building. When I find Xiong, he is alone. His pretty, raven-haired wife, Nou Vang, is not around making us tea, or giving me useful lessons in eating Hmong food. The absence of his family allows me to see for the first time how scant the keepsakes are up here. There's a picture of his dad, standing rigid in his army uniform, with that particular orange-tinted blue sky you see only in 1970s snapshots. There's a picture of Xiong as a rocking 1970s teen, with a certain lean, pop-star glamour, gazing at the horizon above a polyester disco-splayed collar. There's a letter from the governor, in recognition of Xiong's efforts to incubate hundreds of Hmong businesses. And there's an award from this magazine for creating the Hmong-Town food court, one of the most important destinations for authentic southeast Asian food in the country.

People often ask me about the most "authentic" Hmong dish I'd recommend from the food court. I have learned, through the experience of years, that this idea of authenticity reveals more about the questioner: authentic to whom? Hmong teens seek out pork belly cooked in a super-hot oven so it's crisp as state fair bacon, and they pair it with red rice and a bubble tea. That's authentic. Hmong grandmothers who aren't feeling too well seek out boiled chicken and greens. That's authentic. Hmong professional women in yoga pants and stilettos come in for half a dozen orders of larb to go, so they can serve the salads of ground meat and herbs to their friends who are coming over for an Emmy-watching party. It's all authentic.

I've fallen in love with a particular mush of long-roasted pork and mustard greens that's a bit like southern collards and a bit like Mexican carnitas. It's something I'd never have tried if Nou Vang hadn't pointed it out to me. At home, beside the jungle, she said, it would have been cooked in a pit, like American southern barbecue.

The jungle is one of the things I've come to ask about. All the Hmong in Minnesota—the current generation or a previous one—have an exodus story. But those narratives don't often leave the family. They're both very long and full of minor points, mainly of interest to the family, such as the true origins of that one chipped lacquer box on the mantelpiece. Outside the family, who would even ask? Xiong's story, which is epic, starts at the tail end of the Vietnam War.

Xiong's father, like many of the Hmong, had fought for the United States. When the Americans left in 1975, after the fall of Saigon, he became a target of communist Lao soldiers and others allied with North Vietnam. Xiong's mother needed to raise food for the family. So she tended plots near the edge of the jungle, where the danger was high.

At this point, Xiong's family numbered five boys, all told. The oldest had just started college, in Thailand. The baby stayed at his mother's side. And the three middle boys hid with other children in the jungle. Xiong remembers keeping special white rocks in his pocket that sparked when you struck them together. His father sent him off with a message: "You shut your mouth. You don't say we have American guns. You don't say anything."

Xiong and the other kids foraged for fruit, moving around in a pack. At night they erected a sort of shelter, with a tarp stretched over the ground and sticks holding up banana leaves to craft a makeshift cover. A half-moon trench, dug at the perimeter, diverted the rainwater. The kids would use tree sap and slingshots to catch birds, strike a fire with those white stones, and try to limit any cooking smoke that would attract bombers. Often, moving from place to place, they'd find the strafed corpses of their fellow Hmong.

"We were chased for four years, everywhere in the jungle, with maybe a hundred families, running and running," Xiong says. He's fifty-one years old now, and when he talks about his childhood, he seems to get caught between rote recitation of a story he's told a thousand times and completely fresh horror. For example, one time, when his father had rejoined the kids in the jungle, Xiong remembers the Lao soldiers appearing, shouting at them, "If you don't come with us to the city, we're going to shoot you." Xiong's dad instructed the children to get low and run, while he drew the fire to himself, shouting back at the communists, of all things, "We don't like your system!"

Years passed. When two of Xiong's older brothers turned fourteen and fifteen, the family sent them west, to walk from the Laotian jungles to Thailand. The Hmong were not unfamiliar with war, and they expected the peace would return eventually. They waited and waited. But when Xiong turned twelve and his brother five, his parents gave up on returning to their former life. And they too began to walk hundreds of miles toward the border. Sometimes Xiong would carry his tired little brother. His mother carried the pots and pans. His father carried the rice.

When they reached the wide, rushing Mekong River, they

bought three tire inner tubes for the family of four. That's all the black marketers on the shore had left. Xiong's mom couldn't swim. They sat her in one truck inner tube and loaded the pots and pans in her lap. His father, the rice, and his brother took the second tube. Xiong took the third. He was the lead swimmer. They held hands. Xiong started kicking.

He remembers starting after dark, maybe around nine o'clock. Fighting the current, hand in hand, sweating, drinking river water, wrists and legs failing, they made it to the opposite shore before first light. Xiong recounts the strange sounds he heard then, which he'd never encountered in all his years in the jungle.

He re-creates it now, in his lumberyard office aerie, his sinewy hands tense on the table, as if he'd just unclenched them after the swim that finally saved his family: "Beep beep beep"—a car noise. To Xiong, "It was the American sound."

. . . .

So began seven years encircled by barbed wire, in a refugee camp. An hour of language instruction in the morning, then killing time, walking in circles all day.

One of the American church aid workers gave the kids a Yamaha acoustic guitar, and the teenagers would sit on what they called "the mountain"—really a grassy rise—and try to strum along to American pop songs. At the conference table Xiong sings a few bars of that 1967 hit "San Francisco": *If you're going to San Francisco, be sure to wear some flowers in your hair.* Xiong tells me he's surprised that I don't read those lyrics as a song of freedom and promise. It was what inspired him to invent his own tunes.

"I'd sing my sadness," he says. "How come we are born to be Hmong people? We don't have a school. We don't have a country."

The music got him through a lot. It also may have been what drew the attention of his fellow refugee Nou Vang. "We were kids dating kids, kids marrying kids," Xiong says. "There was nothing else to do. Every day you take your girlfriend around the camp. What else could you do to kill the time? There was no good schools, no life."

When he was sixteen and Vang was fourteen (or maybe thirteen, he says), the couple married. Now they couldn't be separated by resettlement, a constant source of worry. A year later, Vang gave birth to their first child. Still later, Xiong, Vang, and their two kids got off the plane in St. Paul on May 28, 1986, to join relatives. The older brothers had gotten here first, and bought a duplex in Frogtown so the family would have a home. The photos of that day show Xiong wearing what he calls his "Thai-style rocker shirt," holding his Yamaha guitar.

He was so young, still seventeen, that he could have enrolled in high school. Instead, Xiong decided to attend community college for business administration, then accounting. "I sat there with my Hmong dictionary in one hand, my English dictionary in the other," he says. "I didn't know any of these words: Syllabus? Marketing? Attorney?" He meant to be the first Hmong CPA, but it turned out he didn't understand the requirements, and after graduating, it took an entire year to land an accounting job. And that job paid only nine dollars an hour.

Desperate for a way out, he took a seminar on distressed properties, which soon landed him a portfolio of rentals. These required as much money to maintain as they were taking in. That nine-dollars-an-hour job was the only thing keeping the whole family in rice: his wife, his children, his parents.

The only privacy Xiong and Vang could find was in their car. They'd put their infant in a car seat, buckle him in the back, and circle the Cities and talk. The question Xiong kept coming back to, he says today, was the same one the couple had debated as teens in the refugee camp: Why could the Hmong claim no country, no land, no place to call their own? Visiting his wife's family in California, Xiong found himself riveted by the various Chinatowns. How was it that the Chinese had China, and all these extra Chinatowns too?

Then the worst day of his life arrived: He was getting laid off. Xiong remembers the experience as pure terror. It was almost worse than the jungles with the bullets, because at least there you could run. Now, in America, running with all these babies and dependents? That was no option. He recounts his last day at his job:

"I went to the bathroom. I closed the lights. I said, *God, help me. Give me a direction.* Suddenly my mind said, call your friend."

His friend, it turns out, was having the worst day of his life too. He had just learned his wife was leaving him. *Get me $5,000 cash today, sign a contract for a total of $150,000, and I'll sell you my grocery store*, said his friend. Xiong took a cash advance against every credit card he could get his hands on, and stopped at OfficeMax to buy a blank template for a contract. Xiong and Vang opened the store for business the very next morning and, on that first day, took in gross receipts of eighteen dollars.

Still, Xiong recalls that event as the first step on his road to retail. Some nine years later, with the city looking to redevelop the market he bought that fateful day, Xiong signed a contract for deed to buy up an abandoned lumberyard a little north of the capitol, off Como Avenue. Originally, he thought he could paint lines on the ground and rent stalls: instant market! But then he learned about obstacles like retail codes and fire sprinklers, and what followed was a Tom Clancy–like financial high-stakes tale that nearly ended up with Xiong losing everything. Instead, he succeeded in opening HmongTown.

Enduring so many trials has given Xiong a unique take on the parenting of his five children—one that I, who parents like a typical, middle-class American, can't entirely process. You see, when three of his children turned ages nine, ten, and eleven, Xiong became worried that they'd grown too soft, lolling around and watching television. "They think they're American, but their hair is black and their eyes are brown," he says. "They are Hmong." So he told them they were all going on a vacation to Thailand.

"I lied to them," he explains. "I said, *We go to Thailand to have fun.* They had one-way tickets. I found an international school. I found a Hmong person to keep house. I left them there for a year. I want them to be motivated. I got motivated when I lived in the jungle. They need to feed themselves. They need to heal themselves when they get sick. There's no TV, no air conditioning. When they came back a year later, they were good kids."

· · · · · · ·

Up in the offices, Xiong suddenly fell quiet. He'd covered all the important points of his family's saga. But it turns out Xiong was actually ready to pivot to the topic he really wanted me to put in the magazine. He'd like to see Hmong senior housing connected to HmongTown. He's taking the first step himself, converting some space at HmongTown into a senior day care facility. But Xiong has concluded that expanding the service to something as big as senior housing will require municipal support, and a regulatory and management structure that dwarfs everything he's already created.

Hmong elders need this, he explains, moving into salesman mode. Don't I understand the unique cultural needs of people like his mother, whose lives have wrenched them from jungle to refugee camp to St. Paul?

Actually, with everything he's told me, I really do, I tell him.

Satisfied, he leaps up to show me the architectural sketches piled on a desk. Xiong is currently working with an architect to create a pagoda-like archway at the entrance, like many American Chinatowns have. But different, naturally, because Hmong architecture is not Chinese architecture. He's also building an on-site Hmong cultural center for displaying art and artifacts, performing music, teaching Hmong crafts, and playing Hmong games, such as tuj lub, which requires grapefruit-sized tops.

The transactional part of our conversation come and gone, Xiong finally relaxes. At last I've connected the dots on a story I've been hearing bits and pieces of for years, and he communicated the importance of municipal support for Hmong senior care. He takes out a few more mementos for me to consider. The American flag, furnished by Congress, which Xiong feels his dad, who passed away in 2014, would be especially proud of. Letters from important politicians.

Not bad for a guy who came to this country with little more than willpower and an acoustic Yamaha guitar, huh? Speaking of that guitar, Xiong got onstage with it, to sing for the first annual HmongTown Festival. This is an outdoor community celebration in June, on the HmongTown grounds, with music, dancing, awards, bands, and vendors selling treats. He sang one of his own songs for the crowd.

"The sadness is always burning in me," Xiong says. "We don't have a country. We were chased and chased. I had no reason to be chased into the jungle at seven. I made no mistake. The camps were a prison. I am as capable as any person, but I never had a chance." So he sang a song he wrote about people without a homeland, in the place he made for them in a new world.

Xiong told me I could probably find the performance on YouTube, but in fact I could not. What I did find, a few minutes later, going over my notes in the car, was that my parking spot afforded a perfect view of Xiong and Vang leaving the office, having wrapped up their workday. They ran to their car, holding hands, laughing, their heads dipped together like lovestruck teens who had promised each other a hideaway, and then made it.

Maria Bamford's Tough Year for Laughs

· · · · · · · · · · · · ·

Mpls.St.Paul Magazine, January 2021

> I think the word *genius* is used too readily, especially when it comes to people making a lot of money or guiding a ball to a destination. In equal opposition, the term is used too rarely when talking about women who live outside easy categories, like ingenue or scientist. Maria Bamford, to my mind, is a straight-up genius, the Lucille Ball of the antidepressant era. I'm so grateful I got to talk to her for this feature in 2021.

Duluth-raised comedian Maria Bamford was working from home and dealing with anxiety before COVID. Here's her survival manual.

"When I'm feeling anxious, I listen to you to hear you talk about your anxieties," Stephen Colbert told Maria Bamford in the early days of the pandemic. He recorded his show in his empty theater, having summoned the great comic to help guide him through the beginning of our collective anxious times. Little did Colbert know how long these anxious times would drag on or how much Bamford, whom he calls his "favorite comedian on earth," has to offer any of us willing to listen.

You know Maria Bamford, right? Born in 1970, daughter of Duluth, proud graduate of Chester Park Elementary, star of more comedy specials and series than just about any comic of the last decade—*Lady Dynamite*, *Weakness Is the Brand*, *Old Baby*, *The Special Special Special!*, and more, more, more. But Bamford isn't just funny. She's brave and tragic and wise *and* funny—which is why people like Colbert call on her in a crisis.

This is because Bamford has battled mental illness, including suicide attempts culminating in a bipolar II diagnosis, since grade school in Duluth. For college she headed out to Maine but came back to finish at the University of Minnesota when anxiety called her home. It was then that she began, in Minneapolis, while serving up slices at Pizza Lucé, to build a comedy career around her particular feminist fight to be exactly who she is—smart and fragile, brilliant and quirky, original as the ocean.

A lot of people call her a genius.

Marc Maron calls her a genius. Mike Birbiglia and John Mulaney too. Mitchell Hurwitz, creator of *Arrested Development*, calls her a genius and also that rarest human: "a real artist." She's often called a comedian's comedian because of her many high-powered comic admirers. Like the comedy of Andy Kaufman, Richard Pryor, and Robin Williams, her comedy works in many simultaneous layers, not just funny but also pure absurdity and heart-wrenching pathos, all of it so complex and interrelated it can feel like your mind is cracking open and learning new ways to think as it chases after her while she gallops along. I personally find her work gives me courage, so much so that I really don't like to talk about her too much: If you insult her, it will be personal to me, and I won't like you anymore.

Which is absurd because I don't really know her! But such is the complexity of art.

Bamford puts so much of herself and her struggle out front that I, like so many of us, feel I know her. Her mom and dad, Marilyn and Joel Bamford, are such important voices in her work, and have been for so long, that you almost start to feel you know them too. From her social media last summer it became clear that Bamford was back in Minnesota, doing Zoom shows from Duluth. I caught one called *Help Me, Help You, Help Me!* in September; it was delightful. She was in a child's bedroom, rehearsing some of her own material and also answering Dear Abby–type questions from the audience. The whole thing felt like the funniest and most supportive slumber party of all time.

And yet.

Since Bamford had shared her mom's stage IV lung cancer diagnosis, it was easy to jump to conclusions about why she was in Duluth. Those conclusions were correct. Bamford was here all

summer, for her mother's last three months, working on a memoir and saying goodbye. Marilyn Halverson Bamford died the day
after that slumber party of a show, in her own home, surrounded
by her family.

Marilyn was a huge part of her daughter's work. Played by Mary
Kay Place in both seasons of *Lady Dynamite*, seen by her daughter's fans clapping from Bamford's couch beside Bamford's dad as
the audience in *The Special Special Special!*, Marilyn Bamford will
always be remembered as the Minnesota Mom—sharp as a flint
knife, judgmental as a fashion editor, kind and loving and reliable
as gravity. Maria Bamford had a very public breakdown in Chicago
in 2011, and it was her mother she called for help. Marilyn Bamford
lives in comedy as the person you call for help.

Was Maria Bamford going to be okay?

This seemed like an issue of statewide importance, so I caught
up with her while she was in a car wash in Los Angeles, not long
after she left Duluth, in the hour before she was going to go do
something top secret with Sarah Silverman and Seth Rogen.

"I'm so sorry about your mother," I began.

"Thank you," she replied. "My beloved mother. This may sound
creepy, and if it does, everyone can go to hell. But I can do a very
good impersonation of my mother. Now, to comfort myself, I talk
to myself saying what I think my mother would say. Sometimes I
skew a little bit more supportive than she may have been on certain issues, but—it's totally devastating." A silence of car wash and
the impossibility of conveying or consoling grief briefly takes hold
of the call, till Bamford tames it. "Also, I want to celebrate what an
incredible person my mom was. She was not a saint—she spanked
us, and in the seventies, as my friend Jackie Kashian says, that was
the golden age of hitting, and we got hit a tremendous amount.
The point is . . . " and Bamford breaks off, indicating the point is
that Marilyn Bamford was both bigger than language and smaller
than infinity.

"The great thing was, she just kept saying to us as a family, with
more eye contact as she said it," continued Bamford, switching
into her mother's well-known voice, all quavery and affectionate
but also impatient and getting-on-with-things: "*You guys are going*

to be fine." She switches back to her own voice. "What's hard is my mom *loved* life. I'm always on the fence about life. I could really take it or leave it on a regular basis. But she loved everything about it. My mom could wax poetical about this car wash bench I'm sitting on." She switches to her mom's voice again. "*Honey, it's got breathable circles in it so you won't get too hot when you're sitting. This is just wonderful. I wonder if we could get one of these for the backyard. I mean, they're sort of industrial looking, maybe Germanic, not exactly Scandinavian. I'm going to ask the guy inside.*"

Bamford turns back to her loss, and how she will be okay without Marilyn. "My mom would be irritated if I lost my mind—and I really thought I would when she left the bounds of earth—but I actually felt okay. Obviously, I'm weeping uncontrollably whenever I think of her and I'm alone or if I listen to a voice mail message she left me, but I felt okay [then]. Because I'm on my meds!"

Bamford relates that grief is best experienced on different psychiatric meds: "Laughter is actually not the best medicine; medicine is the best medicine."

Then I ask her the questions I imagine every creative in America wants to answer right now: How to work without a live audience? (Bamford has done shows just in her living room for her parents, or just by herself, for herself.) How to navigate a world of such intense anxiety it seems like it could swallow us up? (Bamford knows anxiety so overwhelming you fear you might hurt someone or yourself.)

But Maria Bamford has to leave the car wash to go do her top secret Hollywood comedy thing that will doubtless delight both Stephen Colbert and me in 2021. Happily, I was informed the advice is actually all in an audiobook Bamford worked on throughout her mother's last year, released just after Labor Day. As near as I can tell no one knows about it but you and me. It's *incredible*. Because it's called *You Are (A Comedy) Special: A Simple 15-Step Self-Help Guide to Forcibly Force Yourself to Write and Perform a Full Hour of Stand-Up Comedy*, you will think you don't want to listen to it, as it seems far too vocational. Actually, it's not much about craft at all; it's, in fact, a lot like Anne Lamott's *Bird by Bird*, a self-help book about how to do creative work when life seems too much.

I have listened to it ten times. Allow me to scoop out three of the fifteen steps and insist that if you listen to the audiobook, wherever you encounter the phrase "stand-up comedy," you insert whatever creative endeavor engages you: *managing a small business in a pandemic* or *raising kids in a pandemic* or *making pottery in a pandemic.*

Do what you like; like what you do.

Bamford explains in detail the fallacy of trying to please anyone but yourself. "Me, I like telling stories," she says in the book. "I like the six voices I can do. I like my family! I like being physical and making faces, and I love words. Thus, my comedy is heavily story-driven, six-voice-filled, family-based act-outs that could probably use some editing. *But Maria! You ignorant cow. What if I don't get love, adoration, all the laughs? What if I don't get what I want?* Yes, I know. That is painful . . . but have you gotten to do exactly what you wanted to do creatively for minutes, months, or even years? I'd argue that's a huge win. Congratulations on your Daytime Emmy in Useful Happiness."

Ask for help.

"I know it can feel impossible to ask for, much less get . . . help. Call an ambulance, call the fire department, call your local pizza provider. Domino's always picks up. In Minneapolis in 1995, I dialed 0 on a pay phone. I asked the operator, would they still love someone who was flunking out of remedial math? They said yes. I got a total stranger to basically tell me that they loved me—for free! You deserve all of the human kindness available. There is a weird phenomenon where people get wrapped up in trying to find *the right help*, that there is some best help out there. There might be. But somehow it's always someone two thousand miles away that charges $1,400."

That pay phone in 1995, by the way? Coffman Memorial Union. Instead of *the best help*, Bamford explains in depth how to get your friends to text when you need help doing a task, how to get people on Twitter to help you rehearse, or how to get the people who work behind the counter at your coffee shop to assist you, personally, in exchange for helping them! It's a revolution in getting through, literally together.

Keep at it.

"While this book was being written over the course of a year, I rehearsed my stand-up show at least fifty times, with friends, co-workers, strangers, and only sometimes onstage. It has been easy, and boring, and sometimes like pulling out a front tooth directly attached to my brain-heart. You are not alone."

· · · · · · ·

If this self-help book were in paper, I would take it through a time machine to my high school–aged self, who would then underline and star parts of it till the pen sliced through the pages. But since I can't do that, I'm doing the next best thing, which is telling you. I suspect that after thirty years of reading self-help, Bamford could easily spend the next thirty writing self-help, and I hope she does, because she's gone into the scariest places, shone a light, and come back to tell tales—and I know the rest of us could use a guidebook.

"I do feel like the one use I have in life is an almost compulsive honesty," Bamford told me, in goodbye, from the car wash bench her mother would have loved. "If I can use my compulsive honesty to make people feel less terrible, wouldn't that be good?"

The Splendid Prequel

Mpls.St.Paul Magazine, September 2015

What is a celebrity? I'd guess most people today recognize that celebrities are people we have parasocial relationships with; that is, by dint of frequently being in our line of sight, and because of the things they say or do when they're there, we think these people are our friends or, more rarely, our foes. I've interviewed hundreds of celebrities, and I'd add that celebrities are people about whom we carry a lot of unexamined thoughts. We think they're like this, or like that; we think they prefer one thing or another based wholly on ideas we came up with all on our own.

As an extremely minor celebrity, I've come up against some of this myself. I used to keep a running text-joke with a friend about all the people at my public events who would show up with the gift of lovingly prepared raw chicken—seriously. Like, this happened more than five times, eventually causing me to realize: A significant number of people think I am at all times stove adjacent. (In reality, I am *often* heading toward my kitchen, but sometimes I am going to a store, or to a meeting, or for a hike.)

A public persona is a hard thing to navigate. On the one hand, it keeps a roof over your head. On the other, it can start to feel like you worked really hard to get a role in a play, and then some mild curse descended, and now you can never, ever take off your costume or makeup. I've used this insight to get good stories again and again—who's the person behind the celebrity? The answer never surprised me more than when I talked to Minnesota food luminary Lynne Rossetto Kasper.

Lynne Rossetto Kasper has been broadcasting America's top food radio show for twenty years—but she's even more interesting than that.

I've known Lynne Rossetto Kasper—host and cocreator of *The Splendid Table*, the most important person in food radio, icon, Minnesotan—for a decade. But I never knew that the fork in the road that led a young Kasper to food radio was the day she hit Shelley Winters with a broom.

I learn this during the first of two nice, long lunches Kasper and I had on the patio at St. Paul's W. A. Frost. Kasper has the ivory skin and honey-hazel-brown eyes of a northern Italian Renaissance noblewoman. In the world of food, she's bigger than mere nobility; she's a celebrity-demigod, a little like Johnny Carson: bigger than life, universally known, but not actually known. A little like Athena, having stepped fully formed from the head of Zeus, born knowing everything in the world about pappardelle and finger limes. This is partly because she is intensely interested in everything. Simple questions can elicit very long, thoughtful, and interesting responses, and the net effect is that rare is the interview with her that goes beyond extremely thoughtful conversation about pappardelle. Until now!

I decided to take the occasion of the twentieth anniversary of her St. Paul–based, American Public Media–produced show, currently on more than four hundred radio stations around the country, to find out where this local treasure, and powerhouse, really came from. The answer took two bottles of wine, and I was awfully surprised when Ava Gardner came into it.

You see, Gardner was one of several women sometimes sleeping with Shelley Winters's then-husband Tony Franciosa. Winters was in rehearsals for a play being staged in a brand-new theater in New Jersey at which young Kasper had gotten her first job. "And [Winters] was on a phone near the stage, just whining and whining," recalls Kasper. "She was always on the phone whining. 'She's not as pretty as I am.' That sort of thing. I'm just an embarrassed kid, with my first job in a real theater. I'm sweeping. Trying to keep my head down. I swept right into her! That was the end for me. The owner of the theater called me into his office. He said, 'I'm very sorry. She's demanded you be let go.' It was the end of the world to me." So Kasper, in her ballet flats and black culottes and turtleneck, which she recalls as her uniform in her Broadway-aspiring adolescent days, was out on her ear.

Did Shelley Winters know her diva fit would change the course of American food radio? Of course not. But to any historian of American food it's a very interesting fork in the road; Kasper is to radio what Julia Child was to television, the pioneer of her generation, the first to make the medium modern and take it away from the happy-homemaker pattern that dominated a generation before.

For me personally, Kasper has always been a reassuring, eternal lantern on a high, but not too far, mountain: If she could climb it, I could too. She's had that same aspirational effect on millions of Americans listening as they planned the night's dinner. If she could make a stump-the-cook dinner from spaghetti and a lemon, why couldn't anyone? If she was interested in everything from the pepper grinder to cottage cheese, surely getting dinner on the table was not drudgery, but a grand adventure!

That spirit of adventure was obvious in Kasper at the youngest age. She grew up in Paramus, New Jersey, the only child of Italian parents (a Venetian father, a Lecchese mother). Kasper's father worked various aeronautics jobs, and doted on her while teaching her the ways of the world. For much of her childhood he worked on a vast home-construction project, building retaining walls to prevent the family's house from sliding off its hilltop. He deputized his little girl as assistant mason. She helped stack bricks, mix mortar, and haul rubble for infill for four years. "We called it, 'The Walls of China and the Ruins of Pompeii.' I thought he could fix anything; we could do anything."

Soon Kasper took her general feelings of strength off the hill and down to the pastures below, where the horses roamed. She'd creep under fences to ride unattended steeds bareback. "That was what everyone knew me for. I could ride any horse I could get to. . . . Those were my *Black Stallion* years."

Her father taught her more: to surf-cast for sea trout and bluefish in the tides along the Jersey shore, to swim in the ocean, and how to float on her back if she got tired. She must have been six or seven, she remembers, when she put two and two together: "I didn't know a lot about Europe, but it sounded very interesting. And I knew if I got tired I could just float. So I started paddling. Just paddling due east for Europe. The story goes, the lifeguard was just getting into the water when he saw the fin. Then, I seem to remember the semi-rough skin of porpoises. They were tossing me up and tossing me. They swim up and down the coast; they always have. The next thing I remember I was on the beach and everyone was terrifically upset."

Her first European journey stymied, Kasper turned her sense of adventure to the theater. Paramus High School was brand-new at the time, built to educate the baby boom in the new suburbs. It boasted a staff of well-connected young theater actors and a full stage to funnel kids into the flourishing world of Broadway just across the river. Kasper was one of the stars of the school. She saw Anne Bancroft on Broadway and then retreated to Bancroft's dressing room with a group of fellow students to learn about acting.

Young Kasper began spending her Saturdays in the city. If she had enough pocket money for a round-trip bus ticket, a knish for lunch, and a student rush ticket, her life was complete. She saw *My Fair Lady* two weeks after it opened. She saw *Skyscraper* starring Barbara Harris. Then, the tragedy that defined her young life: Her beloved father died of cancer when she was fifteen.

Things went poorly for a while after that. She got a job to help with her grief—and then the Shelley Winters incident happened. All the adventure she used to have drained out of her. When she didn't make the final cut for the theater program she wanted to attend, she ended up at a small, conservative college instead, but left the school soon after.

Her mother eventually enrolled Kasper in secretarial school, where she was required to wear white gloves. Secretarial certificate in hand, Kasper embarked on a series of early 1960s New York secretarial-skill-adjacent jobs, including a stint as assistant to a wealthy artist and collector of surrealist art. The art collector's wife was skilled at Chinese cooking and hosted dinner parties for the city's elite. Before long, she asked the young secretary to help out at the soirees (Kasper thinks she probably sorted chrysanthe-mum leaves for Jackie O. at one such party).

Kasper started to get her groove back during those Chinese feasts. She found friends who would go with her to eat all over the city. She remembers heading into Harlem after the 1964 riots to eat at an Indian restaurant with a bunch of girlfriends (a group of concerned cops saw them walking to the restaurant and promptly gave them a police escort home).

One of her girlfriends introduced her to her future husband, Frank Kasper. He gave her a present of Time-Life books about world cuisines. She carried the Chinese volume into Chinatown, seeking ingredients and guidance. Soon she got another book, then a whole shelfful. This evolved into her teaching in-home classes about Chinese cooking. She called her business "Have Wok Will Travel."

"I'd take three or four shopping bags and schlep them through the subway," she recalls. Word spread through the city, and she was approached by the department store A&S, which housed New York City's leading demonstration kitchen, to teach her cooking classes there and to lead their cooking program. That's where she met everyone who was anyone in American food in the 1960s and 1970s: Julia Child, James Beard (she remembers him as Jim), Jacques Pépin, and many more.

She also finalized her views on marriage: "After you have done it all, after you have explored and had your adventures, find some-one who wants to continue exploring and have further adventures with you. That's when you get married." So she did. She and Frank were married in their Park Slope apartment, which they filled with pails of daisies from the flower district bargain bins. Kasper cooked the wedding feast herself.

Frank, who worked for Honeywell, was transferred to Denver, then Europe, and Kasper went along for the adventures. In Europe she had a eureka moment, fueled from years of seeing cookbook author after cookbook author come through her A&S kitchen. She realized that everything in food had a reason for being what it was, and that Italian food could use the sort of book that Julia Child had given French food. What followed was years of exploring the region of Emilia-Romagna, making friends, being handed on from cheese producer to butcher to winemaker (not to mention historians, anthropologists, and scientists)—all of whom trusted this Italian girl from a distant Italian outpost in Paramus with their secrets.

In 1985 Frank was transferred yet again, this time to Minnesota. Kasper went along, reluctantly, but found the sudden isolation helpful for writing. And so it was that she produced one of the twentieth century's greatest cookbooks: *The Splendid Table*. It won a career-making number of awards in 1993, and prompted Julia Child to invite Kasper to stay with her in California, where she cooked her mentee dinner. Kasper recalls sitting at the table and Child leaning in to her and saying, "Lynne, you know you've written a seminal book, don't you?" Kasper sat there dumbstruck, and Child said, "Lynne, you do know what *seminal* means, don't you?"

It was soon after that a young producer in public radio named Sally Swift approached Kasper and asked her whether she'd like to try her hand, or rather, her *voice* at a radio show. They'd use the same name as her important book and approach food through her spirit of adventure and inquiry.

And the rest is the rest: biggest food radio show since Betty Crocker ruled the AM airwaves in the 1920s. Plenty more cookbooks. Plenty more adventures. And plenty more to come. Kasper has begun stepping away from the show now and then. She does fewer promotional appearances, and other voices introduce segments more often. She's spending less time there to spend more time with her husband. "Three years ago I sat up in bed and I said to Frank, 'You know what? People die at this age! Holy cow! There are so many things I am intensely curious about. We need to explore them.'"

As a longtime fan of one of the biggest luminaries of American food, it makes me happy to know Kasper's explorations are off in fresh directions—because after talking to her for two days, I realize who's really behind all that food knowledge: a spirit who is happiest swimming for Europe or sneaking under fences in pursuit of stallions. And this time not even Shelley Winters can stop her.

Minneapolis Made

Mpls.St.Paul Magazine, September 2019

I read to my kids every night, and some of the happiest memories of my life are sitting in the middle of my wine-colored velvet couch, with a five-year-old on one side, a seven-year-old on the other, as we methodically worked our way through all of Harry Potter, and at dinner I'd explain mudbloods and Hitler in a way kids could understand. Then, a six-year-old on one side of me, an eight-year-old on the other, and we read all the Narnia books and talked about Aslan, belief, faith, and free will. *The Hobbit* and the Lord of the Rings books, all of Lemony Snicket, *Harriet the Spy*, *Alice's Adventures in Wonderland*—too many more to list.

I'll never forget reading Kate DiCamillo's *Tale of Despereaux*, a Narnia-descended story of such tender emotion and awe-tugging poetry that I started uncontrollably crying as we read, and my little boy would take the book out of my hand and read for a few pages. If you've never read *Tale of Despereaux*, do. I know it's one good moviemaker away from being as big as Lord of the Rings, and literally millions of kids are walking around with heads full of DiCamillo's astonishing oeuvre. Also astonishing to me is the fact that children's literature authors are not taken seriously and don't get the lit-world profiles that even minor novelists for adults do. This was my effort to right that wrong.

Kate DiCamillo has 30 million books in print and a cultural footprint bigger than Paul Bunyan's—but do you know the story behind the juggernaut?

Name a living cultural figure in Minnesota with a bigger national footprint than Kate DiCamillo. She's got bestsellers at the top of the charts; a backlist as reliable and as popular as municipal bonds; and plays, musicals, operas, and movies as numerous as mushrooms in the fall. Disney, Queen Latifah, Sigourney Weaver, Matthew Broderick—you know the game Six Degrees of Kevin Bacon? You can get within one degree of just about any massive celebrity using just Kate DiCamillo projects. Her work is recommended by Oprah.

Wait, you say you've never heard of her? Well, that must mean you live in that gated cultural community known as the Land of Adults. In these days of YouTube stars, Instagram stars, video game stars, and unwrapping-packages-while-whispering stars (don't ask), it's not unusual to find folks who are a very big deal in a world you're not familiar with.

But DiCamillo is different. Her body of work is so original, mythical, courageous, spiritual—wait!

Do this. It's important. Next vacation, pack your duffel bag with as much of the lifework of Kate DiCamillo as you can, and take it with you. I did this in July, and it was revelatory.

I'd long been aware that DiCamillo lives here in Minneapolis. I'd also heard that she's intensely private, like seemingly all Minnesota superstars: Bob Dylan, Prince, Louise Erdrich, Jessica Lange, Garrison Keillor. Private: Do not disturb. It probably is self-evident that if you're a celebrity who has decided to make your home in Minnesota, you're prioritizing peace and quiet. But still, a fellow south Minneapolis resident such as myself does get to wondering: Who is this neighbor of ours, and why is she here of all places?

When her publisher announced she'd be doing a few media interviews in conjunction with her newest book, *Beverly, Right Here* (out this September [2019]), I about broke my neck replying as fast as I could: Yes, please!

I met with DiCamillo at the French Meadow Café on Lyndale, one of her favorite restaurants. DiCamillo has big eyes and a shock of pale platinum curls, lending her the appearance of a downy baby bird. She's slight, reflecting a childhood spent with recurring bouts of pneumonia, which is what inspired her mother to move her children to Florida from the family's original Philadelphia.

"I'm old enough that they were still prescribing geographic cures," DiCamillo says, with a laugh, over her iced coffee. (She was born in 1964.) Her father was supposed to sell his orthodontia practice and join them, but he never did, and that's the emotional core of much of DiCamillo's work, and the reason I cried a few times reading *Louisiana's Way Home*, her spiritually soaring and wildly underrated 2018 novel from the Raymie Nightingale series.

Now, if you've previously been tricked by the fact that the literary establishment has hidden these books in the children's section of the library, DiCamillo's major works are these: *The Tale of Despereaux* (an abused girl and a brave mouse molder in a dungeon); *Because of Winn-Dixie* (a lonely girl and a dog unite a southern town); and *Flora & Ulysses* (a girl and a superpowered squirrel grapple with the aftermath of divorce).

That takes us to the Raymie Nightingale series, the reason for my sit-down with DiCamillo. These intertwined novels center on the adventures of a trio of best friends: a lifeguard-training tween; the granddaughter (?) of a lovable con woman; and feisty Beverly Tapinski, the star of DiCamillo's new book, who runs away from home, moves in with an old lady in a trailer, and takes a job as a busboy. It's delightful to read the three in a row: like *Breakfast at Tiffany's*, without the sex.

DiCamillo is a writer of light Southern Gothic—a noble style—and good enough to stand in the ranks of Eudora Welty, Truman Capote, Tennessee Williams, and Harper Lee. What do I rest this analysis on?

The settings, for one. Save for the fairy tales, all of DiCamillo's major books are set in the north and central Florida of her real-life childhood, among the pitch pines and crows, the neglected motels and marshmallow salads. Southern types, like preachers of unclear intent and generous southern cake queens, peer in from the screen doors. Mostly though, you see DiCamillo's Southern Gothic in the way she paints everyday life with romance, mystery, generosity—and, always, extra sparkle.

"It was all citrus," DiCamillo says of her childhood home—seemingly an inspiration for the not-quite-contemporary world she evokes in her novels. "Walt Disney was surreptitiously going around buying all the cow pastures, but it was before that."

· · · · · · ·

After college DiCamillo moved home, and, adopting a fine southern tradition, she "languished."

"It got to be, I'm almost thirty," she says. "I've got it in my head I want to write. But people see my mother in the grocery store and ask: 'What's Kate doing?' Nothing. She's just dreaming of doing something."

This is where Minneapolis enters the story. DiCamillo credits her success entirely to Minnesota—because she is unduly modest and would rather not talk about herself. Still, it's a feel-good story for all of us, so I'll relay it here.

While she was languishing in Florida, DiCamillo had a good friend from Minneapolis who was moving home. "I knew nothing except what I read in the library about how Minnesota was as close as anybody had ever gotten to a perfect democracy," she says. The two moved into an apartment in Uptown. "It was an act of desperation, and the best thing I ever did. I call up my friend every now and then and say: thank you."

DiCamillo landed a minimum-wage job at the Bookmen, a distributor for publishers. She was assigned to the children's floor. This assignment did not thrill her. "I went into that like a lot of adult readers do, thinking: *Duckies and bunnies. That's nice. Maybe I can make my way down to the adult floor.* But I started to be around those books all the time, and then I started to read what I was pulling off the shelves. Then I thought: I want to try this."

In the five minimum-wage years working at the Bookmen, DiCamillo also wrote short stories and sent them to literary journals, placing a few. She was mastering the story arc intrinsic to short stories, which is how she builds chapters today.

Her big break came through a McKnight Artist Fellowship for Writers grant in 1998. "They didn't know me," DiCamillo says. "It wasn't my friends reading. It changed everything. One, the money was fantastic. I was making $4.80 an hour at the Bookmen. Two, it was: You can do it. You can write. It was a vote of confidence, and it mattered."

The next critical step involved an uncharacteristic moment for DiCamillo. "Now, I am shy. I'm the shyest person in the world. I was the kind of kid who would buy my own Girl Scout cookies so I didn't have to say: 'You don't want to buy any Girl Scout cookies, do you?'"

Nonetheless, when a sales rep for the publisher Candlewick stepped into the Bookmen, DiCamillo spoke up. "I said, 'I love everything Candlewick does, and I've never been published, I don't have an agent, I don't know how to get a manuscript to somebody.' This rep was about fourteen months pregnant and had a screaming toddler hanging off her, and she had a cold. And it was also the only time in my life I've ever asked anybody for anything."

This outreach paid off for both of them: Candlewick has been DiCamillo's publisher ever since. The trade magazine *Publishers Weekly* reported that the publisher bought *Beverly, Right Here* for seven figures.

· · · · · · · ·

Today, DiCamillo, when she's not traveling, can be found in one of the wood-frame houses in south Minneapolis that fill the middle-class world between I-35 and the lakes. She writes in the mornings and walks some eight miles a day with her mini goldendoodle Ramona, named for the Beverly Cleary character Ramona Quimby. That's how she figures out plot points and writing problems.

"Sometimes I have to pull the dog off the couch," DiCamillo says. "She's like: 'What?! Again?' Yes: We're going again. People, if they're not from here, say you can't walk in winter. No. The lake paths stay plowed all winter long. I finally got the cleats you put on over your boots. They're fantastic."

DiCamillo's nightlife mainly involves friends who invite her over, and sometimes the playing of Scrabble. The next morning she gets back to it: writing, walking, grocery shopping at the co-ops.

She loves the co-ops: "When I got here it seemed revelatory to me, that you could stand in there and shop with people who really believed they could change the world by doing good things."

If you live and lake walk and drink coffee and grocery shop in south Minneapolis, you probably see DiCamillo ten times a week and never know it. She wears hats. She's quiet as can be, private, the shyest person in the world.

Why Minneapolis? Now I had an answer. Imagine a bird's nest: It is not sufficient in itself to create baby birds. But it is necessary. No nest, no baby birds. Was Minnesota the necessary nesting site and nest? You might be able to make an argument that Kate DiCamillo's career would have happened anywhere. But she says this southern writer's career could only have happened here in the North, and being a Minneapolis superfan myself, I'll take it.

The Donut Gatherer

· · · · · · · · · · · ·

Minnesota Monthly, May 2009

This article—the only one I truly love from among the few hundred I wrote when I was at *Minnesota Monthly*—was the first and last time I wrote about my real-life children in any depth. I cannot describe to you the wave of nasty, meddling mail that followed publication of "The Donut Gatherer." Plenty of hate about how fat I must be, unasked-for medical advice about the various mental maladies I had and my son had. It was an absolute nightmare, and I'm still scarred. And yet, this is also the piece that, years on, gets people to write to me, and many of them say the same thing is happening to their kid.

The update? As of this writing, Beans is sixteen, and he eats banh mi, tacos, spicy pork bulgogi, bubble tea, and everything else an urban teenager eats. He turned the page from non-eating to eating when he was in about third grade. The change from non-eating to eating came as mysteriously as the change from eating to non-eating. I imagine it had something to do with his physiology, with, as Ignatius J. Reilly often mentions in one of my favorite books, *A Confederacy of Dunces*, "the mysterious valves of digestion."

Shirley Jackson, the famed horror author and a hero of mine, wrote about her family often for magazines; the anthology *Life Among the Savages* is phenomenally good. Years after I had my single foray into writing about my family, I read Jackson's letters and the Ruth Franklin biography of Jackson, and I learned that the same thing happened to her. I humbly suggest Americans stop writing to mothers to tell them how awful they are, and I humbly suggest that all women who think they might want to write about their families get a pen name and hide.

What happens when a restaurant critic gives birth to a child who won't eat? Failure, icing, sprinkles, journeys among dinosaur road diggers, tears, and a little bit of triumph.

Is there such a thing as a bad donut? Until very recently I would have said: "Yes. Most of them." The gas station donut. The grocery store donut. The big-box store donut. These are mere vehicles for sugar and grease, and Americans would be better off if we ate gas station carrot sticks, biding time until we happen upon superior, thoughtfully made donuts.

I would have said this because I say it about every kind of everything: nachos, pizza, chili dogs, Chardonnay, and so on. Get the better version; it's *better*. It's not hard. If you want to know what the best donut in town is, you simply go to twelve or twenty of the likeliest places and find the best. And you want the best, don't you? That's self-evident, right? Everyone wants the best.

I do. Or I did. Before I got pregnant, before I had kids. Now I've got a one-year-old who will eat anything—shabu-shabu, red curry, sand—and a three-and-a-half-year-old who will eat almost nothing. Consequently, this food critic has learned a few things about food.

I'll call him Beans. That's not his real name. But I used to sing him a lullaby about bumblebees when he was a baby, and over time, bee turned to beans.

Beans was born colicky and beset by acid reflux. Tilt him off an upright axis and his stomach acid would bubble past a little poorly functioning valve and make him scream. Until he was eight months old, he had to be held upright at all times. My husband would stay up walking and holding him until 3 AM, at which point the alarm clock would ring and I would wake to hold him.

Things have gotten better, though not much. His stomach still hurts all the time, and he doesn't like food. He eats about a dozen things, all white, all things you'd want if you were recovering from stomach flu: pears, apples, saltines, white bread, pretzels, Cheerios, string cheese, poached chicken meatballs, butter, and ice cream (rarely). That about wraps it up.

If you read the foodie press, you'll know it's a point of pride among today's parents to brag about what arcane foods their child delights in: Japanese nori paper, capers, Roquefort cheese. Ideally, the sentence you want to drop at the playground runs something like this: "Little Gabriel is such a snob, he won't eat cassoulet with truffle oil—only real truffles. I'm going to go bankrupt!"

Not us.

This is painful. As a food critic, it destroys the dream I had when I first got pregnant, that of running around to obscure taco holes and barbecue dives with my little sidekick. More urgently, as a parent, it means I have no way to bribe him.

Other children consider being sent to bed without supper punishment. Being sent to bed without supper would be Beans's preferred evening. (My husband and I have twice taken our pediatrician's advice to simply offer food, without insisting Beans eat it. Both times, after two days, when not a single morsel of food had crossed his lips, we buckled.) Other children can be coerced into all sorts of activities by offering or withholding dessert. We're as likely to get Beans to eat a cupcake as we are to get him to eat a block of soap. A few weeks ago, I got a bag of jelly beans in the mail as part of some promotion. I brought them home. We got Beans an egg carton, into which he happily sorted the jelly beans by color. Over the next week, he did this several more times—and not one jelly bean went missing. He has a bag full of Dum Dum lollipops from which he has removed all the wrappers. He sticks them into modeling clay to make sculptures. Child-rearing experts tell us that one of the chief predictors of a child's future success is the ability to delay gratification, to choose two cookies in fifteen minutes rather than just one cookie now. There are no studies on children who want no cookies ever.

Now, you may be thinking: *Why don't you just cut the kid some slack and let him not eat?* Isn't the ultimate state of enlightenment to live without desire? Hasn't Beans achieved this at the tender age of three?

If you are thinking this, it is probably because you are an idealistic fourteen-year-old without kids. I know this because I was once an idealistic fourteen-year-old without kids, and that idealistic voice still echoes in my head. I find myself incredulous how deep and dark my desire is to lure or coerce my kid into eating. This uneasy part of me, however, has been pummeled into submission by the panic-stricken part of me, the part of me that can't shake the memory of being at a friend's vacation house in Wisconsin where we met another family with a child beset by the same cluster of acid reflux symptoms. This child's family didn't force her to eat. She was five years old, but she was the size of a slight two-year-old. Her family explained that her teeth were so soft, from lack of nutrients and vomiting, that she would probably soon get child-sized dentures.

So we force him to eat. Here's how: We turn on the television. There have been studies showing that sugar is more appealing to rats than cocaine. In my experience, television, to a curious toddler, is more powerful than either. We turn on a screen and sit behind him popping bites of meatball and cheese in his mouth. It's a terrible option, except for all the other ones. I've heard other parents call television "the zombie machine." Exactly.

Then there's YouTube. For a while Beans was obsessed with church bells, and we would watch videos of ringing church bells, as well as glockenspiels, carillons, and handbells. Later it was marble runs and domino constructions falling down. Then he discovered a show that airs on the Discovery Channel called *How It's Made*. The show consists of five-minute segments explaining the construction of crayons, novelty ice cream treats, push brooms, and everything else. Beans's favorite was about donuts.

At first, I didn't think too much about it. It's not atypical for Beans to watch a two-minute YouTube clip hundreds of times. There's a 1979 *Sesame Street* abstract animation, set to a piece by Philip Glass, called "Geometry of Circles" that he must have watched a thousand times. But one night, I found him in his bath, shoving bath toys through the water, reciting: "A high-speed mixer works the yeast dough, then workers pull it off the machine into bins. From there, it goes into a hopper that extrudes the dough as a sheet. . . . " Not long after that, I found him shoving his favorite blanket into a drawer, slamming the drawer shut, then extracting the blanket and transferring it to a space beneath a footstool, all while providing this commentary: "Donuts used to be called 'oily-cakes' because they were deep-fried in pork fat. They were ball shaped when Dutch pilgrims brought them to America. . . . "

"Beans, are you making donuts?" I asked.

"I am," he said. "I am making donuts. . . . A high-speed mixer works the yeast dough. . . . "

Was this the thin end of a wedge?

I thought so—if donuts could somehow become more than a mechanical process to Beans, that is. I ordered some books.

· · · · · · ·

Children's picture-book literature involving donuts is limited, but uniformly excellent. There's *Arnie the Doughnut*, by Laurie Keller, about a young ring of dough, "chocolate-covered with bright-colored candy sprinkles," who is made through a series of numbered steps. Beans particularly enjoys step two, "Deep-fried," which involves Arnie swimming in oil and saying, "I'm soaking in boiling grease but I LOVE IT!"

After Arnie meets his fellow donuts in a pastry case, a rude donut hole points at a jelly donut and shrieks, "Eeeooo! His brains are leaking out!" To which the donut replies, "It's not brains, silly. It's jelly!"

Arnie is nearly eaten by his purchaser, Mr. Bing, which horrifies Arnie, and so he phones his baker to warn him, at which point he is informed that donuts are, in fact, made to be eaten. Arnie can't believe him.

"Are the other doughnuts aware of this arrangement?" he gasps.

There's also *The Donut Chef*, by Bob Staake, which details the war between "two donut shops on one small street! For customers they did compete!" This competition first involves discounts and extra frosting, but it soon devolves into something else: "Some were square and some were starry, some looked just like calamari!"

Eventually, after all the peculiar shapes have been mastered, bizarre flavorings are brought to bear, until the day a small girl named Debbie Sue ventures in, looking for a plain glazed donut. There is none. "We've donuts laced with kiwi jam / And served inside an open clam!" Staake writes. "Donuts made with huckleberry /

(Don't be scared; they're kind of hairy) / And donuts made from spiced rum pears / So popular with millionaires!"

I bristled the first time I read *The Donut Chef*. (Were children's picture books really going to criticize molecular gastronomy? Really?) But over time it's grown on me, especially when I hear Beans reciting the donut-positive messages in the book: "Then all the people sang in praise / Of simple donuts dipped in glaze!"

But my favorite donut book is a recent reissue of 1973's *Who Needs Donuts?* It's an odd, psychedelic-looking pen-and-ink-drawn book by Mark Alan Stamaty, a famous illustrator whose work has appeared in the likes of the *Village Voice*, *Slate*, and *New York Review of Books*. The book tells the story of a boy who can never get enough donuts, and so one day he rides his tricycle to the city to get his fill. He pairs up with a professional donut gatherer. As he and his pal roam the city, they often cross paths with a bereft-looking woman.

"Who needs donuts when you've got love?" she asks.

The answer? The bereft old woman herself, of course. After an escaped bull pierces a giant vat of coffee that sits above her basement home, she risks drowning until the boy uses his many, many donuts to rescue her—by soaking up all the coffee.

Perhaps what I like so much about *Who Needs Donuts?* is that, aside from imagining a world in which children are unafraid of the city, it features the only professional donut gatherer I've ever run across—besides myself.

In many years of restaurant criticism, I've written about donuts repeatedly. I actually have a sort of road map in my mind of what I consider the best donuts in town: There's Mel-O-Glaze, in south Minneapolis, home to the city's best raised-glazed donuts, as well as the cake donuts that I prefer above all others. Sweet and rich, they're almost like pound cake. Even if I've been to six other donut places first, I can always eat a whole donut when I get to Mel-O-Glaze, which is saying something.

Then there's A Baker's Wife's Pastry Shop, a mere ten blocks north of Mel-O-Glaze. A lot of people argue that they make the best cake donuts in town, and I see that as a respectable opinion.

They're less sweet and crisper, and they seem even more old-fashioned than most plain cake donuts.

I also really like Wuollet's, which has the area's best selection of the usual suspects: long johns, bear claws, and the like. Then there are our other lovable local donut places: Sarah Jane in Northeast, Rosemark in St. Paul, Granny Donut in West St. Paul, Denny's 5th Avenue Bakery in Bloomington, the Old Fashioned Donut Shoppe in New Hope.

· · · · · · ·

On the way to Denny's 5th Avenue Bakery in Bloomington, I fed Beans lines from all the books: "'Scuse me, Mister,' said the tyke / 'But where's the donut that I like? It isn't here, it isn't there—You think it's under that éclair?'"

We zipped down the construction canyon of I-35, between the dinosaur-sized diggers, oblivious to their dusty menace, for the topic of donuts was just that riveting. Denny's 5th Avenue feels like it has been lifted whole from the 1970s; it's all Jimmy Carter bicentennial blue and Naugahyde brown, slick, vinyl-touched, and awkward. Beans stood in front of the pastry case like a pro. There they all were, the long johns, the cream-filled, the jelly. Arnie had prepared him well for this moment.

"Is that brains leaking out?" Beans asked, rhetorically. "Nah, it's just jelly."

I got a dozen, and he got one just like Arnie, chocolate-covered, with bright-colored candy sprinkles. I placed it on a piece of waxed paper and set it on his lap as he sat in his car seat. There it rested for the drive home. I fed him lines from the books all the way home: "Do you doughnuts know you're going to be eaten?" I asked. "Yes, we're delicious!" he replied. "Try us for yourself!"

When we arrived at home, I looked at the donut carefully. To the untrained eye, it might have seemed untouched. But there was one small blemish on the icing's surface, as if a thumb had smudged it, or a little mouse had, perhaps, taken a lick.

A few days later, we went to Wuollet's. The one on Hennepin Avenue that always has a pleasant mix of dog walkers from Lake of the Isles, anti–coffee shop rebel teens doing homework, and construction workers and tradesmen. We got a box of the assorted donuts. I particularly enjoyed the raised yeast one frosted with chocolate. It had a deep real-cocoa taste. However, even to my wishful eye, I knew that the sprinkle-topped donut I got for Beans was completely untouched. I coined a name for such perfectly lovely donuts that went unsampled: They were Holders. Beans liked holding them. In fact, he liked them so much that he would spend twenty-four hours holding on to them, moving them from plate to bag repeatedly. But if any icing got on his hands, he'd demand: "Mom, can you clean it up?"

We made a trip to Mel-O-Glaze. Sun twinkled from the wide parkway outside and into the vintage bakery. I thought the donuts were great. The raised-glazed was light and dewy within; the cake donut was sweet and buoyant in just the right way. But it too was a Holder.

We went to A Baker's Wife's, a tiny bakery cluttered as a church sale with baked goods, but the crisp little gem there was also a Holder. We even made the trip to Granny Donut, a nowhere-looking chain in West St. Paul. The donuts there were, at best, average, cold, and greasy tasting. I wished I had made mine a Holder, instead of a Taster.

Donuts, it turned out, were not the thin end of the wedge. In fact, donuts were starting to become a lot like parenting itself, which in my experience is a series of minute, constant, intolerable failures, interleaved with exhaustion, and punctuated by moments of heart-rending cuteness that somehow add up to general success. The success, of course, comes not from anything one does, but because of nature's plan: The kids grow. Before I had kids I'd hear things like, "Parenting is humbling," and I'd put that in the same basket as, "Life is sweet" and "Happiness is worth pursuing." Whatever. Now I know that parenting is humbling because you can put all the mighty force of your heart and mind into it and you will still be failing. Where'd I put that remote control?

Still, while donuts were looking to be a series of failures, they also had become a habit, and when I picked up Beans from preschool one day, he asked for a donut. It was the end of the day when we stopped at Wuollet's, and they were cleaned out. So we crossed the street to SuperAmerica. I hoisted him up so he could peer inside the plastic doors at the plastic-looking donuts on their plastic trays, and Beans chose a raised-glazed and a vanilla-iced with bright candy sprinkles. Such donuts are the heroes, respectively, of *The Donut Chef* and *Arnie the Doughnut*. Beans put them in a plastic bag and carried them around like carnival goldfish all evening. The donuts even came with us when we walked the neighbor's dog to the neighborhood garden. And as we sat in this garden, next to an old wishing well, Beans turned a handle.

Ka-thunk, ka-thunk.

"Mom," Beans said, "Mom I want to make a wish in the wishing well."

"Yes," I said. "You can make a wish. What do you want to wish for?"

"I wish for *donuts*," he said. He looked at me intensely, a little smile tickling his mouth with its little baby teeth slightly too far apart. "I wish for *donuts*," he said again.

I took the donut out of the bag and, to my astonishment, Beans actually tried *eating* it. Of course he didn't know how, and went in icing-first, from the top. In the process, he gave himself a clown nose of white icing, and a matching goatee and mustache too.

All I could think was: *Really? A SuperAmerica donut?*

I redirect your attention to the central tenet of my professional existence: namely, that good food is better than bad food. This could not stand.

We went back to Mel-O-Glaze. Those donuts were still Holders. Back to Baker's Wife's. Holders. But then one day we were heading back to the house from the playground when Beans requested a donut. We stopped at a coffee shop with baked goods straight from some warehouse store. Beans got a pink donut with candy sprinkles—and began eating it straightaway, spinning it until he ate all the sprinkles and icing off the top. His one-year-old sister, sitting next to him in a double stroller, finished her donut, then lunged for his. Amid the tussle, his donut cracked in half.

"Mom!" Beans shrieked, preparing to cry. Until he realized the breaking had revealed a secret inner-nugget of icing and sprinkles. Which he ate.

And now Beans eats donuts. I feel pride, because eating more, and not less, is an enormous triumph in our little world, and somehow we got from eating less to eating more. But more than that I feel painfully amused, because as per usual, triumph comes at the end of a chain of near-total failure. And this chain of failures has even forced me to come to terms with something that readers have been telling me for years, an idea that I have so hotly resisted—that good enough is indeed good enough, that any port in a storm is better than none, and that there may well be no such thing as a bad donut. Sometimes.

Places—and (Edible) Things

What are places? I know that sounds like a silly question, but let me go on. Places, when it comes to writing, are not just a spot you drive to on a map. They're the spot you drive to on a map expressed through *your particular lens*. If you sent me or Batman or a jellyfish to write about Pipestone, Minnesota, we'd each come back with different stories. (Sure, the jellyfish's might be, "*No ocean, pfft, I soon died*," but still.) All you can find when you're travel writing is yourself and the things you're interested in. Batman might go to Pipestone six times and never notice the toddler playground or try the sour cream–raisin pie at Lange's, unaware of the long history of sour cream–raisin pie, from back before refrigeration and airplanes made fresh fruit a part of the northern winter.

It was only in looking at the twenty-five-year arc of my career that I realized: I write about nouns. People, places, things, and particularly edible and drinkable things. What else is there? Plenty. The front page of the *New York Times*, for instance, is rarely about nouns; it's about: *What happened yesterday*. The opinion page is: *What I think about recent stuff*. Nouns, on the other hand, are a little less changeable. Therefore, they go after the front page, and people like me can devote some more time thinking about them, and editors can have more time tinkering and thinking too. Temperamentally, I need that additional time. Temperamentally, that which makes the front page is not well suited for my talents.

I was in the WCCO newsroom once when a sought-for child was discovered dead, and merely watching the coverage I started to weep. Across the newsroom, one of the men who had been onsite and interviewed the parents stolidly typed. I always knew I was the last person who could do that kind of reporting, and that morning proved it. If I had been at the scene I would have been an additional problem, and no kind of help, not remotely able to write down details. This is because I feel and think deeply. Sometimes I think of myself as a water glass filled to the absolute top with thoughts and emotion, and any little tremor starts to make the whole thing spill over. This is a very good way to be for a noun writer, because when I tune in using my particular lens, when I consider a croissant or a glass of wine from Cahors, I come back with all kinds of big thoughts and feelings, and some of those will be amusing or insightful for my readers.

There's a scene in *Catcher in the Rye* when Holden Caulfield's awful roommate asks Holden to write a descriptive composition for him to submit for an English class. Holden writes about his brother's baseball glove, his brother who died of leukemia, his brother's baseball glove covered in poems in green ink. His roommate hates the composition, rejecting it as too emotional. That's me, except everyone likes my compositions about baseball gloves *because* they're too emotional! I also select nouns about which I feel emotional. If I taste thirty wines at an event, and twenty-nine are meh, or fine, or technically appropriate, but one reminds me of thunder and makes me feel like a twang has plucked in my soul like a loose bass guitar string, guess which one gets written about?

Sometimes I will go on a scouting visit to a bakery or a restaurant and come back to tell my editor, "It was fine, it was meh, it was additionally fine." We don't write about that one. Because where's the story? If I do have to write about a place that's fine and meh, I'll do whatever I can to make a story. I'll pull in history, my morning drenched in the rain with water filling up my raincoat pockets, a child smearing sticky fingers on the glass in front of the croissants—anything to make the dull noun into a *story* that will make your world more interesting and comprehensible.

Some of the most difficult writing I do is disambiguating similar nouns—eleven Chardonnays, nine burgers, three river towns, four metro DJs. To manage that, I do what I always do: I pop into the mind of an imaginary reader and try to make 'em laugh, make 'em cry, make 'em think, and never be boring. But at the end of the day, what a Chardonnay, a burger, a river town, or a DJ have in common is only two things. One, they're nouns. Two, they're being described for the current moment by me, in my words, using my lens. Sometimes people on social media will write posts to the effect that as soon as they read the first line of a story they knew it was me. Yup. Wherever I go, there I am. Me, and some nouns.

A Fisk Called Lute

. . . .

City Pages, November 6, 1996

After moving to Minnesota I acquired a Norwegian last name, from an eight-year marriage to a local blue-eyed rock star. I also acquired a profound love for Sweden and Norway, or what I picked up about them from hanging out at Ingebretsen's, the hundred-plus-year-old Scandinavian market on Minneapolis's Lake Street. Over the course of my twenty-five years as a food writer, locals have constantly tried to get me to write about lutefisk. I won't do it, because I said everything I want to say here, in this *City Pages* piece from 1996. It does occur to me that if I wrote it today I'd be a lot nicer, which would make the story worse. What's the use of a writer being a prickly, underinformed jerk? There's a lot of value, actually: It helps the reader clarify their inner world, through reaction, for one thing. The choir talking to the choir has its place, but it can't be *everything*.

"If you ask most people what lutefisk is they'll tell you it's cod. But that's not true. When the Scandinavians left the old country, they got on the boat and packed up all their belongings, came across the ocean, got here, got off the boat, but when they unloaded all their stuff, well, they found out they'd forgotten their lutefisk. So they wrote home to the relatives, and said: 'send lutefisk.' They didn't have a problem sending the lutefisk. But they didn't want to pay the freight. So they sent it COD. When it came through customs— you know, those guys aren't the sharpest knives in the drawer— they read 'COD' and said 'cod.' And that's the way the story's been ever since."

Tim Furlong is a big man with a big beard, but he's not about big enough to let the chance for a groaner go by. He claims to be the last maker of "lutefisk lures," jokey decorative fishing lures for the lye-cured cod. One is topped with a wild-haired purple troll. "That's a trolling lure," he pointed out, at the seventy-fifth anniversary of Ingebretsen's Food, Gifts, and Goods. His eyes danced around the room filled with the audience of his dreams: hardy Scandinavians who had come for a lutefisk-themed party. Lutefisk was on sale, lutefisk was free in little paper sample cups, and lutefisk eaters' prowess was applauded. The culmination of our day would be a lutefisk eating contest, with only the bravest contestants, only the most Scandinavian in-joke-aware spectators.

For the uninitiated, "lutefisk" is salt cod; that is, cod gutted, salted, and dried in the sun, but then rehydrated using lye, and finally rinsed with water. The process creates a yellow, mucousy glob that's trimmed with cream sauce or butter. It's an ancient food of poverty, but to modern palates raised on plenty it tastes foul, like ancient cold cream—slightly salty, with a chemical tinge and overpowering odor. But that didn't seem to stop the feeding frenzy: At the celebration, folks threw open the door, hooted "this must be the place!," and yanked their turtlenecks over their noses.

Clearly the only reason anyone ever ate this stuff was for brute survival, during famine or at the tail end of a fruitless winter. But it seems these cultural K rations have staked out new and glamorous life as a delicacy. "It's a big tradition here," says Furlong, "but native Norwegians won't eat it; nor will any Scandinavians who lived through the World War II era—it's all they had, dried cod. The older people won't touch it. When people ask me my feelings about lutefisk, quite bluntly, I tell them I wish I was a dog—because if I was a dog I could lick my ass to get the taste out of my mouth."

But! The women clustering around the free lutefisk table begged to differ. "You either love it or you hate it," one of them said. "We eat it at Christmas every year; it's like a treat. We actually have it over mashed potatoes with a white cream sauce." While they talked, the klatch, all in their fifties with clean purses and sensible windbreakers, spooned up the goo.

Ingebretsen's has been having such lutefisk reveries since 1921, when the meat market was part of the vibrant Scandinavian community centered around Cedar Avenue. Cedar was then known, derogatorily, as "Snoose Boulevard," and do-gooders regularly traveled the avenue to cluck over the Swedes' heavy drinking. Today Ingebretsen's stands on the same block as the infamous Pizza Shack, near DO Me Nails. After a spell of relative calm, east Lake Street is once again a stretch that doesn't have cordial relations with the law: In the final minutes before the lutefisk-eating contest, a cop pulled over three teenage girls, ordered them to throw their hands up on a wall, and patted them down. A dozen Ingebretsen's patrons, pink-skinned and plump, stepped up closer to the front window to watch, still holding their helpings of lutefisk.

As the frisking continued, the games inside got started. Darkened by the shadow of a giant wooden Viking in front of the herring case, the contestants took their marks—Bob Paulson, a Scandinavian calendar maker; Roger Moe, of Minnesota Public Radio; John Lundberg, whose mother, grinning, and daughter, grimacing, were on the sidelines; Pastor Haug, of Gethsemane Lutheran Church; and our own Tim Furlong. Each was handed their own steaming tub of lutefisk.

"We're going to ask you not to call out, or cry out," judge John Anderson warned. "You'll be judged by how well you hold in your emotions, like a good Scandinavian. If you finish your plate we'll give you more." The four judges, including Olsen Fish Company president Bill Andresen, who unloads about 500,000 tons of the muck each year, took their positions. "We will judge you entirely subjectively," announced Anderson, "on how well we think you are holding up under the pressure of lutefisk."

With that verbal shot of the starting gun, the contestants took to feeding. Suddenly, as promised, Furlong went wild. He removed a cloth from a formerly insignificant looking pile, revealing a baggie of boiled potatoes, buttered lefse, and lingonberries, and also tubs of ice cream, and also a blender. As the crowd watched, aghast and laughing, Furlong dumped the ingredients of a traditional lutefisk meal, including the steaming fish itself, into the machine, blended, and decanted the hellish beverage into a wine glass. But, while Furlong was providing the theater, Lundberg and Paulson quietly polished off their portions. The lady behind the counter nuked another round. They polished that off. Together, in seconds flat, they'd eaten two pounds of chow that seemed to have come from a plumbing mishap. ("You know what Drano is?" Furlong asked in a quick aside. "You know what the primary chemical in Drano is? It's lye.")

Because the judges claimed to be distracted by Furlong's antics, they awarded two crowns. Lundberg, using the Swedish pronunciation, shared the glory as the day's "loot-fisk" king, while Paulson, using the Norwegian, took the "lute-uh-fisk" title. Paulson clammed up about his winning secrets, but Lundberg was more expansive. "I just like lutefisk. And I'm a fast eater. I could have eaten more."

A Tribe Called Lucy

City Pages, August 12, 1998

I'm pretty sure I kicked off the national Jucy Lucy media craze with this *City Pages* article from 1998. Well, I publicized it, anyway. Ju(i)cy Lucys were of course a well-known phenomenon in south Minneapolis and had been for many decades. But the art of magazine feature writing is to listen to the chatter around you and pull out the threads that people will want to hear about in six months or a year. This story also happened to hit the internet about a year after cable food TV really got going, and producers around the country were looking for stories that were fresh (to them), easy to sell to higher-ups, and cheap to produce. Nothing was cheaper than flying in a host, hiring a local crew, and eating burgers at restaurants a couple miles apart on the same road. I distinctly remember standing in a fur hat in the screaming cold in front of the 5-8 Club taping various takes for a food TV spot as a local expert, imparting wisdom like, "the cheese is *inside*." Overhead, in a big cottonwood tree, a bald eagle peered down at me, and I'm pretty sure we shared a thought: *Funny, funny thing, this life.* Eventually President Barack Obama came to visit, and the burgers-with-cheese-on-the-inside were such big news they have now spread to Buenos Aires and New Jersey. Rereading this piece now, I see it was also from the years I had one foot in New York and one in Minnesota, freelancing in both places, and I was struggling about whether to leave Minnesota or buy a house. I'm glad I bought my house.

So where exactly in Michigan is Minnesota? Living in Mindiana-polis, is it difficult to get tickets to the big car race? Oh, I've been to Minnesota four or five times, I just love it, all those geysers, they just take your breath away.

I thought I'd heard it all—East Coasters, happily clueless about the world on the far side of Philadelphia. I was wrong. Witness today, when an editor called me from New York to clarify some questions about where exactly the Twin Cities were: So we were a suburb of Chicago? And our main industry was Hormel? So there were a lot of feedlots? How exactly did Milwaukee and Fargo fit in to it all? And mostly it was like the movie? I stammered something incoherent. Later, lying in the dark, headachy, with a cold compress on my head, I imagined all the witty things I could have said.

Yes, yes, of course! Think of the Twin Cities as a cluster of igloos by Wrigley Field. We all look like Loni Anderson in a parka, and we spend our time shoveling handfuls of fire-roasted Spam into our ChapStick-caked maws. The most important thing to remember is that the buildings you see are mostly underground. You see, the snow piles up so high—hundreds of feet in winter—that building vertically is just about impossible. Some do still call us the Twin Cities, but mostly we're known as the Subterranean Cities. So come visit Minnesota, the only state that hasn't yet repealed Prohibition. We're lucky the sun doesn't set all summer, since it makes it easier to shoot the roving packs of timber wolves and polar bears that daily raid our trash barrels. Primary industries? Cod fishing, lace tatting, ice chipping—come to the land that time forgot!

When I pulled the cold compress off my brow I realized my headache was still there, and the only possible cure was to take a couple of Juicy Lucys and sleep it off. Now Juicy Lucys are south Minneapolis's contribution to world cuisine. They're made by crimping two beef patties together around a hunk of cheese and grilling until the cheese melts. Served on a white, seed-free bun and usually topped with onions, grilled or raw, and a slice or two of pickle, the Juicy Lucy works on a couple of levels.

First, it keeps the meat inside near the cheese very moist. Second, keeping the cheese apart from the bread makes for a pleasant separation of meat and bread tastes and textures. Last but not least, the Juicy Lucy effectively separates members of the tribe from outsiders. Those in the know bide their time and wait for the cheese to cool, while rubes, hicks, New Yorkers, and other social misfits scald their tongues on the excruciatingly hot mixture of grease and cheese that pools inside the burger, poised to escape through any opening.

The idiosyncrasies of the Juicy Lucy allow for the development of personal technique: Some people like to dump their liquid cheese over their fries, some carefully nibble the cheese-free edge away while waiting for cheese cooling. Some even claim to be able to stanch the flow of cheese through the careful application of a frosty beer glass.

Did the Juicy Lucy originate at Matt's Bar? That's like asking: Is there a Santa Claus? You can only answer in the affirmative, even if there aren't any scientific documents to prove it. Cheryl Bristol, daughter of Matt Bristol, the bar's founder and namesake, tells the well-known tale. "The whole story goes like this. There was a bachelor customer who used to come in every day and order a burger. One day, in 1954, he told the cook to seal up some cheese in the middle. So the cook did, and when he bit into it the hot cheese spurted out, and he wiped his mouth and said, 'Oooh, that's one juicy Lucy!' They used to talk goofy like that back then." The name went up on the board as "Jucy Lucy," and they've been serving a couple hundred a week ever since. (Was life more fun in the age of creative spelling—Krispy Kreme, Jucy Lucy, Uneeda Biscuit?)

Matt's Lucys sizzle upon what might be the best-seasoned grill in the universe. It's been on for about twelve hours a day since that fateful 1954 experiment. Burgers come off with a gorgeous crust of char; onions are grilled to a lightly caramelized summer blond. Most importantly, when you're tucked into one of the booths, waiting for your cheese to cool, beside a gold-vinyl wall covering as wholesome, slutty, and American as Annette Funicello's beach blanket, with points of light poking through from the perforated

brass lamps like so many stars, you know you're in Minneapolis, deep in Minneapolis, in the Minneapolis where everyone knows what 3.2 is, where *the crick* goes, when the Aquatennial is, who Sven and Ole are, and how you become a butter queen. No explanations required.

Meanwhile, twenty-three blocks south, you can find more Lucys at the 5-8 Club, a one-time speakeasy and current neighborhood 3.2 bar filled with small reproduction tin signs and nostalgic film posters. The 5-8 serves an upscale Juicy Lucy. The meat is ground daily, and the buns are baked every morning for Lucys stuffed with your choice of thick American cheese or—and there's genius here—Swiss, pepper jack, or blue cheese. At $3.85 for a big, sizzling, dense, and tender burger filled with good cheese—or $5.45 in a basket with fries and some homemade coleslaw—if you consider yourself any sort of a Lucy connoisseur you owe it to yourself to give the 5-8 a whirl.

The rivalry between Matt's and the 5-8 is rather charming. "The Juicy Lucy has been around for many, many years, and there's always been a dispute between Matt's and ourselves as to who invented it," says 5-8 owner Jim Emison judiciously. "We try to outdo them, and I'm sure they try to outdo us." Not so, says Cheryl Bristol. "I haven't eaten their burgers, so I don't know what they're like."

Which is the better Lucy? I could tell you what I think, but then I'd have to leave town, because offended Lucy partisans would surely rip me to shreds. And I'm not ready to go back to New York, the obnoxious homeland which fills me with such alternating bouts of love and horror. Thankfully, my headache's gone. With a gut full of beef, onions, and cheese, thoughts of the East Coast dissolve like tears in my 3.2. Such are the pleasures of life in Mindianapolis.

In Search of Hot Beef

. . . .

Mpls.St.Paul Magazine, April 2019

I will never forget how this story of Minnesota's obsession with the hot beef sandwich came about. I had been pitching it since my *City Pages* days, and no editor ever thought it would have enough to it to publish. Years later, my *Mpls.St.Paul* editor at the time, the brilliant Michael Tortorello, also passed on it. "Too bad for you," I said. "I'm going to just write it and send it to *The New Yorker*." Michael said something to the effect of, "Are you serious? It's that important/good?" Evidently I hadn't been making clear that I was talking about a *story*, not a *topic*, and my passion made him realize that yes, I was serious. And thus I offer you one of my favorite northern food tales of all time.

The other Juicy Lucy, Minnesota's signature sandwich that you never heard of.

One of the great vexations of writing about northern cuisine, as opposed to southern, is our lack of iconic restaurant foods. The South has so much, like biscuits, pimento cheese, barbecue, fried chicken. We have—what, exactly?

Our small-town cafés served pie; we can all agree on that. Eggs and bacon and hash browns. Toast. At some point in the mid-twentieth century, we got hamburgers and fries. These are not exactly foods that lend themselves to Faulknerian rhapsody among the tupelo trees.

Yet one particular northern food-culture question has been tickling at the edges of my mind for years. It has to do with something that's sometimes called a "beef commercial sandwich," sometimes called "hot beef." I decided this year to get to the bottom of it. Where did it begin? Where is it now?

I got a ping back from the news archives, and the summer of 1952, when the *Minneapolis Tribune* took a few inches away from the dire issues of the day to reprint an editorial from the *Christian Science Monitor*. "Much was my consternation the first time I sat down in a modern American eatery and ordered the advertised 'Hot Beef Sandwich,'" the author started. "What I got was a perfectly straightforward Beef à l'Angleterre"—an intentionally pretentious phrase for roast beef.

The author went on to describe the sandwich: beef served between two pieces of bread, with mashed potatoes *inside the sandwich*(!), and the whole beef–mashed potato brick smothered in gravy. But here was the author's problem: It was impossible to eat with "the fingers, on account of the gravy, among other things. . . . I do not want to carp, but let us have some respect for tradition."

Why did the *Minneapolis Tribune* choose to run this, when the hot beef sandwich—bread, mashed potatoes, some form or other of roast beef, gravy coating—had been common for at least a generation? I suspect that reprint fits in a noble Minnesota newspaper tradition: calling out *what these boneheads on the coasts have to say now*. (See: grape salad.)

I'm pretty sure that I am the specific human being who first wrote about the Ju(i)cy Lucy—our burger with the cheese inside—after noticing it on a couple of local menus. (See "A Tribe Called Lucy," in an August 1998 issue of *City Pages* [page 133].) Nowadays, there's a small juicy lucy chain in Lima, Peru, and a brand-new juicy lucy restaurant in Staten Island—yes, in New York City.

I'd seen what it looks like when a northern food entered the canon and became famous. So I went out in search of hot beef. Or the hot beef commercial. At the outset, I really didn't know what it should properly be called.

I first got in touch with Tracey Deutsch, an associate professor of history at the University of Minnesota, who has a great interest in food and Holmesian powers of inquiry and research. By the 1910s, she reported back, hot beef sandwiches were common throughout Minnesota.

With that lead and time frame, I took to my telephone to quiz the Women Who Would Know. Women like Marilyn Hagerty (born in 1926), the features editor for the *Grand Forks Herald*. (You may remember when she leapt to viral fame after giving a positive review to a local Olive Garden, which led to *Today Show* and Anderson Cooper appearances and a whole circus.) When did Hagerty first encounter this gravy-drenched hot beef? The date escaped her: It was already utterly common around 1940, when she started writing for the *Capital Journal*, in Pierre, South Dakota.

"If you lived in the country and were going in to town, especially the men, they'd order that," Hagerty told me. "Bread and meat, with the gravy over it. Often there would be some vegetable on the side: carrots or corn, a basic thing. There was the same plate with pork, with pork gravy. That's what most restaurants had. In my experience, it's always been this way."

Men on farms get hungry. That's the rough shape of what I heard again and again. Beatrice Ojakangas, the James Beard Award–winning Minnesota cookbook queen, was born in 1934, on a farm in Floodwood, Minnesota. "It was what my dad would get when he went into town," Ojakangas said of the sandwich.

I reached Ojakangas on the phone when she happened to be visiting with a group of older friends. And she called out my question to the group: When did they recall first seeing hot beef sandwiches? One man remembered his dad ordering them when he hauled pulpwood to Cloquet. Another recalled his dad ordering them in Duluth. The group burst into laughter, which broke like the sound of waves on a rocky beach through the cell phone line.

"What's so funny?" I asked.

Ojakangas answered me in the tone of a mom trying to tell a blundering child, *We're not laughing at you; we're laughing with you*. "We all remember hot beef, hot roast beef, whatever you want to call it," she said. "It was so popular."

"When?" I pressed: in the 1930s, 1940s, 1970s—did anyone in the group know?

"What's the difference between the fifties, sixties, and seventies?" Ojakangas answered. "Those years have all blended into one big mush."

. . . .

It wasn't hard to find the hot beef. Once you start combing local menus, you see it everywhere. The only difficult aspect of the search? When I started looking in February, I planned to visit the distant farm towns of southeastern Minnesota. But blizzard after blizzard made that impossible. (And what's more Minnesotan than finding your hot beef blocked by the cold?!) I made do with what I could get in the Twin Cities, and an hour outside it.

A few things I discovered. First, a working definition: The "hot beef" or "hot beef commercial" is not two things; they're two names used for the exact same thing. That is, a sort of Thanksgiving-leftovers sandwich, where the main meal is beef, potatoes, and gravy.

That said, two variations exist, one made with deli-style roast beef and the other with pot roast–style beef. But either one can appear under either name. The name "hot beef commercial" is more popular in southwestern Minnesota, bleeding toward South Dakota. Mankato is roughly the epicenter of the "commercial" name. In the rest of Minnesota and in North Dakota, look for "hot beef."

We could decide as a state to call them all "commercials," and I'd be fine with that. It's a nice name. If we do that, we can embrace the story I've most often heard about the name. The commercial, in this version, referred to commercial travelers.

As Eileen Popelka, co-owner of Bump's Family Restaurant in Glencoe, told me, "There was a train depot here in Glencoe, and traveling salesmen came through. That's how the story goes. If you want a fast, hearty, relatively cheap meal, you'd ask for a commercial."

Traveling salesmen, traveling for commercial business, eat commercials.

However, Tracey Deutsch, the historian, helped me find a great number of 1950s and 1960s newspaper advertisements for beef. Here, "commercial" and "beef" appear to be inextricably intertwined—a classification akin to "prime rib."

It turns out the beef grades we eaters all know today—categories like prime (best!) and choice (still really good!) and standard (oof, not good)—became codified only in the 1960s. In the decades before, "commercial" meant a federally guaranteed label of quality, somewhere in the upper middle of the beef-grade spectrum. If you wanted really good—but affordable!—commercial was your grade. The way contemporary eaters hear "prime rib" as an indicator of quality and tenderness, our great-grandfathers similarly understood "commercial beef."

(Sadly, for the purposes of this story, in the post-sixties classification system, "commercial" grade beef is among the lowest. Think elderly stud bulls.)

· · · · · · ·

Whatever you call it, the very best beef commercial sandwich can be found at Bump's, in Glencoe, Minnesota, an hour west of downtown Minneapolis, on Highway 212. Drive toward Minnetonka and keep going.

Order one and you get a diner plate heaped side to side with heaven can tell what. It's a brown quivering mountain that could just as easily be bread dough, a brownie overfrosted by a child, or a platter of beer wort. Just a brownness that glistens. Explore it with a fork and you'll uncover a whole lot of very tender pot roast, homemade and robust mashed potatoes, and some very soft white bread that has soaked up a considerable quantity of gravy. Imagine a midcentury American Yorkshire pudding.

While beef gets the marquee billing on the menu, it's the gravy that is the beginning, middle, and end of the dish.

"There's twelve ounces of gravy on every one," Mike McGuire explained to me. "We have a six-ounce ladle; every sandwich gets two scoops. It's deceptive, because it spreads out."

McGuire, who has co-owned Bump's since 2006, estimates the restaurant goes through two thousand gallons of gravy a year.

Speaking of gravy, do you know what it's like to eat twelve

ounces of gravy at a sitting? I don't, because I couldn't finish it all. But let's talk about eating six ounces of gravy, plus pot roast, plus mashed potatoes, plus bread. I learned something about early twentieth-century life you can't learn any other way: What was it like to haul pulpwood to Cloquet by wagon? What was it like to work in a Minneapolis sawmill? It required *calories*. As many as you could get on a plate.

After tasting a dozen hot beef sandwiches, I'm here to tell you the success (or lack of success) of this particular sandwich depends on the gravy. In that mode, the other best hot beef plate I tried came from the Keys Cafe and Bakery mini-chain, where they also make a from-scratch gravy. The Keys hot beef has been on the menu since founder Barbara Hunn started it in 1973, she told me. It begins with drippings from the beef (also roasted from scratch).

"The younger group doesn't order it," Hunn said. "They go to your trendy restaurants, your fast-food restaurants. That doesn't really have anything to do with me. I've had hot beef on the menu here for forty-seven years. You have to have a chef or someone on staff who can do the whole thing from scratch. That's the way we've always done it. After you decide to do it all from scratch, it's easy."

Here's what's terrific about the Keys hot beef: everything. Again, it's soft pot roast–style beef, fork tender, with a good beefy gravy, real mashed potatoes, bread and—because why not?—a scoop of stuffing as well. I'd probably been to Keys twenty times and never even thought of ordering one. It's glorious. Every forkful mellow and beefy, mellow and potatoey. The essence of country farm food. If you live in the Twin Cities and love pot roast and don't avail yourself of one of these sandwiches, you are missing out.

It's important, I think, that both Bump's and Keys went into their projects as a reaction of sorts against the cooking of the time. That would have been dehydrated gravy packets and boxed-and-rehydrated potato flakes or buds—which I regret to tell you remains the norm.

Barbara Hunn opened her first Keys on Raymond Avenue, in St. Paul, determined to do things the right way, and based her whole restaurant on ideas like mashed potatoes made from potatoes.

At Bump's, McGuire and Popelka took a conscious leap into real mashed potatoes around 1992.

"Do you remember when we did that?" Popelka asked McGuire, when we all spoke on the phone. "We used to use potato pearls. That was a huge move at the time. It was the best thing we ever did."

Back to the beef. There are two ways of making a hot beef commercial today. One way involves roast beef, like deli meat from a slicer. The other way takes beef that has been roasted in an oven. If it sounds like those are the same thing, that's because Americans lack an agreed-upon vocabulary to differentiate between the dozens of wildly different inputs and outputs that all mean beef-from-an-oven. (Someone get on this.)

Beatrice Ojakangas suspects that the whole concept of a Minnesota hot beef sandwich evolved out of the home-cooking staple of a big Sunday roast. Think something like a chuck-arm roast. The next day, homemade bread would stretch the leftovers.

After Sunday roast dinners at home became less common, roast beef sandwiches made by a deli that roasts its own beef became more popular. A few spots continue this deep history of Minnesota deli-style, house-cooked roast beef and make truly stellar roast beef sandwiches: for instance, Maverick's Real Roast Beef, on Lexington, in Roseville; and Wally's Roast Beef, in Bloomington. However, they don't make good gravy. Please take my advice: If you order the gravy at Maverick's or Wally's, you will ruin an otherwise delightful roast beef sandwich.

Where else should you go for a hot beef sandwich? Good question.

Once you start looking, they're everywhere. At some point I became convinced there was some cutoff year—say, 1980—and every Minnesota restaurant that opened before then offered the sandwich. There it was on the menu at Milda's (excellent), in the Bryn Mawr neighborhood of Minneapolis. At Manning's (meh), near the U. I loved the one at Emma Krumbee's, in Belle Plaine, perhaps in part because I had a delightful conversation with a couple of elderly men in seed caps about their best caught-in-a-snowdrift story. (Answer: It took three days till the plow found her! And she popped right out of the driver's seat window, saying, *I was getting worried about you.*)

I learned other things I hadn't set out to know. For instance, wherever you find hot beef, you will also find the semi-endangered species that is the cream pie with a meringue top. My whole life I have seen sour cream–raisin pies only in old church cookbooks. Yet I encountered one in real life at Emma Krumbee's, and it was just a surprise and a pleasure. Sort of savory, a bit tangy. British somehow?

I'll confess, when I started this story, I thought it would be like any other food roundup. You research who makes the donuts, you taste the donuts, you judge the donuts. But finding the hot beef commercial ended up raising more questions: How did we lose it, in plain sight?

My theory, which I ran past all my food matriarchs, is this: For the first half of the twentieth century, Minnesotans lived—and ate—modestly. We made our bread at home, we mashed our own potatoes, we bought the second-best beef. And, with a little flour and a lot of time, we made something wonderful for it: gravy.

The food technologies developed for World War II, like powdered gravy and dehydrated potatoes, came right for the heart of our northern food culture. We forgot what a scratch roast beef platter could be. Fast forward from 1950 to now, and you find a South that has preserved and even mythologized its country ham and red-eye gravy. While we in the North mostly lost our hot beef.

But we didn't entirely lose it. My plea? Take the same journey I did, in miniature. Make this the year you start seeing hot beef. Go to Keys, visit Milda's, road-trip to Bump's. While you're at it, why not hit our heritage purist deli roast beef spots too? Try Wally's; try Maverick's.

When people ask you what's the Minneapolis food, have a second answer after the Juicy Lucy. Our food is hot beef. Your out-of-town friends will look at you to see if you're joking. Keep a straight face. Tell them: *Imagine a Thanksgiving-leftovers sandwich, but it's beef.* For a hundred years it was the meal country folk ate when they came to town.

Tell them: *There's almost nowhere left that has a good one. But you can still find it—and I know where.*

The Brown-Plate Special

What does it take to make Minnesota's greatest sandwich?

1. Bake a loaf of bread, the soft, fancy, weekend-sandwich kind. White, brioche, sourdough? Your call.
2. Season and roast a giant hunk of beef. Like a five- or ten-pound boneless beef rib roast. Gather the drippings.
3. Make a great deal of real gravy from your beef drippings. Use homemade roast bone broth if you've got it.
4. Make mashed potatoes, any variety, from scratch. Don't skimp on the butter.
5. Enjoy a nice Sunday dinner with all of the above.
6. Wake up on Monday. Finally, it's sandwich day! Take out your leftovers and make the best sandwich in the world. Bread goes on the bottom, then mashed potatoes, then beef, then another slice of bread up top. Finally, dump enough gravy over the plate to get gravy in every bite. That's living!

How to Review a Restaurant

Restaurant reviews have long been my bread and butter, so to speak—even though I wrote zero restaurant reviews before 1997 and only about one a month since 2008. I'm very good at them. To date, I've won six James Beard Awards for my restaurant reviews and different bits of food writing out of fifteen nominations. Chefs and restaurant owners mostly love my reviews, even the negative ones, because finally someone is taking them seriously and seeing all that they do. Readers love them because I deliver delightful, fresh nonfiction and am reliably right—if I do say so myself.

Still, restaurant reviews are actually understood by very few and are most misunderstood by restaurant people. Everyone thinks restaurant reviews are about the grade or the stars or the thumbs-up or thumbs-down at the end. Absolutely not. Restaurant reviews are nonfiction prose a writer quilts up to create joy, or some other emotion, in the minds of their readers. Many of these readers will never go to the restaurant; you must serve them. Some readers will; you must serve them. How? Let's take a step back. What is a restaurant review, really? It's a piece of nonfiction for which the writer must juggle at least half a dozen necessary elements. Here's how:

1) You have to make your readers laugh, or cry, or think.

2) You must not be boring.
I cannot emphasize this enough. People read a restaurant review expecting certain things, and if you give them a formulaic checklist of what they expect, they're bored. Not only do you have to not be boring, in a restaurant review you must leap over an additional hurdle, which is that so many other restaurant reviews your reader has encountered are formulaic and boring, so they are pre-bored before they read your first line.

3) You have to write about what you see, taste, feel, and hear.
There's a phrase people use to talk about how bonkers it is
to use words to express things that are non-words: *Dancing about architecture*. Food writing is always dancing about
architecture, but it's also doing so with a paucity of useful
words. *Sweet*—I hate that word so much. It's so inadequate.
Words you can use in, say, novel writing to convey sweet, such
as *honeyed*, *saccharine*, and *treacly*, those mean very specific
things once you're talking about food. You can't say a croissant
is honeyed, because that means it has honey in it. Sometimes
it'll take me half an hour, a thesaurus, and staring at the
ceiling in exasperation to come up with a mere six words to
describe one cookie. But that's what you have to do if you
want to be clear and also not boring.

4) You have to be right.
Being right has three parts. A) You have to put in the work in
the restaurant itself. I've been to restaurants as many as five
times, trying to uncover a few conclusive insights. Three visits
is standard. B) You have to put in the work in research. Unless
you spend a few hours brushing up on the history of Trinidad, you will not be able to write even a single useful clause
about a flatbread sandwich from Trinidad. Ditto for an opera
cake such as they make in France, a Cornish pasty in the style
favored in Alexandria, Minnesota, and everything else. C) You
have to put in the work in interviews. I've spent hours on the
phone with chefs or owners trying to learn about what they
were trying to accomplish; what this bread or that sauce says
to them about their grandmothers, or mentors, or a farm.
Sometimes I do a big interview and don't use much of it in
the final review, but it still informs the story.

5) No fear.
If you can't say that a restaurant is awful, and then stand up
to the blowback, quit the field. All you have as a critic is your
honor, your work, and your truth. If you can't stand behind
those, just quit. Yes, if you say a restaurant is bad people will

call you a snob. Yes, they'll sit around on the internet and fantasize that you have relatives running competing restaurants. It's all part of the territory. Sometimes you're Champagne Barbie; sometimes you're Champagne Cruella de Vil. Welcome to the life of a critic.

6) Every review you write is also a review of you, the reviewer.
Declare a mediocre restaurant great, and people will rightly blame you for their wasted hundred bucks and their wasted time, and your reputation will never recover. Never. No pressure!

7) Trust the process.
Once you have been to a restaurant three times, have done the research, and have the intention to make a dazzling piece of writing for your readers, the skills to pull it off, the patience to stare at the ceiling until the right words come to evoke a cookie, and no fear of what happens after you hit "send," you will write a great restaurant review.

I have written hundreds of restaurant reviews over the years, but I haven't selected many for this anthology, mostly because I think they don't age well. I set myself the challenge of picking my top three.

Sooki & Mimi Isn't an "Authentic" Mexican Restaurant—It's Authentically Ann Kim

. . . .

Mpls.St.Paul Magazine, May 2021

If there's anything in my restaurant-reviewing life I'm most proud of, it's knocking the concept of "authenticity" off its pedestal. This journey started in the 1990s, when I'd hear various Asian chefs trash other Asian chefs for their "inauthenticity." Typically this was delivered to me in a phrase like, "you can't print this, but they're not really Thai." Over time I noticed there was some kind of anti-Lao or anti-Vietnamese thing going on, and I recoiled at being dragged into it. By the 2010s I started seeing very talented millennial chefs tarred by know-nothings for their "inauthenticity." It was then I realized the food world had been using "authentic" as an unexamined synonym for a whole range of concepts—from "good" to "outgroup" to "newfangled" to "place-based" to "someone told me a thing and I'm parroting it."

Honestly, "authenticity" as typically used in food writing is so lazy, it's essentially beneath contempt. How can anyone cook "authentic" Sardinian food in San Francisco? Without the fish from that morning's catch out of the waters of the Mediterranean Sea, without the local greens, without local bread baked in local sea air, without the local olive oil, without a dining room full of Sardinians who speak the same language and have a basket of shared feast days and seasons and other experiences? And authentic to when? Precontact, before that murderer Columbus and his contemporaries brought tomatoes to Europe from the Americas? Before or after commercial pasta factories? Before or after Sardinian Jews were handed over to Hitler for extermination? Before or after commercial fertilizer was introduced to local farming? At the point you discover you must anchor your authenticity in a particular time in a particular place, you quickly find that you now have to anchor it in a set of culinary choices. (Chicken? Wood fire or gas stove? Feast day foods or workday foods?) And suddenly you have created the inevitable perspective of a single person. Authenticity can never be anything but: A person, in time, making choices.

I started writing against this unexamined idea of authenticity in about 2013, and the fullness of my thought is best exemplified in my 2021 review of Ann Kim's Sooki & Mimi in Uptown Minneapolis. As of today, I believe my various arguments against "authenticity" have percolated through elite food circles, such that I don't think any self-respecting major critic today will use the word *authentic* without defining it first. Or at least I hope not.

Ann Kim's new Sooki & Mimi marks the James Beard Award–winning chef's leap to a next level.

The emerald pool of aguachile appeared before me, and I was transported. It glowed like the proverbial leprechaun's pile of jewels at the end of the rainbow, sparkling with sapphires of mango, ruby petals of Beauty Heart radishes, golden segments of the cauliflower variety called cheddar for its bright-orange color, pale green Japanese quick-pickled cucumber namasu, flamingo-pink fractals of romanesco, and a black glitter of preserved lime peel scattered across like the fairy dust the dish required. I pulled back my face mask, dipped in a spoon, experienced an ecstasy of lime, freshness, vitality, earth—and knew at once to where I had been transported: San Francisco, or maybe New York. So this is why dinner for two was pushing $500!

What I found on my first visit to the new Sooki & Mimi was not dinner, exactly. This was Art with a capital *A*—and every course thereafter further proved the Art beneath my fork. A delicate and fragrant madeleine made from corn grown and milled by Native Americans from Ute Mountain in Colorado, paired with butter made with the United States' only native wild chili pepper, the chiltepin. A "taco" of olotillo blanco Mexican heirloom corn pressed with a hoja santa leaf so that the tortilla resembled a preserved flower ready to frame. Upon it, piled high, a fine shred of kakiage vegetable tempura and bright school bus–yellow wheels of sweet-pickled kumquats, and beside it on the plate, a white smudge of pure ivory just-grated horseradish. Here was something uniquely Minnesotan—our great local chef Ann Kim, using the products evangelized by another local luminary chef, Sean Sherman of the Sioux Chef and Owamni, in the whimsical and erudite fashion of Gavin Kaysen's tasting-menu restaurant Demi, and in the manner of a few dozen other of the world's Top Best Extreme Magnificent Lofty Empyreal (got it?) restaurants.

Well, well, well, I considered, glancing around this thing that had been Uptown's landmark restaurant Lucia's and was now a recognizable sister to Ann Kim's Northeast restaurant Young Joni—tropical parota wood, chunky tile, sage-green succulents, a general aura of the nicest possible home of married professors in the late 1970s. *You get it, girl*, I thought. *You bring home those international awards.*

"Are you going to bring up the anger?" asked my co-critic Steph March as she held one of bar star Adam Gorski's smoky and ripe mezcal creations up to the light.

"Oh yes," I promised as a tostada arrived, topped with white beans in brown butter and set with a ribbon of honeynut squash whorled into a sculpture of a ranunculus blossom.

• • • • • • •

Ann Kim moved to the Twin Cities when she was four and grew up the child of Korean immigrants in and around the Twin Cities. "My mother lived through the Korean War and other traumatic events. I wonder if it's passed down epigenetically, why I have constant fear and I always worry," Kim said to me when I talked to her on the phone for this story. "They were ashamed of themselves, my mother and father, because they didn't emigrate as doctors or lawyers—my mother cleaned nursing homes; my father started on an assembly line and worked his way up to the post office."

Kim grew up eating Korean food; her mom was renowned in the family for her particular unique gift—called *sohn mat* in Korean for "hand taste"—the special elevation of food that came about as a result of her touch, her hands. But Kim also grew up eating what we'd call fusion today, throwing together Korean foods and whatever was currently available. For instance, the family used the Korean bean paste gochujang that her mother would make and American condiments like ketchup. They made potato salad for picnics with Miracle Whip and fermented vegetables. "I called it pseudo Korean midwestern food. I went back to Korea five, six years ago, and my mother didn't even recognize the street food anymore, dishes had changed so much. Food is evolution."

Fed on Miracle Whip and improvised gochujang, Ann Kim grew up mainly in Apple Valley, at the knees of her beloved grandmother Sooki (a nickname for her mother's mother, Sook Young Kim) and her white adopted grandma, Thelma Lange, known as Mimi. (Thelma was Kim's aunt's mother-in-law, for those keeping track.) "Mimi was a huge influence on me. She wanted us to fit in, to not be bullied. She'd buy us books—*The Legend of Sleepy Hollow*, Dr. Seuss—take me to the Children's Theatre. I think I became an actor because of her. And when I think of her, it's her scotch and water, every day like clockwork, at four o'clock." Kim became a superachiever, an Ivy League student. After graduating from Columbia, she worked at a law firm for a year, then moved back to Minnesota to start a career as an actor. When she was cast in *Cinderella*, it was on the same stage and beside the same actor, Wendy Lehr, she had seen as a child. Now that's a Cinderella story!

But of course everyone in the Twin Cities knows what happened next. Kim saw herself drifting toward a career in the back office of an arts organization and decided to make a change and open a restaurant—to her parents' horror, because restaurants are where immigrants work because they don't have a cushy Ivy League–grad job. She studied pizza and opened Pizzeria Lola in 2010 with her husband, Conrad Leifur. The two began a journey that was both, somehow, meteoric (a James Beard Award for best chef within a decade!) and measured. And so, even with the success of Hello Pizza (2013) and Young Joni (2016), she's opened no second locations of anything, despite the offers. Instead, creative growth and brand stewardship have been prioritized over all.

Then in 2019, soon after Kim won her Beard Award—the first Twin Cities woman to ever do so for cooking—rumors began to swirl that she and Leifur were opening something inspired by a trip to Valle de Guadalupe. All hell broke loose on the internet, as usual. Accusations of "cultural appropriation." Social media swarms on Kim's restaurants' sites and other media sites. Angry Instagram comments. Pleas to critics to *stop Ann Kim from making tortillas*. Then came the pandemic. A year of racist monikers surrounding the virus and of anti-Asian hate crimes. A week after I talked to Kim for this story, the massacre of Asian women outside Atlanta.

I told Kim I thought it was strange that no one objected when Roy Choi burst to international prominence cooking Los Angeles street-style Mexican and Korean at the Kogi BBQ trucks in LA, starting in 2008, birthing a whole niche of fast food known as K-Mex. (For more on K-Mex, see *American Tacos*, an excellent book by José R. Ralat, taco editor for *Texas Monthly* magazine.) I told Kim I thought it was ahistorical to locate corn in Mexico, when Indigenous people grew corn all over North America for thousands of years. And not just in places you intuit, such as California, but as a staple food throughout Minnesota, Wisconsin, Michigan, southern Ontario, and as far east and north as Maine.

Kim refused to join me in my outrage, but said, "This whole social media call-out culture—it's been difficult. At first I wanted to tell people, *I've been the victim of discrimination; I've been the victim of racism*, and so I'll admit at first all the outrage surprised me. But then I thought about it, and then it didn't surprise me. People are angry, they've been pent up, they don't have places to go, they're struggling—and the one thing they have is their phone and their screen. So they're responding to hearsay, to sound bites."

She went on to add, "I will say I keep responding to people: *Let's have a real conversation, over the phone or face-to-face*. And they vanish. Someone who called me out was being racist at the same time, telling me what 'lane' I could stay in, saying I could cook Chinese if I wanted. What? I'm not Chinese. So I'm 'allowed' only to cook anything Asian? Says who? At the same time, I'm very sensitive to these issues. Cultural appropriation exists. The idea suggests abuse of marginalized cultures by dominant ones for profit. But that's not what I'm doing here. I've tried to make very clear that Sooki & Mimi is not any kind of 'authentic' Mexican restaurant. I hope to celebrate nixtamalized corn in a way that's authentic to Ann Kim, a Korean immigrant raised in a Twin Cities suburb."

· · · · · · ·

Kim told me a story of the person who taught her to make tortillas and told her hand tortilla–making was a dying art, along with the dying art of growing heirloom corn. He begged her to help carry the ancient ways forward. "He was elated!" she said.

No matter how elated he was at the time, he'd still probably be surprised to find Kim using those learned skills to press nixtamalized corn into a sort of tart shell for labneh cheese made neon pink with smoked beets. Or to create a taco base to support a beautiful, slick whole maitake mushroom confit, seared till glossy, and meant to dunk into an intense, smoky vegan birria broth. Who eats like this? No one, ever before. This is very much Ann Kim food, which I tend to think of as very intense, paired with a companionable breathing space of quiet.

So at Pizzeria Lola, the intensity is toppings; the breathing space is that uniquely airy and meaty crust. At Young Joni, the intensity is everything on the plates; the breathing space is the room, which feels like you are within an alive aesthetic thing—lifted up and held in it. Some rooms are like that. It is the same at Sooki & Mimi, which I suspect will quickly be known in town as Young Joni South. In the middle of the restaurant is a ten-seat tasting-menu area for communal dining or special-occasion tasting menus, for people who want them—rare though they will be, she insists. Kim tells me the expensive tasting menu she opened with is temporary, but I don't believe a word of it.

In fact, the tasting menu is something she never wanted to do,

Kim says, despite building a whole area of the restaurant ready to do just that. "As frightening as it was, it turned out to be kind of a blessing. I could have died and never done a ten-course tasting menu. Now I know I can do it."

Even after all the awards and success, it seems as though Kim continues to surprise herself. "This whole time, it felt odd to be called a chef," Kim told me. "I think I've gotten better about it, owning that. It's like: Hey, I've been in this business for ten years; I have three, now four successful restaurants. We've built strong systems and structures. I have this imposter syndrome—*I'm not really a chef.* After a while, it's like, shut up and own up to it!"

· · · · · · · ·

What most people will get at Sooki & Mimi, says Kim, once the real menu is in place, is a whole fish or Peking duck served Korean ssam wrap style, with all kinds of sides and tortillas to create the actual wraps. Maybe a heap of shrimp with salsa macha with tortillas. Maybe a few of her samosa-like Indian paneer-stuffed triangles, where the outside is tortillas. Maybe those out-there tostadas pressed with leaves.

I really loved my one single meal at Sooki & Mimi. It felt like the rarest of all things, an artist coming into her own. We used to argue about whether food could be art. At first, we concluded *food was not art.* It was a craft. Grandmas and drive-throughs made food too, and if they didn't call it art, how could we?

But over time, consensus drifted the other way. If a checker-sized gel of avocado inset with cubes of pickled mango served on a porcelain antler before twenty more checker-sized bites on the theme of *spring recalling oranges* was food, was it not also art? It certainly wasn't what grandmas or drive-throughs did. If creatives like Lee Bul, one of the most important Korean artists of her generation, could use fresh fish to talk about identity and history and desire, why was what chefs were doing so different?

So we were left with: Food was not art—unless the chef was trying to accomplish art or unless the receiver of the food decided it was art. Humans make idiosyncratic judgments like this all the time, so it's fine. If the artist Jeff Koons makes a balloon animal, it's art. If your kid makes a balloon animal, it's not. If a Greek potter makes something to hold wine, it is not art—unless it lasts four thousand years and a museum buys it, and then it is.

• • • • • • • •

Sooki & Mimi feels like an artist claiming her right to make art, or to be recognized for making art. This has not been easy for Kim. Personally, I have found the chorus of internet voices telling her to be quiet, stay in her lane, take up less space, and stay off the microphone to be infuriating. I, a longtime critic, believe anyone can criticize work—but if you try to keep someone from making their work at all, that's a dirty trick. Actually, it's unforgivable.

So far, Sooki & Mimi is not particularly Mexican. Kim's pozole is more like a Korean hot pot, despite the slaty Michigan Potawatomi flint corn. There's enormous Japanese influence here, as well as that through line you find in all Minnesota restaurants working with our excellent local farmers who are raising specialty ingredients—a practice, of course, kick-started a generation ago by chefs like former tenant of Sooki & Mimi, Lucia Watson. Kim's menu is original. I'd never had hot little spheres of Korean sweet potato mochi donuts stuck to a plate with dulce de leche caramel and served with a spicy, bitter, and lively Mexican drinking chocolate. I'm glad I have now—they were surprising and delightful.

"Who is Ann Kim?" Ann Kim asked me as we spoke. It's a question she's not asking me, she's asking the rhetorical space between us, where Ann Kim is an idea in the mind of strangers, not the only soul she's got. "So many times as a child, I did what I did to survive. I don't know if I was able to identify who that person was till recently. But I see now. I feel alive. I feel like I'm doing something that has purpose and meaning, like I'm contributing to my community. And I'll be damned if someone's going to suppress that in me. I didn't work this hard, and my parents didn't work this hard, to be silenced."

Spoon and Stable

· · · · · · · · · · · ·

Mpls.St.Paul Magazine, January 2015

Don't be boring, tell the truth, and love everybody. Those are
some mottos I keep in my mind when I write a review. Writing
a critical review might not seem like it's "loving everybody,"
but I think it is. It's an act of love to take someone that seriously, and it's an act of love to tell the community the truth, or
as close as you can get to it. This 2015 review of Gavin Kaysen's
Spoon and Stable was one of three restaurant reviews that
earned me a James Beard Award nomination that year. When
I look at the review now, one thing that jumps out at me is
that I was swimming against the social currents in town at
the time. Every single person—and especially all the powerful
ones—were enthralled, enraptured, delighted with Spoon and
Stable. So first thing in the review, I wanted to knock back
everyone's expectations and bring them into a different head-
space. That's why the gangly, gear-grinding intro. Semiotics!
What an awful word. But it acts like a jousting lance, clearing
a path in the mind.

*In which we try to neutrally evaluate Spoon and Stable, the restaurant
that is hotter than the mighty and incorruptible sun.*

Semiotics is the study of how images and words—a phrase like
"hottest restaurant ever"—derive meaning from their context. For
instance, if I were to write, "old fashioneds are hot," it would have
a very different meaning than "the surface of the sun is hot." A
headline stating "Soup Is Hot" would contain an embedded wink,
while "Venus Is Hot" sends us in an entirely different orbit. Semio-
ticians would posit that all communication is, in fact, the human

mind using bits of whatever is at hand (paint, sturgeon, E-flat, lace) to create meaning in the mind of the beholder by summoning context. Without context, not only can meaning not be clear; it can't even exist.

So let me tell you! I was in the Hottest Restaurant Ever, having an old fashioned, and thinking about how to put this review into useful context. Spoon and Stable is, of course, the Hottest Restaurant Ever, opened by Gavin Kaysen in late November in the North Loop neighborhood of Minneapolis.

For context: Kaysen grew up in Minnesota and left to have the starriest cooking career imaginable, winning a James Beard Award, being named a *Food & Wine* Best New Chef, competing on *Iron Chef*, and coaching the US team in the Olympics of cooking: the Bocuse d'Or. The chain of conquered summits year after year prompted whispers in his home state. Will he come back? *He says he might, he says he might. He has kids now, and everyone comes back to raise kids.* Then the announcement: He would come back. Then, he came back. Then the poaching commenced from Minneapolis's finest restaurant, La Belle Vie. First went the sommelier (Bill Summerville), then the pastry chef (Diane Yang), and local media (myself included) turned all eyes, all blogs on Spoon and Stable. Headlines gushed forth: The front door was installed, plans for pot roast were announced, Thomas Keller and Daniel Boulud flew in for the opening! Kaysen was featured in this very magazine before he had served a paying customer a single dish. The day the phone line opened, reservations booked solid, for months. Customers lined up outside in the falling snow in late afternoons hoping to get bar tables, which are first come, first served. I was one of those customers. I ordered the pot roast.

The menu comprises half a dozen appetizers, three pastas, which come as main courses or served in smaller portions, and half a dozen entrées, priced $25 to $39. There's a bar menu of casual snacks as well (the full dinner menu is also available at the bar), and an elaborate dessert program. I tried most of the menu and found a few things that were very good and a great many that were very dull, and came away with little idea of how to put this all into a meaningful, useful context for a savvy Minneapolis restaurant-goer. Do you like hot restaurants? Then you'll certainly like going to Spoon and Stable. But you already knew that. Do you mostly chase extraordinary plates of exquisite cuisine? Then Spoon and Stable may strike you as faltering.

There were some extraordinary plates: Scallop crudo was a sensuous intensity of fresh scallops firmed up a bit with lime zest and salt, then decorated with charred scallion vinaigrette, a chiffonade of shiso leaves, compressed vinegared green apples, and crackling slips of garlic and Fresno chili peppers. Each bite was like a waltz step of lush pleasure followed by a tap dance snap and crackle of vibrant spice. Delightful. The variation on salmon gravlax, with dewy but taut salmon paired with jewels of roast beets and orange was just as lively and engrossing. Pasta and risotto dishes were excellent. The perfectly chewy ropes of bucatini glistened with sea urchin cream and were studded with sea-fragrant clams, culminating in a charmingly highbrow and peasant-soul-satisfying combination that is so hard to achieve. Crispy potatoes, thrice-cooked in a process of baking, tearing, butter, garlic, and best-kitchens-in-the-world magic, are so good they could become a modern classic: Eat those right away.

But there were more dull dishes than magical ones. Dorothy's Pot Roast (named for Kaysen's beloved grandmother), which I tried again and again, tasted unseasoned, despite the fancy chanterelle mushrooms tucked beneath it, the raw slices of gossamer-thin carrot on top, and a fancy rosemary broth poured tableside. The slow-cooked cod, seared Arctic char, and poached sturgeon were all too subtle, inducing yawns from the table. I didn't have an entrée from the dinner menu I can honestly recommend.

Likewise, most desserts were forgettable. The apple crisp with elements of olive oil cake and coconut sorbet came together as little more than sweet; a grape frangipane with white wine sorbet was so delicate it tasted like nothing in particular. The exception was a buttercup squash custard with a pumpkin pie–like ring of delicate custard containing a tiny lake of luxuriant sauce: Pierce the wall of custard and the sauce tumbles out among quince balls and toasted marshmallow cream hillocks. It's charming, and the tartness of the quince plays beautifully with the different flavors of sweet cream and pie spice. Why does the food here tend to want to erase itself so much of the time?

It does this less so in the bar. There, arancini, Italian-style, breaded rice balls, are filled with a liquid fontina cheese that oozes out, making it easy to blot up the black truffled crumbs that act as the little nest on the plate. Duck meat loaf sliders, made by combining duck meat and foie gras into a succulent, beautifully seared puck, then sliding them onto tiny brioche toasts, are indulgent and crave-worthy. They go well with the restrained but darn-near-perfect cocktails by bartender Robb Jones. His roasted pineapple accent to the old fashioned is clever, adding a twist without the clutter.

The wine list, by Bill Summerville, is a wonder of adventure and economy, with $26 bottles of good Chianti as well as extensive offerings by single houses, such as the Austrian Weingut Prager and Italian Emidio Pepe. I particularly enjoyed the ease of "Bill's Pick," a nightly wine by the glass that lets diners spelunk through the wilds of Summerville's educated taste, without risk of bottle cost. Summerville appears at most tables a few times during the evening as part of the service in the dining room, which is both courtly and gracious. Securing a table here does lead to the satisfying sense that you are in the center of the world, and possibly its king. This feeling is quadrupled when the kitchen sends out a tuft of fresh cotton candy the size of a cheerleader's pom-pom to celebrate birthdays and anniversaries: Every eye turns to the huge pouf, and however much you felt like the king of the world, with the cotton candy you feel it more so.

Poufs and kingly feelings notwithstanding, I'll probably return with greatest excitement to the bar, to pile up appetizers and eat duck sliders. The restaurant's food really is at its best when it's riffing, playing, and being relaxed. While I'm in the bar, I'll no doubt get to think more about context.

One night, I sat beside a table of Medtronic executives who compared each and every course with Bar la Grassa. Okay, I thought. That's their context. Another night I was beside a pair of very pretty young twentysomethings, one of whom went positively bonkers, sending things back: "I thought this was going to be better!" she sputtered. The kitchen graciously offered to replace her food, even though there was nothing particularly wrong with it. I happened to stand next to her later at the valet, and she was still ranting in disbelief. That's her context, I thought. Kaysen told me later that he's talked to customers who thought the menu would be structured as a tasting menu, like at La Belle Vie. Another context. I've tried and tried to imagine what I'd think if Spoon and Stable was a new restaurant by a comparative nobody, some promising sous chef from Tilia, let's say. If that were the context I'd think: *This kid shows lots of promise; he really can cook; he is one to watch!* Is that, in the context of Kaysen's career, a withering insult?

There's a lot of promise here. At its best—in the bar—it seems to thrive because it doesn't have any baggage. Baggage, of course, is another word we use for context when it's bumming us out. Because even context has a context, and I think it's inarguable that no other restaurant in the history of Minnesota has opened with so much context, throwing a spotlight on the complications of modern life, in which we all are trapped in a cultural quicksand of our own creation, with nothing to save us but our shared experience in the insistent human condition of needing to eat every day. But now we can do that eating at Spoon and Stable, which is The Hottest Restaurant Ever, and more—and less—than that too.

The Sioux Chef, An Indigenous Kitchen

· · · · · · · · · · · · ·

Mpls.St.Paul Magazine, August 2016

My journey to understanding that which I do about Indigenous people in Minnesota has been piecemeal and generously given by many people. It started, for me, talking to a woman named Jackie Dill for a 2013 story in *Saveur*. She spent maybe three hours telling me about her Cherokee ancestors trying to make a new life for themselves after the Trail of Tears and suddenly needing to use the landscape of Oklahoma as a supermarket. She led me, plant by plant, through what there was to eat in what is now Georgia, and what was the same and different in what is now Oklahoma. During that conversation I had *aha!* moment after *aha!* moment: How people used prairies and rivers as their supermarkets and medicine cabinets, and what a holocaust the Native American experience was. I really didn't understand, until that day, that there was more than one holocaust that wrapped around my present life. I now know that the myth that Native Americans disappeared a long time ago is a foundational part of white supremacy. In New York City, I grew up not far from the Ronkonkoma and Rockaway train stations, and I spent years in Manhattan, but I didn't know until I lived in Minnesota that all these names were from Native American people, people who gave those places those names and were then . . . what? Removed, killed, absorbed, all three? How could I grow up in such a place and not know? I was at first racked by the enormity of my failure of understanding. Then I realized something also obvious: I'm not omniscient. We all know what we've studied, what's been communicated to us, and then when we learn more, we learn more!

I had already been given this gift of understanding by Jackie Dill by the time I met Sean Sherman in person. I had written about him before, in maybe 2010, when he was the chef at an affordable and competent tapas bar, but when I met him, everything changed. A dark sushi bar, inside a hotel, me and a visiting food writer and David Treuer, the famed Ojibwe novelist. Sherman was setting up tiny plates on the sushi counter in the pinpoint-lit dark: a bit of wild rice, a bit of whizzed-up berry sauce—basically the food you see at Sherman's acclaimed Owamni restaurant today. Right then, I started writing more seriously about him, and about the Indigenous cuisine almost erased by genocide.

I'll never forget the first time I put the word *genocide* into print. It was a blog post, and I could feel the skin from my skull to the base of my spine tremble and crawl. Was I going to just start saying *genocide*, and then recommend lunch? It reminded me of the Eddie Izzard sketch about cake or death, but in this case: genocide or lunch? And then I'm supposed to come in and say, *Why not both?* Is this not wildly offensive? After wrestling with it for a while I decided that pretending the genocide didn't happen, that was the offensive part. I made a plan: I won't pretend genocide and lunch don't coexist, and I won't pretend there's some easy solution. I think one of my greatest contributions to American food culture was making it okay for the food press to say, cake *and* death. Lunch *and* genocide. Because the absence of cake, the absence of lunch? That's perpetuating the genocide. Food is part of culture, in all its everyday ways.

I had a hard time choosing from among the dozen pieces I've written about Sherman over the years; his rise has been the most consequential happening in the Minnesota food scene in my lifetime. I picked this one discussing Sherman's plans to open the restaurant that would come to be called Owamni.

A slew of farms, restaurants, and education initiatives are galvanizing Minnesota's Native and Indigenous foods movement.

By early next year, Minneapolis could be the site of the first Native, Indigenous, tribal foods restaurant in the whole country. While the location was, at press time, still being narrowed down, the idea is clear. It'll be called The Sioux Chef, an Indigenous Kitchen, and it won't serve any European grains like wheat, modern inventions like soybean oil, or Asian sweeteners like sugarcane. What's left?

Owner and chef Sean Sherman let me taste a preview: thousand-year-old varieties of teosinte, a corn precursor, pulverized into a cracker boasting a certain rye-like earthy quality, paired with a bean-and-smoked-trout spread, mashed ripe blackberries, and sour wild sorrel. A salad of diverse wild greens looked generally like the things I'm often weeding out from the tomato plants. Dressed with tamarack pine bud and honey and covered with a flurry of bonito-like shaved dried rabbit, it tasted like nothing I've ever had before, entirely tangy and alive.

Sherman, a member of the Oglala Lakota Sioux, made his name cooking in Minneapolis restaurants including Three Muses and Common Roots. Sherman tells me his restaurant will be affordable and family-style, a bit like Brasa, with platters of bison, walleye, and wild rice for a family to share, sourced whenever possible from Native people and tribes. "We want this restaurant to be the flagship for a model that can be done all over the country, to get everyone to think about the history of their lands," says Sherman.

Speaking of history, what was food like in and around the Twin Cities a thousand years ago? Let's jump in a time machine. The food scene in Minnesota, Wisconsin, and the Dakotas was booming. Native people had raised-bed gardens literally everywhere, distributed on diverse sites around each village—for instance on south-facing hillsides, and on meadows and valley bottoms, to ensure that whether a given year was cold and wet or hot and dry, enough harvest would come in at the end of it. In these raised beds were bottle gourds and many different edible squash, sunflowers, corn, and beans. There were also plants modern iPhone jockeys might not recognize as crops, though ancient people did, such as goosefoot, a local cousin of quinoa grown for its seeds and leaves.

Food also came from lakes and streams. Native people had a

special way of tying down wild rice seed heads to differentiate one family's wild rice from another's. They'd weed, plant, and tend the wild rice as a garden. Forests, too, produced an abundance of food. Bill Gartner is a senior lecturer in geography at the University of Wisconsin–Madison and one of the country's few specialists in the archaeology of Native farming. Typically, Gartner says, "there was a sort of humanization of the forest itself through time, resulting in something like an orchard." When people went into the forest every day they'd make choices about what to harvest for firewood and what to let grow for food. "In the upper Midwest there were about three dozen fruit and nut trees that Native people relied on for a long, long time," says Gartner.

Gartner has combed through the records left by voyageurs and other explorers. "They were amazed," he says of the French traders. "The forests are full of food; it's the land of milk and honey; it's incredible! They never seemed to realize that it was intentionally created by Native people." It was also a foodscape a modern person has to stretch to imagine. Picture a forest full of chestnuts, for instance. Chestnuts were once the predominant tree in North America, and passenger pigeons, which once numbered in the billions, were big chestnut eaters, leading to indigenous dinners of wood-roast pigeon and chestnut. Of course there was also fish (smoked and fresh), venison and wild turkey, and local fruits including chokecherries, Juneberries, blackberries, and raspberries.

Since we're time hopping, we may as well visit the nearly opposite time, Native food-wise. When cultural genocide forced tribes from their historic lands and onto reservations, Native people were no longer allowed to hunt and fish traditionally and thus had to make do with the commodities the federal government gave out as a way of fulfilling treaty obligations—foods like flour, cornmeal, oil, canned meat, and sugar. The Indian taco, a simple flour batter fried in oil, topped with ground beef, was born. It was the best thing that could be done with the only ingredients to be had. (Not surprisingly, diet-related health problems exploded. Today, an estimated 15 percent of Native Americans have diabetes, some 80 percent are overweight or obese, and Native people die of heart disease and stroke at a rate 20 percent higher than non-Hispanic whites.)

One more stop in the time machine: A generation ago, Native writers like the Minnesotan Winona LaDuke articulated what was lost with the disappearance of Native foods, and a great many people took action. We're seeing the fruits of that work today, with the Twin Cities becoming the center of the Indigenous and Native foods movement. The Sioux Chef is poised to be its crown jewel. Sherman and his Sioux Chef team's first public foray into Native foods was Tatanka Truck, the country's first Indigenous-health-foods food truck, owned by the Little Earth of United Tribes community. The Tatanka Truck specializes in simple Native foods—polenta-like cornmeal discs topped with roast squash, for instance. Today it's not the only Native foods quick-serve in town.

The Gatherings Café opened quietly last winter in the Minneapolis American Indian Center. It's a little counter-service spot offering a walleye melt made with fish caught on the Red Lake Reservation and a warm wild rice, kale, quinoa, and mushroom bowl that tastes pure and healthy. In Prior Lake, the Shakopee Mdewakanton Sioux Community (SMSC) now runs a nineteen-acre vegetable garden and native orchard called Wozupi, which fills the country's first "tribally supported agriculture" boxes for tribal members and also fills the shelves of Mazopiya, the country's first Native foods grocery store (imagine the Wedge or a small-footprint Whole Foods, but one of the hot items is always bison chili, and instead of cod in the frozen case it's reservation-sourced native walleye). Seeds of Native Health—another SMSC project—is a Native foods and wellness think tank that's hosting the country's first national Native nutrition conference this month. In Hugo, Dream of Wild Health is a ten-acre garden growing out a tribal seed collection passed down from a Potawatomi elder.

One of the architects of this Native foods movement is Lori Watso of the SMSC. It began simply, she recalls. "I had my own garden, and was trying to feed my own children well, with good, clean foods. I was working with patients as a nurse, so many people with so many difficult issues, and I knew that every Native community is a food desert. One day I had that light bulb moment—that's what we could do that could address all of these health disparities." A $5 million commitment from the SMSC followed in 2015, giving birth to the Seeds of Native Health.

"It all fit into the philosophy of the tribe as a whole," says Watso. "To restore and maintain a healthy environment for our community, to provide state-of-the-art holistic health care, to be good stewards of the land, good neighbors, and good employers, while supporting our small community." The farm and the store are just the beginning. Seeds of Native Health is quietly developing policies and guidelines that will make the Twin Cities the policy capital of Native foods. "Say a tribe in Wyoming is harvesting buffalo and wants to trade with the Senecas in New York for white corn, how can that be done?" says Watso. "Native people have 112 million acres, and while most of that land is not under their control for agricultural purposes, I think it's possible that Native entrepreneurs can feed Native country."

For that vision to become reality, Native people are going to need to learn how to farm again. Part of that work is being done by Diane Wilson—an enrolled member of the Rosebud Sioux tribe of South Dakota who is the executive codirector of Dream of Wild Health in Hugo. Wilson began working at Dream of Wild Health to help Native people recovering from addiction.

"We started with a tiny little garden and a handful of different seeds," she remembers. "Then a Potawatomi elder, Cora Baker, heard about what we were doing." Baker donated her lifetime collection of seeds, which grew into the ten-acre garden Dream of Wild Health is today. For Native people, says Wilson, a corn seed is more than a seed. "It's an indigenous food, and the seeds have been handed down through families and tribes for many generations. It's your legacy. You think of your ancestors growing out those seeds. There are songs and ceremonies which go with the food, with planting and harvesting. If you change your diet, what happens to the songs that go with the foods? The food isn't just food; it's central to culture." Dream of Wild Health now offers Native youth in the Cities opportunities to learn Native foodways, job skills, and some language. In earlier years, it had 120 applications for twenty-eight spots.

The poet Heid E. Erdrich, an enrolled member of the Turtle Mountain Ojibwe who wrote a book about Indigenous foods, says it's a mistake to look at food independently. "It's the resurgence of culture," she says of the Twin Cities' burgeoning Native foods movement. "Language, art, dance, spiritual activities. . . . That's where this comes from."

The Twin Cities has been uniquely poised to recover their knowledge, says Erdrich. While many tribes were relocated a thousand miles from their ancestral homeland, tribes here were pushed to one side or another of their native homes, where they were still familiar with the plants, animals, and climate.

"There were a couple generations where people were really distanced from their own food, their own traditions, but I'm really influenced by the idea that a place influences how we behave," says Erdrich. "How could we live here and not connect with what was always here?" So it was a thousand years ago, and importantly, suddenly those connections are being made again.

The Cheese Artist

· · · · · · · · · · · ·

Mpls.St.Paul Magazine, September 2012

This 2012 story about the LoveTree Farmstead in Grantsburg, Wisconsin, earned me a nomination for the most prestigious of all food-writing awards: the M. F. K. Fisher Distinguished Writing Award from the James Beard Foundation. I wish the universe would give me space and time to write a dozen more four-thousand-word stories about the natural world and food. I am convinced that the only thing that matters in food in our climate-changing, animal-and-everything-extinction time is land use. Support everyone who is supporting birds and bees, please. Also: Mary Falk still makes some of this country's best cheese. Get some.

What would a great horned owl want with a lamb? Just the brains, really. One will fly in over the flock of dairy sheep and grab a young lamb in its talons, then make like a zombie, and fly away. Eagles eat the whole lamb. So do black bears, wolves, and the primary problem, coyotes.

But to lamb guardian and artisan cheesemaker Mary Falk, co-owner of LoveTree Farmstead in Grantsburg, Wisconsin, the predators that target her prized Trade Lake sheep—the creatures that provide the milk from which she makes her exquisite cheese—aren't the true danger. The real danger lurks in the cities, where people don't understand what complex ecology means, where people think you can kill your way to abundance and pleasure. Because if your pleasure is cheese, you should know that Falk makes what many call some of the finest cheese in the United States—maybe even the world. And she does it by nurturing a complex ecology of top predators, gentle grazers, and many much smaller creatures. "The University of Wisconsin sent a guy out here who was doing a predator count in the state," she says. "He counted ours and said we were crazy."

Falk doesn't look crazy. She looks like Jane Fonda playing the role of a farmer who has been out in the sun all day. Her hair is the color of honey, her eyes like a light-green leaf in a sun-dappled forest. She came to the Twin Cities as a radio host, and she has the perfect voice for it, gravelly like Kathleen Turner's, the kind of voice that makes you lean in to hear more. And when she laughs, her voice broadens and deepens into a welcoming boom. It even does this when she's telling a rueful tale, like the time she let coyote hunters on her land and they mistakenly took out "the alpha bitch," disrupting a long-established hierarchy. "She had been running things around here for ten years, managing two packs of coyotes, keeping them away from the sheep. Once she was gone, all hell broke loose. We went from having perfectly well-behaved coyotes, as those things go, to civil war."

There are many reasons for the great number of predators on LoveTree Farmstead, where Falk and her husband, Dave, have been raising dairy sheep since 1989. The St. Croix River isn't far, and it's a major reserve for great birds such as bald eagles and red-tailed hawks. The land around LoveTree holds eight lakes that act as a water road to the river, attracting all sorts of critters, and there is a string of state forests and wildlife reserves just north of LoveTree. Then there's the fact that Dave and Mary like predators, insofar as they support the grand balance of nature. That's why they keep half of their 130 acres as their very own "wildlife refuge." This gives trumpeter swans, osprey, otters, and several less benign animals free run of the spring-fed ponds and rolling hills covered with lavender clouds of bluestem and yellow sparks of birdsfoot trefoil.

To combat the predators without actually waging full-scale war, Mary has assembled a sort of Dr. Dolittle–style SWAT team of protective animals. There are the lookouts: tall, shaggy llamas who spy predators at the perimeters no matter which way the wind is blowing. If the llamas see something, they let the guard dogs know. Mary's guard dogs are a special crossbreed of Spanish Ranch Mastiffs, American-bred Italian Maremmas, and Polish

Tatras. They are the size of a timber wolf and are fiercely committed to their lambs and ewes, among whom they live twelve months a year. On any given day, these impressive dogs can be seen poking their heads up a few inches above an ocean of wool, like seals in the sea. They can easily take down a coyote, and they can make a wolf think a lamb is more trouble than it's worth. The final members of the SWAT team are the border collies, who take on crowd management in the event of an attack, rounding the sheep into a tight flock.

By nature, the LoveTree dairy sheep don't flock; they eat, outside, year-round, making the sweet milk that Mary gathers and turns into cheese. On Saturdays, she sets up shop at the Saint Paul Farmers' Market and sells cheese to people who, curiously enough, have no idea that they are buying some of the best-tasting cheese in the world.

The Taste of Genius

Tami Lax is the founder of Madison's Slow Food chapter and owns two of Madison's best restaurants: the famous white-tablecloth Harvest and the casual Old Fashioned Tavern. Before that, she was the chief buyer and forager for an even more famous Madison restaurant, L'Etoile. That's where she encountered Mary.

"To this day, I've never had a cheese culinary experience like the day I met Mary," she remembers. "I was at L'Etoile, and she brought in all these little samples. I don't want to say it was life changing, but I was absolutely speechless at every sample of cheese. The word 'genius' is the first thing that came to my mind, and it's the word that has stayed."

As the chief cheese buyer for her restaurants, and a former American Cheese Society judge, Lax has tasted as many Wisconsin cheeses as anyone. "Mary's easily one of the top three cheesemakers in Wisconsin, there is no doubt in my mind," she says. "The originality of what she does—each of her cheeses has such a unique flavor profile. Such depth, such texture—her cheese is always a mind-blowing experience for me, even years later."

Steven Jenkins, another fan, wrote the book on cheese, literally.

His 1996 book, *Cheese Primer*, is the definitive reference for Americans who want to understand cheese. "Mary is the most talented, drop-dead cheesemaker of my career," he proclaims. "Her Trade Lake Cedar is an American treasure. What she does to get her sheep's milk—my God. Her sheepdogs have to protect that flock from eagles, bears, wolves—it's a wild wonderland. That she's not a superstar and as rich as some bogus so-called 'celebrity' chef is criminal."

Jenkins's beef with celebrity chefs is this: He feels that artisans like Mary do all the work, and chefs get all the credit. "All chefs do is pick over and buy what artisans and retailers have spent twenty years working on." In Jenkins's view, these poseur chefs are aided and abetted by "hackneyed food writers who keep talking about terroir. What lunacy this idea of striving for terroir is! Cheese is either well made or it's not. It's either made by somebody who has that magical spark or it isn't. You can't actively imbue your foodstuff with terroir. That happens by God and the supernatural, and it's a natural outgrowth of your talent as a cheesemaker."

Terroir is indeed a popular idea in food right now, and it looks to be growing in importance. The idea is this: If a food is from a specific place, and only that place, it will taste of that place. What makes Italy, Bordeaux, and Wisconsin different are the plants, trees, soil, bedrock, rain, rivers, ponds, and lakes there, all the way down the life chain to the tiny microscopic molds and microflora that, incidentally, make cheese possible.

The idea of terroir finds its fullest flower in wine writing: Austrian Riesling vines plunge their taproots forty feet under the ground to retrieve water, and in the process somehow come back with the taste of slate. That idea of terroir is almost entirely responsible for the difference between $10 and $400 wines. But terroir is a critical underpinning of cheese as well. For instance, Roquefort, the famous blue cheese, came about because of the specific natural interactions of a certain little part of southern France, called the Larzac Plateau, where there is a plain of red clay that isn't much good for tilling but is very good for grazing. Sheep were fed there, and their milk turned into cheese, which was stored in natural limestone caves of the region that happened to provide an excellent medium for growing a wild, bluish mold indigenous to those caves, a mold now named *Penicillium roqueforti*, which is cultivated and distributed worldwide.

Cheddar cheese came from a similar but different interplay between the milk of cows from a certain part of southwestern England and wild molds in the caves of the Cheddar Gorge. Gruyère cheese has the same story in Switzerland. Today, around the world, and especially in the United States, most cheeses are a sort of fortieth-generation carbon copy of that original moment of lightning in a bottle: They're made with commercially cultivated strains of the original molds and bacteria and milk that has been pasteurized, then named after that original tangle of animal, plants, and cave.

An American Original

To make an American cheese with the significance of Roquefort, Cheddar, or real Swiss Fribourg Gruyère is not easy. It requires three things: one, a belief that making such a cheese is possible; two, the willingness to do what it takes to make it happen; and three, an essential erasure of the modern world.

LoveTree Farmstead is where Mary effectively erases the modern world. There are the wolves and great horned owls, of course, but more germane to cheese production are the untilled, herbicide-free, pesticide-free fields of wild grasses, nettles, sedges, and assorted plants on her land. The dairy sheep rotate through the fields, contained by mobile electric fences—her one concession to modernity. The Falks move the sheep into one meadow, with their attendant animal SWAT team, then the sheep and lambs advance, often standing single file like a herd of munching Rockettes, slowly chewing. At the end of the day, the Falks retrieve them, milk them, and then move them into another field.

I toured these fields with Mary one day—fields with names such as Little Eden and Beer Can Stand—and with each footfall a hundred little bugs would hop and skitter: grasshoppers, crickets, odd little leaf jumpers. It sounded like we were walking through a bag of potato chips. "A guy from the USDA came out here to take soil samples for a statewide census of what's living in the soil," Mary says. "He said we had more worms than anybody."

It's easy to imagine why. Many plants need animals to distribute their seeds by physically carrying them through their digestive tracts or on their fur and by tamping seeds in the soil with their feet, piercing the top crust of soil and pushing the seeds into the earth. In the LoveTree fields, chomping, pooping sheep play the roles that deer and bison did on the prairie. Then the sheep turn those wild plants into milk. The milk retains the taste of fringed blue aster, Indian paintbrush, and purple prairie clover, making it much different from the milk of cows raised in Switzerland or California or on a confinement dairy cow lot down the highway.

Mary gathers that milk and, in its raw state, separates the curds and whey.

The importance of making cheese from the raw milk of ewes who graze one particular patch of land can't be underestimated. Humankind's understanding of the microbiome—the cloud of bacteria, yeast, protists, and fungi that circulate in, on, and all around us, from the deepest cave to the top of the tallest building—is in its infancy. Recently, scientists from the Human Microbiome Project announced that each and every one of us has 100 trillion microbial things living in and on us, turning food into usable nutrients, moisturizing our skin, and defending our lungs against invaders. Without them, we'd be dead.

Without the right ones, or enough of them, we might just be sick. Research into whether our microbiome plays a critical role in human health is just beginning, but preliminary results suggests it has a part in everything from obesity to asthma and autoimmune diseases. Analysis of the flavor complexities of aged foods such as prosciutto, salami, wine, and especially cheese suggests that microbial complexity correlates to the complexity of the finished product's taste. But how does the native complexity of a stand of predator-filled woods in northeastern Wisconsin affect the taste of cheese?

To find out, Mary had her husband take out part of a hill with a Caterpillar. It was a red clay hill, and Dave is comfortable doing things like that because he used to build silos for a living. "She

looked at me and said, 'We're going to put cheese underground,'"
Dave remembers. "I had never heard of that."

Once the hill was gone, Dave constructed a concrete room with
ventilation leading out to the woods. Over the years he took that
hill apart with a Caterpillar several more times, eventually discovering that the best shape for a cave was round, like a silo. It's best
because of the way the air circulates, in a circle up to a ventilation
hole, and for the way the moisture drips down from a pitched,
round roof, keeping humidity even throughout the space.

When Mary shapes her individual cheeses, she brings them
to her cave to age. (The whey from the cheese production is also
blended into the guard dogs' food, perhaps strengthening the
dogs' attachment to their flock.) Many of Mary's cheeses are pure
sheep's milk, but some are a blend of sheep's milk and her outdoor-
pastured cows' milk. The cows are descended from a Scottish
Highland-Angus-Jersey cross and are majestic animals with soaring horns that make them look like bulls, but they're actually milk-
able ladies. In the cave, the young cheeses are hand-rubbed—a
treatment that encourages a rind to form on the outside—and
are then flipped every day or so, sometimes for weeks, sometimes for many months, depending on Mary's own personal sense
of when a cheese is ready. It is inside this humid, refrigerator-like,
woods-connected silo of a cave that the cheeses become what they
will become.

What they become is absolutely unique, a true American original cheese unlike anything that has ever been made, or tasted, on
earth. Her Trade Lake Cedar looks like a rock or mushroom; the
rind tastes earthy and ashy, an umami non-fruit world of hay and
mineral, whereas the interior is tangy and chalky and meadow-like.
Her dry Gabrielson Lake tastes a little like Parmigiano Reggiano,
but is flecked with little crystals of concentration and tiny red lace
points of mold.

The cheeses come and go, and Mary often makes one-of-a-kind
batches that reflect some event on the farm, some week of too
much milk or too little. "When I think of Mary's cheeses, in terms
of a world analog, what comes to mind are principally the cheeses
of Sardinia and the Pyrenees," Steven Jenkins tells me. "Though

Mary's are more graceful and unctuous." And they're essentially only available to people in the Minneapolis and St. Paul metro area. But she isn't very well known, even among foodies. In fact, an informal poll of people I know outside of the restaurant industry suggests that almost no one has heard of LoveTree.

"It's funny, there's a sort of Minnesota paradox when it comes to something on this level," says Lenny Russo, chef at Heartland and owner of the only market to which Mary will sell. "The Minnesota paradox is, people who live here think it's the best place in the world, even if they've never been anywhere else. At the same time, there's this inferiority complex, where something not from here immediately gets a leg up. If you say this is one of the best cheeses in the world, there are a lot of people here who just won't believe you. But they'll pay a super premium for something from France or Italy that essentially comes from a factory. This indigenous inferiority complex is what will probably keep her from succeeding the way she should. If she was making this cheese in California or New York, she'd be world famous."

But Mary isn't even as famous here as she should be. The only places to buy LoveTree farm cheeses are at the Saint Paul Farmers' Market (year-round), Heartland Market, the summer Kingfield Farmers Market, and the LoveTree farm, at their new farm store. You can also taste them at the LoveTree farm on Pizza by the Pond days. Every Sunday, from 2 PM to 8 PM all year long (weather permitting), Mary trades in her shepherd's crook for a pizza peel and melts some of her LoveTree cheeses on top of her four-day-fermented pizza dough, made with flour from Great River Organic Milling, just down the river, and mixed with a sourdough culture developed from her cheese.

Before the pizza-farm events, she forages for such idiosyncratic toppings as fiddlehead ferns or wild wood nettles, or she trades ingredients with neighboring farms or friends from the farmers' market. Try the plain cheese—it's as bold a plain-cheese pizza as you'll ever have in your life. I've also tried the wild watercress, which tastes like something straight from Sardinia, iron-y and green and fresh. I've also had the Old Man Dave, which comes with different sausages from the day's farmers' market or is topped with meats from a neighboring farm, Beaver Creek Ranch, and vegetables from nearby Burning River Farm. The pizzas are delicious, but more than that, they're exquisitely true to their place. The whole scene reminds me of one of those ridiculous magazine features where writers are eating some salad of wild-foraged greens and locally grazed but unnamed cheese on an island in Corsica that no one could ever get to. But this is in Wisconsin, not too far from a Dairy Queen. The pizza oven is located in another part of the hill that Dave bulldozed, then lined with tire bales, built out with logs from the property, and roofed.

The Politics of Cheese

I talked to Mary in the pizza enclosure one hot day, as some strange beetle gnawed loudly on a log overhead, occasionally sending down a shower of sawdust. She was terrified about the raw milk crackdown that's happening nationally and in Wisconsin. She's convinced that they're coming for the cheesemakers next.

Currently, raw milk cheeses are allowed in the United States if they're sixty days old or older. She'd of course like to be making younger cheeses, as she has now and then and sold as "fish bait: not fit for human or animal consumption." She has sold it at the Saint Paul Farmers' Market, where presumably avid fisher-people snap it up. "We don't have much money or many material things. All we have is what comes from nature," she says. "And that's a good thing. All you have to do to have raw milk and raw milk cheeses is regulate it. I'm not afraid. My milk is much cleaner than pasteurized milk."

The way the state of Wisconsin regulates its milk is by counting absolute numbers of bacteria, the standard plate count. Milk, after it has been pasteurized, can have an SPC of 20,000 bacteria per milliliter. Milk destined to be made into cheese is allowed to have an SPC of one million bacteria per milliliter. Mary says her raw milk is consistently measured with an SPC of less than 10,000 bacteria. If any, or all, of these numbers sound high, you might have an incorrect notion of how many bacteria actually surround you and everything you see. Adults have two to three pounds of microbes—that is, bacteria, yeast, and other tiny creatures—in and on us at all times; they're also currently in your garden and on your walls and on everything you can see, except the moon, sun, and stars. Heavily pregnant women's whole microbiome changes, with digestive microbes moving to the birth canal; the act of being born is also a biological christening with necessary bacteria.

The way Mary sees it, good cheese does not repudiate its connection with nature; rather, it is the land from which it comes, from the wolves and eagles to the invisible microbes, that makes the caves of France taste like the caves of France and the caves of Wisconsin taste like the caves of Wisconsin. "I remember that first time I felt the cheese in the vat: What is that? That's the curd firming up. And that understanding: This is the milk I have, so how can I get to the flavor I want? Why are people so afraid of nature?"

She launches into a complicated scientific argument about how the cheesemaking process destroys pathogens, about how the fact that food has microbiology at all is a foreign idea to many. We understand antibacterial soap, but we don't understand that without the microbiome of bacteria on our very own hands our skin wouldn't work; it would crack and split. We understand killing bacteria in food. We don't understand that bacteria are not an outside thing; they are part of the thing—they are part of the wolves and the flowers and us. She leans back and listens to a blue heron baying from a nearby pond. "But I don't know if most people even understand where cheese comes from," she muses. "It's easier to be afraid than to learn something. Between the politicians and the coyotes, I prefer the coyotes."

King of the Roast

. . . .

Mpls.St.Paul Magazine, July 2016

I've gone to the Minnesota State Fair every year since 1995 in search of stories on the fairgrounds, ever since Elizabeth Foy Larsen—then an editor at Microsoft Sidewalk, now famous for her Unbored series of books—pressed a wad of cash into my hand on the first day of the fair and said something like, "Go find stuff and write about it." Since then, I've dipped in and out of the fair, unearthing the stories, digging deeper, deeper—and there's always deeper to go. The Minnesota State Fair is its own world, its own culture; literally millions of people bumping into each other over a tiny area for twelve days, then going their separate ways.

I have always loved the paintings of the Dutch Renaissance artists Pieter Bruegel, both elder and younger—you know the ones, tiny bodies on a big ground, everyone with their own agendas and private experiences, but also all together. That's what the state fair is to me. It's *place* and *people* as one thing, including me, and including you too.

Brad Ribar isn't just the creator of the Corn Roast at the Minnesota State Fair—he's as close as the fair gets to born nobility.

Imagine an amazing land far past, a land very much like ours but also so unlike it as to be unrecognizable: a land with no roast corn at the Minnesota State Fair. You can't fathom it, right? The charred ochre-yellow ears, the brittle green husks, and the fire-and-butter smell are such core parts of the fair today. And yet the Minnesota State Fair Corn Roast has an inventor. His name is Brad Ribar, a lean, green-eyed, laconic, and no-nonsense man who is a living link to a world few of us today can imagine, one where the state fair was not just pre–corn roast, but pre–food frenzy.

Here's what it was like, says Ribar, now sixty: People would drive right into the fairgrounds and park on the streets. They'd park on Machinery Hill. They'd throw their cigarette butts out the car window. When lunchtime came, they'd pop the trunk on the Chevy and haul out a picnic basket.

Today, packing in food to the state fair seems as mad and improbable as hauling your own Tilt-A-Whirl down to the Midway, but Brad Ribar knows this was true because he didn't just see it with his own eyes, he swept it. He started sweeping it all in the 1960s as a preteen paper picker with the sanitation crew, stabbing paper with a pointed stick and sweeping up cigarette butts. Next, he was promoted to "turdsman," cleaning the livestock judging arenas and readying the barns for the mid-fair shift from, say, sheep to goats. After success as a turdsman, Ribar graduated to life on the service crew, cleaning up when folks drank too much and came to grief in the Grandstand. Finally, when he had a driver's license, he vaulted to the ultimate position—garbage truck guy.

"None of it was glamorous, but it was all fun," remembers Ribar, who grew up in Eagan and graduated from Henry Sibley High School. "My brothers, my cousins, my friends from school, we were all there." They slept in sanitation crew dormitories under the Grandstand bleachers. His cousins and brothers were there because Ribar's grandfather, Jim L. Libby, was the state fair ground superintendent. The state fair was an all-hands-on-deck situation for the family. The Libby Conference Center at the fair is named for Ribar's uncle John E. Libby and also his grandpa Jim, and the fair and family estimate that someone in Ribar's family line has been working at the fair since around 1919. (The very first state fair, by the way, was in 1859 in downtown Minneapolis; the fair moved to its present permanent location in 1885.)

Ribar's first memories of the Great Minnesota Get-Together predate the Haunted House and the Activities Building, and mainly involve things kids would remember, like snow and popcorn. Snow, because in the winter, his grandfather would haul the grandkids through the deserted and unplowed fairground streets on a toboggan; popcorn because his family ran a couple of pop-corn stands near the cattle barn, and he was sometimes pressed into service running popcorn up to people in the stands.

The family popcorn stand was an extension of the Corn Cabin, a popcorn and root beer stand owned by Ribar's grandfather near Hiawatha and Lake in south Minneapolis. When Ribar was a kid in the 1960s, the state fair had a new vision of people spending money on food at the fairgrounds rather than bringing their own meals, with the fair getting revenue from vendors (today, the fair takes 15 percent of every food vendor's revenue). This led to Grandpa Libby and his family re-creating the Corn Cabin popcorn model on-site.

Little did Ribar know that as he was hopping around the cattle barn and popcorn stand, his future wife was just a few blocks away in a hot dog stand. Yes, in 1982—in the manner of a prince from the royal House of Windsor marrying a princess from the royal House of Orange, but Minnesota State Fair–style—Brad Ribar fell in love with and married Lori Peters, descendant of the house of Peters Wieners (now Peters Hot Dogs), the anchor state fair Food Building tenant that began selling hot dogs in 1939 and continues to this day. Ribar reports that more recently, when his and Lori's kids were married, in attendance were the families of Tom Thumb mini-donuts, Dippin' Dots ice cream, and Granny's Caramel Apple Sundaes. His son Matt Ribar now runs Duke's Poutine at the state fair, not far from the original family popcorn stand.

Brad Ribar leapt from popcorn to roast corn because he was such a state fair sanitation fanatic that he'd spend his free week-ends traveling to other state fairs to look for new sanitation best practices and innovations. On these journeys he saw a lot of things that confused him—the Florida State Fair had bathroom matrons and porters who worked for tips—and one thing that changed his life forever: a stand at the Wisconsin State Fair where corn was roasted in the husks over an open flame. He tasted it, and it was so much better than any corn he'd ever eaten at Minnesota's fair that he immediately volunteered to work at the stand, and he asked questions and wrote down everything.

He took the idea back to Minnesota and developed it for his business school final project at St. Thomas. But when he pitched the project to the state fair, it was rejected again and again, over the course of five years. "They just kept saying they couldn't see it; no one would pay good money for corn on the cob," says Ribar. Finally, in a fateful move, the O'Neill family decided to shut down their meat loaf operation near the Grandstand, and Ribar put in a bid to buy the building. He had a vision that was about more than corn. He wanted the corn roast to be an event, for people to be able to see the corn roasting and smell it. He tore out the building's walls.

"When she saw what I did to it, Mrs. O'Neill said, 'Son, you'd have been better off just putting that money in the bank,'" Ribar remembers. The first day he sold only three hundred ears. Then the television duo of Steve Edelman and Sharon Anderson from the local show *Good Company* came by and raved about the corn on television, and the rest is corn legend.

Today, Ribar tries to sell 200,000 ears every fair—at three dollars a pop, a price that hasn't risen in thirteen years, that's a harvest. They can sell as many as 2,400 ears an hour, and, for the duration of the fair, they go through 4,000 pounds of butter supplied by Wisconsin's Ellsworth Cooperative Creamery. Ribar has a great sense of how difficult it is to time a harvest in Minnesota to a particular date, because in a cold year, your crop might be a week late, and in a hot year a week early. That's why he pays the Untiedt family—yes, those Untiedts, of the very many metro-area roadside veggie stands—an ultra-premium price to plant some twenty acres of sweet corn just for the Corn Roast at time-staggered intervals. Most years, some of that corn comes ripe too early or too late, but that's just how it has to be to get the corn sweet enough. Every ear of corn sold at the stand is harvested the day before it's eaten.

The favorite part of the state fair day for this ex–paper picker is cleaning up at the end of the night. "I love the evening, once the fair is shut down and everyone is gone from the Grandstand," says Ribar. "I've got my cleaning crew, just a couple guys who come in at night, and we power-wash the whole stand. I love to be here and hear the sanitation crew, to hear the backpack blowers up in the Grandstand. The whole fair, it's so dirty by the end of the day, and it looks brand-new in the morning. I don't know if you can appreciate how amazing the state fair is, how absolutely amazing it all is, if you haven't worked sanitation."

Speaking of amazing: Can you imagine a land where someone who was practically born and raised at the Minnesota State Fair—whose business is as synonymous with the fair as the Skyride—still finds the whole thing amazing, every night for the twelve nights leading up to Labor Day? Brad Ribar is living in that amazing land, and power-washing it too.

Above the Clouds and Crowds on the State Fair's Skyride

. . . .

Mpls.St.Paul Magazine, August 2018

I fall in love a little bit with everyone I've ever written about. I used to think this was a failing; weren't real journalists tough and objective and kind of like blind justice, roaming around but not knocking into things? Over time I've realized that falling in love with everyone and everything everywhere is what makes me me. To me, this story about the state fair Skyride is the epitome of that moment. How can anyone fall in love with a funny old gondola machine run by a little guy and a gigantic dog? I spent so much time thinking about it, learning about it, marveling at all the work put into it that I fell a little bit in love with the whole thing. Maybe that's the only way to make a story come alive.

A revolutionary transportation system can ferry passengers in and out of crowded cities with almost no pollution, traffic, or infrastructure. Try it this summer, for $4.50, at the state fair.

Back in fifth grade, I read a lot of books about inventors: geniuses who'd spent their childhoods building radios and restoring clocks. When my parents' digital clock radio broke, they bought a new one. I carefully spread a bedsheet across the floor and removed every wheel and transistor from the old one. I imagined the eureka moment that would come when I reassembled the device, demonstrating my affinity with the greats.

Instead, I was overwhelmed by the heap of undifferentiated nonsense. I could never fit all that junk back in the casing. A week later my mom made me dump the whole mess in the trash. Instead of learning to fix clocks, I learned once and for all that I was not a quiet, clock-building type.

This memory came to me a few weeks ago when I was hanging out with Don McClure, who is a clock-building type of the highest order, and turned that temperament into a life running one of the most iconic machines in the state.

Now, Don McClure didn't quite fit into his household dreams either. He grew up on the edge of Lake Harriet in Minneapolis, in a family of speed skaters. They'd shovel a big circular path on the lake and zoom over the ice flats. But McClure only liked zooming at speed down a slope, and so he became a regular at Buck Hill.

When McClure turned fifteen, his parents informed him that all those lift tickets were getting pricey; he should get a job. He did, and found out what I'm told many working ski people discover: The lift is the weak link in the operation. If you learn how to fix the lift, you'll never lack for work. You'll also get to ski more.

Eventually McClure worked his way up to co-owning Buck Hill. And he developed a reputation as the guy who knew his way around a lift system. That's how he became acquainted with the owner of the Skyride, Ed Hjermstad, who called him up for help.

Have you ever asked yourself what the Minnesota State Fair; Medellín, Colombia; and Walt Disney World have in common? It's aerial transportation systems, of course!

Aerial transportation is what people in the business call machines like the Skyride. At the state fair, it's a 1964 Von Roll 101. When Hjermstad wanted to sell the concession, in 2003, he knew he wanted to sell to a friend who didn't see the Skyride as requiring more maintenance than it was worth. That same year, McClure stepped up.

Having only fifteen years of experience with the Von Roll 101, McClure insisted I phone up someone who knows aerial transportation even better than he does: Red Blomer. He grew up in Anoka and subsequently spent thirty-eight years working in the world of aerial transportation, currently as a technician for one of the few remaining big players, the Doppelmayr/Garaventa Group, which took over the original Von Roll company in 1996. Blomer visits Minnesota every year to examine the Skyride on behalf of McClure.

"For some reason, every amusement park or state fair that got one in the 1960s and 1970s called it a Skyride," Blomer said. To aerial transport experts, he explained, ski chairlifts, funiculars, tramways, and gondolas are all basically the same but different— the way boots and shoes and sneakers are the same but different. What do all these aerial systems have in common? Ropes.

Here's how the Skyride works. A motor turns one giant loop of rope. A rope is both bigger and stronger than a cable. The rope that powers the Skyride has a synthetic core wrapped in woven layers of galvanized steel wire. It may look like a cable, but that's not the word they use in the industry.

That rope turns and turns. The motor that moves it lies on the west end of the fairgrounds, near the cream puff stand. This is a giant metal wheel called the motor bull wheel. The rope must be kept at a certain tautness: too slack and the gondolas, the things you ride in, will sag. Too taut and the whole system stops.

The thing that keeps the tension just right? That's the counterweight, which is governed by a tension bull wheel over on the east end of the fairgrounds, by the Ag Building, where you see the crop art.

You could make a decent replica of the basic mechanism of the Skyride with two spools and a big rubber band. Spin one spool and the rubber band would move, turning the spool on the other end. Now imagine clamping a matchbox onto the rubber band as it travels between spools. That's the gondola that carries the passengers. An arm above the gondola locks onto the rope when it leaves a terminal and comes loose when it enters the opposite terminal.

Europeans in the Alps devised this system some 150 years ago, Blomer said. They were struggling to get a steam locomotive up a mountain: At a certain grade, the feat became impossible (picture the steel wheels sliding backward on a steep track). One solution: Attach a rope.

That same mechanism—with a little refinement—will apparently power what could be one of the world's most expensive tramways, rumored to be opening in about a year at the Disney World Resort in Orlando. Each tram car will contain characters, maybe holograms, while leaping over cars, into the heart of Epcot and Hollywood Studios. This design will allow for easier entry into the parks and enable new development at more distant Disney sites.

The twenty-first century has also brought new state-of-the-art aerial transport systems to South American cities such as Medellín, Colombia; La Paz, Bolivia; and Caracas, Venezuela. The gondolas and trams hop over traffic, ravines, and rivers, depositing people right where they need to be—reducing traffic, pollution, and poverty in the process. As infrastructure goes, it's actually relatively simple: no roads or bridges necessary. All you need to add a tram is a place to put the two terminals, and a post every four hundred feet or so.

In the post-Sputnik era of the 1960s, Skyrides seemed to represent the transportation of the future. Now, I told Blomer, they look like they could be the transportation of the future again.

"They were always the transportation of the future," Blomer replied.

· · · · · · ·

Going back to the future, then, the Von Roll 101 came to the Cedar Point amusement park (outside Cleveland) in 1961; the Tulsa State Fair installed a system in 1965; and the San Diego Zoo added one in 1969. Minnesota got our iconic system in 1964. McClure guesses about a dozen remain in operation (he maintains the Tulsa system now too).

As he led me through a tour of the parts, he explained that just about everything has been replaced in what he calls "the machine"— by which he means the entirety of the system. The exception here is the big bull wheels, the counterweight, and the gondola cars themselves.

"This machine runs fifteen days a year," McClure said. "It has to meet all our inspections, all our code requirements. It has to be a perfectly running machine. If this machine loses one day, it's like another business losing a month."

A few years ago, McClure installed a backup system to provide electricity, should the city power go out. Then it did, and he was happy to not miss a minute of business. (Riders were also presumably happy not to dangle while the electric company worked out the problem.) McClure keeps a double for just about every part of the machine. "It's my philosophy that if you have to buy one part, always buy two," he said.

To the extent that McClure hasn't managed to clone himself, during the fair he lives in a tiny studio apartment inside the west terminal. (His beloved—and truly gigantic—Newfoundland dog, Malcolm, must stay with friends for the fortnight.) On-site, McClure keeps a close eye on the weather. High winds and storms are two of the only forces that will stop the Skyride. He conducts safety drills before the fair with the St. Paul fire department, so the operation stands ready for anything.

He's figured out how to staff the Skyride to a suitably high standard: McClure hires Boy Scout summer-camp counselors over the age of eighteen, just before they go back to school. He keeps morale high by grilling pork chops behind the terminal and shepherding any employees who look like they might be overheating into air-conditioned booths. It's a big job, and it's big money. On a busy day, the Skyride sells tickets for around 20,000 rides, at $6 round trip, or $4.50 one way. (The state fair claims 30 percent of the ticket price.)

"My friends and family, they all give me grief," McClure said. "'So you're a carny now.' Well, there isn't a machine down there," he gestured to the Midway, "worth less than a million dollars. And none of them are easy to run."

McClure is a slight man with pale blue eyes, and he is much more comfortable talking about the care and feeding of his machine than about himself. But he did let slip one small note of satisfaction. "I got my first job at Buck Hill in 1975," he said at one point, contemplating the giant clockwork of gears that make the Skyride turn. I peered into the dark hole where the counterweight lurks, and he added, "Look at me now."

The Pride Behind Pride

Mpls.St.Paul Magazine, June 2020

In magazine world we typically work months ahead, so this June 2020 story was actually reported in April of 2020. In those early days of the 2020 coronavirus lockdown I thought it would be a good idea to do a big Pride story for *Mpls.St.Paul Magazine* celebrating the importance of the Twin Cities in the establishment of gay marriage, and Pride as an international phenomena more generally. Huddled isolated in my tiny office, as my kids were doing school from home in the next room, I took solace in talking to elders in the gay community. The parallels were strong between fear of AIDS in the early days and fear of COVID in those early days. Unfortunately, one of the difficulties of magazine writing is that you think you're going to have so many pages for a story, but then if something unexpected happens—like wedding and hotel advertisers canceling their ads because of pandemic lockdowns—the stories have to be cut to fit the available pages. Fortunately, this anthology came along, and now the story can be told in full!

Jean Tretter died in December 2022. He was a one-man historical force, collecting the warehouse-worth of ephemera from the gay scene in and around the Twin Cities that went on to become the University of Minnesota's Jean-Nickolaus Tretter Collection in Gay, Lesbian, Bisexual and Transgender Studies. He was everything I like in a person: wry, witty, wise, painfully aware of the fleeting nature of our days (who else would collect ephemera?), and hence committed to enjoying the moment. I'm profoundly grateful for the four hours we spent together on the phone in those strange days.

Do you remember The Dugout? The Noble Roman? A Woman's Cof-
feehouse? A Brother's Touch? Long before Queer Eye and RuPaul's
Drag Race, LGBTQ people built a rich—and often hidden—culture in
the Twin Cities. A glorious (sometimes glamorous) world of bars and
bookstores, hookup spots, and health centers. Many of these places have
disappeared—but not from memory. This June, when we think about
Pride, here are the places and people we're proud of.

It's the year 2020: COVID spring. Pride is cancelled. This is very hard to say out loud. It feels like saying we're cancelling joy and progress. Of course the cancelling of Pride—the festival, the parade, the week when tens of thousands of far-flung LGBTQ peeps come streaming home—represents an act of love to keep people healthy.

But its absence presents us with an opportunity to consider all the profound and important local LGBTQ landmarks that built Pride—and often disappeared. Living in a city is complicated. Each of us lives in a different Twin Cities: We share the Foshay Tower and the Mississippi, but we go home to different bars and bedrooms.

LGBTQ cultures have, historically, needed to hide their bars and bedrooms for fear of eviction, firing, imprisonment, or worse. As Ricardo J. Brown put it in his St. Paul memoir, *The Evening Crowd at Kirmser's*—one of the best mid-twentieth-century looks at American gay experience—the LGBTQ life was "a ruse that kept all of us safe," conducted in "a fort in the midst of a savage and hostile population."

Hiding in forts was useful, important, necessary. But what was long hidden is easy to lose. With that in mind, I called a number of prominent folks in the LGBTQ community and asked, "What would you tell someone who arrived with a rainbow suitcase today about LGBTQ life in the Twin Cities before they got here? What landmarks should we know about this personal, political, geographical Twin Cities we all share?"

And, in a rush of memories, they talked to me about bars and bookstores, softball leagues and churches, theater troupes and travel companies, hookup spots and health centers. Names many of us haven't heard about in years—or decades. The bright, public LGBTQ world we see around us in the Cities today was built on these foundations, the way modern Rome coexists with, and couldn't exist without, its ancient skeleton of roads, monuments, and ruins.

The stories people shared with me were sometimes dark and painful, sometimes light and funny, and always enlightening. And they made clear to me that we can have a different sort of pride this year: pride in our history, pride in our accomplishments, pride in our resilience through tragedy, and pride in our capacity to find new things to love about our home.

The Players

LGBTQ leaders look back and share.

Jean Tretter: Born in 1946 in Little Falls, Minnesota, Jean Tretter served in the navy as a linguist, where part of his duties included intercepting Soviet communications. Back in the Twin Cities, Tretter led a rich gay life and collected a truly staggering quantity of gay ephemera: newspapers, flyers, brochures, etc. His personal collection seeded one of the country's greatest archives of LGBTQ experience, the University of Minnesota's Jean-Nickolaus Tretter Collection in Gay, Lesbian, Bisexual and Transgender Studies.

Scott Mayer: Former AIDS event fundraiser; events consultant and founder of the Ivey Awards.

Russ King: AIDS activist and creator, in the mid-1990s, of drag character Miss Richfield.

Andrea Jenkins: Activist and poet; Minneapolis's first trans Black city council member; former director of the Transgender Oral History Project at the Tretter Collection.

Tom Hoch: Founder of Hennepin Theatre Trust, former Minneapolis Downtown Council board chair; one-time Minneapolis DFL mayoral candidate.

Patrick Scully: Artist and activist most closely associated with Patrick's Cabaret, a radical, brainy vaudeville founded in 1986.

Mary Bahneman: Founder of Ruby's Cafe.

Stewart Van Cleve: Author of the definitive book about Minnesota gay history, *Land of 10,000 Loves: A History of Queer Minnesota.* Currently a librarian at Augsburg University, he previously was an assistant curator of the Tretter Collection.

Lisa Vecoli: Founder of the Minnesota Lesbian Community Organizing Oral History Project, one-time Amazon Bookstore employee, and the second curator of the Tretter Collection.

Kim Hines: Theater artist and a key member of Mixed Blood, Penumbra, At the Foot of the Mountain feminist theater company, and Out and About Theatre.

Gail Lewellan: Former environmental attorney in Hennepin County; member, Amazon Bookstore women's softball team.

Billy Beson: Interior designer, founder of Billy Beson Company.

John Veda: Former server at Minneapolis's first openly gay restaurant, Ye Gadz.

Charlie Rounds: Former president of RSVP Travel, cofounder of gay bar Boom and restaurant Oddfellows.

Mark Addicks: Former General Mills chief marketing officer and senior vice president; an original member of Betty's Family, the internal LGBTQ group at General Mills.

What we now see as LGBTQ+ culture has been in Minnesota forever. In the book Changing Ones: Third and Fourth Genders in Native North America, *Will Roscoe uses "two spirit" to translate a word Anishinaabe/Ojibwe people have long used to describe folks we'd likely recognize today as queer.*

Later, Oscar Wilde slept here—in Minneapolis, in 1882, eliciting a Minneapolis Tribune *headline of none-too-subtle innuendo: "Arrival of This Much-Talked-of Young Man in this City Yesterday Afternoon:*

He Tells a Small Audience in the Evening What He Knows about Decorative Art: 'AN ASS-THETE.'"

Wilde left, no doubt rolling his eyes. Careful perusal of local newspapers in later decades reveals a hidden queer world of cross-dressers arrested now and then, female impersonators alighting on big vaudeville stages, and what seems to have been power-lesbian, essentially married restaurateurs running the downtown Minneapolis restaurant Richards Treat.

Our story picks up after the war.

The Dugout
Minneapolis Gateway District; 1939–59

Jean Tretter: I talked to a lot of World War II veterans out in California, and their best memories of Minnesota were going to the gay bars downtown. At first in Minneapolis, the bars were split in half. [Minneapolis laws forbade same-sex dancing, and anti-prostitution laws barred women from entering bars alone. This is why St. Paul was an early home to lesbian bars in the Twin Cities.] Lesbians sat in front of the bar, gay men sat in the back, and the bartenders had whistles around their necks. When they saw cops coming to raid the bar, they'd blow the whistle, everyone would get up and move, and the lesbians would sit with guys, guys would sit with lesbians. That way when the cops came in it was just a normal bar and everyone was sitting together. Cops leave—*whistle!*—back to it.

Gay 90's, 19 Bar, the Saloon, the Town House (now the Black Hart of St. Paul)
Various locations in Minneapolis and St. Paul; still open

Jean Tretter: The bars were really the only place we could be ourselves, and be more or less left alone.

Scott Mayer: Speaking as a gay man, so much of our community was based around the bar scene. It was where we could congregate and find other people like us. It was the bars that defined becoming an openly gay man. There would always be new places—and then everyone would go back to the Saloon and the Gay 90's.

Jean Tretter: The Town House, in St. Paul, Emmett Jewel owned it. He hired me to work there. His daughter Kelly, who was a lesbian, ran it. The St. Paul cops pretty much left people alone. I had my suspicions Emmett took care of them. The St. Paul cops were not the best in the world at that time.

People don't understand that a lot of the bars in Minnesota were huge—truly enormous. People would come in from New York, San Francisco, they couldn't believe how big our bars are. Because you can't run from bar to bar in the winter! There's no cruising a park in January in Minnesota. That's why the 90's expanded; that's why the Town House is so big.

The Gay 90's itself was originally founded in 1957 as a supper club with, improbable history insists, a coincidentally blessed name. It opened beside the Happy Hour, an already famed gay bar. In 1976 an interior door fused the two.

Jean Tretter: You could start at the Happy Hour, then visit five or six bars inside the 90's without going outside. See Lori Dokken at the piano bar, go to a drag show, go to the hard-core motorcycle bar, and upstairs was a level with all these little shops—and a theater group! They'd do plays up there; gays loved plays in those days. You could buy most anything you needed. There was a souvenir shop with candy bars and postcards, cigarettes, greeting cards; a leather shop if you wanted whips or handcuffs or a leather jacket. If you drank too much you could go out the back door, make your way to one of the bathhouses. You paid maybe five bucks, they gave you a couple towels, you got a locker and a key, and you just ran around with two towels and your key. There were showers, dark rooms. You'd go into the dark rooms for sexual activity; you could go into the side rooms to just rest up. It was cheaper than a hotel. There was never any expectation put on you that you had to have sex with people. It was far more sociable and normal than most people believed.

Gay theaters were also important. There were two or three that played movies all day in Minneapolis. The Adonis was the big one. You pay your money, get your popcorn box, sit down, wait, and see if anyone came to sit next to you. I remember one movie that was the first gay full-length science fiction movie I ever saw, about a guy who visits an all-male planet. They were erotic movies, but they had plots and everything. Gladiators were a big theme.

Scott Mayer: My first professional job, as a lobbyist for student associations for colleges, I got fired because I went to the Saloon. I was at my job for nine months maybe. Suddenly they had an emergency board meeting and called me in: "We have heard that someone saw you go into the Saloon—is that true?" I said, "Yes." They said, "We're sorry, but you're fired. We can't have someone that is homosexual represent us." The thought of challenging it did not even enter my mind. It was like: Shit. Life is unfair. 1986.

Russ King: I remember John Moore, who owns the Saloon, telling me, in the early 1980s, they put in sprinklers because they were afraid someone was going to burn us down.

Andrea Jenkins: The Gay 90's [in the 1980s] was a safe space for a lot of trans-identified people, especially the lounge upstairs. I went there all the time. One of my best friends was one of the hair stylists who would do all the girls' hair. The hospital at the University of Minnesota, they were the second big place to do gender confirmation surgery, after Johns Hopkins. So there were a lot of trans pioneers who moved here. The language was different back then. We referred to ourselves as trannies and queens. That's over.

Back in those days, me and my friends would do a lot of thrift-store shopping, Ragstock, Savers, Gus, Banks, shoes from Payless—all the trans women got shoes at Payless. You came, ready, at the top of your game, whatever that meant for that day. Today you see transgirls in leggings and a sweatshirt; that was not done back in the day. I'd put my heels on. Back then everybody wore heels, dresses, nails done, hair and makeup to the highest level. You did not just throw on jeans and a sweater and go out. Thursdays and Sundays were my Fridays and Saturdays. I'd pregame at the Saloon, then make for the 90's. You came in, took off your coat, and Big Mama would hang it up for you.

Big Mama was an interesting character. She said she was born a boy, lived as a girl from the time she was six. She was part of a wealthy farm family when she started having sex with farmhands. As she grew older she was never comfortable with her body, always presented as a girl, and was one of the first people at the U to get full gender confirmation reconstructive surgery. I got the sense that she wanted more life in her life. That's how she ended up in Minneapolis. She was a sex worker for a long time and had a lot of longtime partners who loved her.

So I'd come in to the '90s, give my coat to Big Mama, tip her, and head up the stairs and into the drag lounge where all the transgirls and the guys who dated trans women were. A lot of smoke and banter. The drag community is very "cutty," super competitive, putting each other down and one-upping each other. Wigs were the thing, especially from Sunny's, Black-owned. Watch the girls in the show, then I might dip late into the Brass Rail, and after that always the parking lot sidewalk sale between the two buildings—a minimum an hour, an hour and a half. It was the scene after the scene, and it was all important. Everyone knew everyone, so it would be friends catching up with friends, also cruising, also drugs and all the nefarious things. If a new girl came, everybody was all over them. I remember being the new girl, and that was an interesting time.

It was pretty fun back in those days. Minneapolis was pretty ahead of its time, relative to other parts of the country, because of the U.

Loring Park

Community hub of gay Minneapolis, locus of Pride. Ask a gay man when they first knew Loring Park was the epicenter of gay male life in the Twin Cities and they will laugh like you asked when they first knew the sky was up.

Russ King: It had such a public reputation. It was like, "How did you know the Gay 90's was gay." *You knew.* I would take my dad's Chrysler down there, just drive around and pick somebody up.

Tom Hoch: It seeped into you. There was always a lot of cruising, cars circling, men hanging out. And it wasn't unusual to open the paper to see someone had been beat up or murdered in Loring Park. And they never said what it was, but you knew what it was. That's why Pride had to be in Loring Park.

Jean Tretter: Whether it was murders in Loring Park or a Pride March in Loring Park, the mainstream papers and the television stations wouldn't tell you anything about that—but our papers would. There were gay gangs that came together to patrol the parks to keep gays from getting beat up. They had names like Pink Panthers and the Third World Gays. I guess that was a seventies type of name. The Third World Gays ended up disbanding after they beat up a couple of cops that were trying to beat up gay people.

Patrick Scully: Those early Gay Pride parades, when we'd start at Bde Maka Ska and end at Loring Park, it was all about having a drag show happen in the light of day *in Loring Park*. It was so important to be out in the daylight. When I was a young man coming out, it was the norm for gay people to live their lives in the closet, in fear. I remember talking to this one woman about having the police come and pound on her door. They came because someone called in a complaint about two women having sex, and the police headed out to do something about it.

The first gay bar I ever went to was the Gay 90's. One of the women I was in a group dancing with, this total Seward hippie, said, "You know, Patrick, my intuition tells me you are a gay man and figuring this out." I was in college; we walked in—I'll never forget that door opening—and it was packed. Not even the kind of crowd you could walk into. I remember thinking: *My God, are these all gay men?* In the nightmarish scenario I had concocted in my head, there were six gay people in all of Minnesota, and they were all hiding, separately, from the police. Not a group you wanted to be part of. Then, a literal door opened. That's why it was so important for Pride to be out in the daylight in Loring Park. A way of saying we're here, we're queer, we're fabulous—get used to us.

Pride
Community event that started as a civil rights march down Nicollet Mall; 1972–present

Scott Mayer: You can tell how old someone is by if they call it a "march" or a "festival." Gay men and lesbians started out marching [down Nicollet Mall in 1972], like a Martin Luther King Jr. civil rights march. They were marching for equality and taking risks. Today it's just a big party, which is wonderful, but it was different when you were going to march. Actually it could be depressing. You'd spend the weekend having this rush of being free and around people like you, then you'd wake up on Monday and be in this horrible depression because you couldn't talk about who you really were.

Mary Bahneman: Pride was so freeing. If you were partnered, you could actually walk hand in hand without fear of getting attacked, which was a real and constant fear.

The Noble Roman
Gay bar and cultural center, Grand Avenue, St. Paul; 1970–76

Jean Tretter: When I was managing the Noble Roman, we had a whole parallel world. We put in the papers: "We're having a Gay State Fair." Other bars, from Nebraska and Chicago, set up tables with advertisements. We sold T-shirts and made-up drinking glasses. It was a long time before the [Minnesota] state fair allowed us to have our own booth, so we had to do our own thing.

We'd put our weddings in our papers too. Some were serious; some were silly. I remember this one silly one, an older guy just infatuated with this younger kid who wasn't too bright but was just enthralled that everyone was paying so much attention. He was the bride, in a white wedding gown; the other guy was in a tuxedo, and they had a big old wedding at the Noble Roman. The guy paid for an open bar for the night, and of course the place was packed.

Before churches like the Metropolitan Community Church actually let you go and have a wedding, we threw them in the bars. Of course the windows were blacked out, and maybe you didn't put your last name in your wedding announcement, but you had the wedding in front of everybody in the bar.

The All God's Children Metropolitan Community Church
LGBTQ-inclusive congregation, Park Avenue and South Thirty-First Street, Minneapolis; 1974–present

Russ King: This one guy, Doug, after we had sex, said, "Do you ever go to church?" Well, I came from a church background, so I was intrigued. I went. It was founded specifically for gay and lesbian people [in California in 1968 and emerged in Minnesota from Gay House in 1974] because a lot of gays and lesbians, ministers and congregants—everyone—was getting thrown out of church. Why not start our own?

It was great. Reverend Arlene Ackerman was particularly great. Her sermons were so smart and poignant and moving. It was all about love, a higher power, and doing these good things. Back in the day, you were gay or you were Christian—you couldn't be both. I mean, Harvey Milk was assassinated in 1978. [Look at] how AIDS was treated in the 1980s and 1990s—I mean, holy shit, people were still very much against us not that long ago. The sad part of today is how acceptance can be a blessing and a curse. Obviously life is good, we have opportunities and families, but there is less glue holding us together. Adversity brings people together.

Gay House
Community center, 216 Ridgewood Avenue, Minneapolis; 1971–79

Steven Endean, who helped craft and pass Minneapolis's early anti–gay discrimination ordinance, credits Gay House as the inspiration for his founding the Human Rights Campaign in Washington, DC, the originators of the ultimately successful national marriage strategy.

Stewart Van Cleve: It was like a drop-in community center—very hippie crash pad, everyone sitting on the floor with paisley shirts—and was used by so many early gay rights groups. That's where Twin Cities Pride began. That's where OutFront Minnesota began. So much activist work came out of there.

Lesbian Resource Center
710 West Twenty-Second Street, Minneapolis; 1972–80

Opened as a counterpoint to Gay House in 1972, the Lesbian Resource Center (LRC) began as a sort of career center and legal services advice spot with a pool table as well as a coffeehouse. The big LRC lending library eventually spun off to become Amazon Bookstore, and a weekly LRC evening gathering spun off to become A Woman's Coffeehouse.

Lisa Vecoli: To anyone's knowledge it was the first lesbian resource center not affiliated with a university in the country. It was so needed; at the time lesbians could get fired from your job, evicted from your house. You'd go in, there was a bulletin board with a lot of information, about concerts or jobs or roommates, you could talk to someone if you were just coming out and get a list of people who would mentor you.

Kim Hines: The women's community, we really looked out for each other and had each other's back. I wouldn't know where to begin to look for that information. I don't know how these young ones do it today, I really don't.

Dyke Heights
Neighborhood, Powderhorn Park, Minneapolis

Gail Lewellan: Just south of Powderhorn Park there were about six houses of lesbians, around Columbus and Oakland Avenues. It was a place where being lesbian was perfectly normal. You didn't have to explain anything. You went to softball games together, concerts together, grilled in the backyard, have twenty people for a meal. We had a front porch, and I could sit out and see people coming and going that I knew were safe and that were friends.

It was like where I grew up in Iowa; you'd see what people were doing and chat—"How's that job? What about that girlfriend?" We were really neighbors. We made our own community. It changed everything.

Amazon Feminist Bookstore
Loring Park and south Minneapolis; 1970–2012

Lisa Vecoli: When I came out in 1981, I couldn't go into a Barnes & Noble to get information about lesbian existence. I couldn't use the internet. Amazon Bookstore, though, it was a place to get books and music, a place that showed you what lesbian existence looked like. The music! Cris Williamson, Holly Near, Deidre McCalla—every lesbian had the same fifty albums, mostly from Olivia Records. And you got them there. You were starving for some reflection of yourself and your culture. Then those artists would tour the country; you'd see the flyer on the Amazon bulletin board and buy the tickets at Amazon. That bulletin board was a thing. That's where you'd find the political actions, the rallies, support groups, who needed a roommate, who had a cat, who needed a cat.

I remember at one point Amazon was on Twenty-Sixth Street and Hennepin Avenue, with a huge facade. It was terrifying. I'd park three blocks away and, as soon as I got inside, skitter to the back away from the plate glass windows. Part of what was difficult about coming out in the 1970s was that you had no family to tell you anything; just books and the people you met at the bookstore. Amazon *was* our internet. I still remember all the little things, like the jewelry case with little silver ax pendants, and the buttons. My favorite was: "So many women, so little nerve."

Kim Hines: I was their bookkeeper. I remember when Alison Bechdel was living across from Powderhorn Park and doing her comic strip [*Dykes to Watch Out For*]. In her first book, that Black character that runs the bookstore is based on me. She'd call me up periodically: *I'm going to do this story line, is this typical, blah blah blah.* When people think "women's bookstore," they really are thinking [the early Minneapolis feminist bookstore] Amazon, whether they know it or not. I was glad to see Alison get her MacArthur genius grant and make it to Broadway [for the adaption of her graphic novel *Fun Home*]. She was just this cute little tomboy with round glasses at Powderhorn Park.

A Woman's Coffeehouse
Plymouth Congregational Church, south Minneapolis; 1975–89

Lisa Vecoli: Woman meant *lesbian*; coffee meant *sober*. Everyone knew that at the time. And it really was woman-only—no men at all, not performing, they don't get in the door.

Kim Hines: You'd never find the little entrance into the basement of Plymouth Congregational Church unless you knew about it. Usually the first couple of hours each night was a performance, music, reading, any number of things. The last half was dancing.

Gail Lewellan: It cost maybe two dollars to get in. First there was this area with old couches, then a smoking area. You could get baked goods, soft drinks, coffee, and tea. Like a bar without liquor. I'd guess we had around sixty people most nights, and a hundred people on a Saturday, all dancing. I remember being there one August, when I was just starting to come out, and a lot of the women started taking off their shirts. I was freaking out. I thought: *Do I need to do this in order to be a lesbian?* But I kept on dancing and pretending I was cool.

It was a safe space, because there were never any men. I remember one time when I first went, there were these two gray-haired women in the corner, and I thought: *I bet they're the ladies auxiliary of the church, and they're going to report us.* But we introduced ourselves, and it was Reverend Elaine Marsh and her longtime partner; it turned out they were the ones that made this safe space for young lesbians. But it was a sign of the times that people were afraid to take pictures. We just didn't do that. If anyone out there has pictures, I'd love to see them.

At the Foot of the Mountain Theater

Revolutionary feminist theater company, Cedar-Riverside People's Center, Minneapolis; 1974–91

Kim Hines: You need to know about At the Foot of the Mountain Theater. Now, I was at Out and About Theatre for a few years. I worked with August Wilson, and I give the Playwrights' Center a lot of credit for nurturing me on many levels. But still, there was a vibe; not that they were overly misogynist, but the guys had a hard time supporting the women. And it was very white—very, very white. And theater is a very patriarchal place; most of the roles are for men.

I can't tell you how many roadblocks I kept slamming up against. I had already been in professional theater for twenty years when I started there part-time in 1983, before eventually becoming new programs director and production manager. It was woman centered, woman designed. There weren't more than five of us, but we became the biggest and oldest feminist theater company in North America.

We made up a multimedia soap opera called *Toklas, MN*. For each installment, I was the playwright and one of the directors, and we had videographers, dancers, singers. We created this town, and it was a multimedia production, with cooking segments featuring the Galloping Lesbian Gourmet, all kinds of flipping-the-channel television things. We started selling key chains and cups. The guys, the gay men, were saying, "how come we can't see it?"—it's for women! People were just loving it. It got so popular people would drive in from Nebraska when we were going to put on the next installment. We were it; we were *it*. Being a boomer, in my generation, women did not feel empowered; we felt ignored and undervalued—"Oh, you can't do that because you're a woman." It's like being a one-year-old; everyone's always telling you: "No, no, don't go over there. No, don't touch that." But we did the opposite. We created a world. It was us, it was us women. That part was way cool. I loved the whole thing of supporting and nurturing female artists.

To the young person, I'm sorry these places don't exist anymore. This is what happens when you integrate and assimilate. I'm a Black person, and I watched my south Minneapolis community fall apart because of integration. Same thing in the LGBTQ+ community. We created these different entities, we created our own world, because we weren't accepted by the dominant culture. The minute they started to open the door, a lot of LBGTQ+ people left the community.

AIDS Fundraisers of the 1980s and 1990s

Scott Mayer: When I think of the 1980s and 1990s, I was either going to an AIDS fundraiser, organizing an AIDS fundraiser, or going to a funeral. That has resulted in a lack of mentors for younger gay men. It has resulted in a lack of history and passing down lessons. And I'm not sure what the long-term repercussions of that are: If young men don't vote and get the elected officials we were able to elect, I don't know what happens.

But the parties we had, to fundraise—wild and phenomenal. There was a formula: Take an empty warehouse, send out postcards—I had a big, big mailing list, and mailing lists are power. Hire some dancers, which were good-looking men without shirts on. Give all the money to AIDS organizations. It wasn't like things are today, where you have to get permits for everything. You could just have parties.

Billy Beson: One minute the whole industry was run by beautiful gay men; the next minute everyone was dead. It was the most heartbreaking time in my life. But we had such huge fundraising parties. Smoke and Gregorian chants in International Market Square, ball gowns. I remember once, *A Midsummer Night's Dream* was playing at the Guthrie. We rented a farmer's field, had a twelve-hundred-square-foot path mowed, put up a tent and a fountain, brought all the sets. I remember Merlin in a costume. All we did was fundraise, but the parties were unbelievable.

Lesbian Parks and Rec Softball
South Minneapolis; 1970s and 1980s

Lisa Vecoli: We had a softball team, the Fesbian Lemonists, sponsored by the Lions Tap. Softball was very significant.

Gail Lewellan: Amazon Bookstore sponsored two softball teams: The green team was the A league; the purple team was the Minneapolis Rec league. Oh, it was so much fun. The City of St. Paul had just voted to revoke a nondiscrimination ordinance for housing and employment, so everyone was saying, "We're not going to live in St. Paul anymore." The world wasn't a safe place then. My first interaction with the word *lesbian* was someone yelling out the car window: "Goddamn fucking lesbians!" And I thought: *Lesbians.* That's a word. For me!

Even coming out of the Town House, which was more of a women's bar, you watched—for the risk of rape, but just because of the hatred for people in same-sex relationships. On the softball sidelines, there would be folding chairs, something to drink, and you'd settle in for a nice evening. It was never a place of conflict. You could just play and be competitive, be fair, have fun. And be normal. Wearing the word *Amazon* across a shirt, or even better, a shiny jacket—that was the best.

Foxy's
Various St. Paul locations; 1968–84

Honey Harold, who died in 1994, was responsible, almost by herself, for lesbian nightlife in Minnesota. As a St. Paul born-and-bred factory worker, she first opened Honey's Roadhouse, north of St. Paul, then relocated to near Dale and Como and renamed it Honey's Barn. When arsonists torched Honey's Barn, Harold opened Foxy's, at 249 West Seventh, the longest running of Minnesota's lesbian bars. When Foxy's closed, Harold opened Castle Royale and, finally, Rumors.

Lisa Vecoli: The first time I went to Foxy's, I left my girlfriend in the car, pulled open this blacked-out glass door, like: *What's inside* *there?* I was nervous. The music was thumping, the flashing lights, the heavy haze of cigarette smoke. I turned around. It's real!

What did we wear? If you were feminine-appearing, then you were appealing to the male gaze. If you were butch you were appealing to stereotypes. You were supposed to be kind of androgynous: a lot of tennis shoes, T-shirts, and flannel shirts. And disco, Donna Summer, Gloria Gaynor, tequila sunrises and gin and tonics. There was nowhere better to wear your cool softball jacket. We'd go to Foxy's and push four tables together. There was a lot of overlap between gathering, entertainment, and political action.

Ruby's Café
First Uptown and then Loring Park, Minneapolis; 1984–95

Mary Bahneman: I was in the closet when I started it, with no thoughts of it becoming a gay restaurant. And then *Equal Times* [an LGBTQ newspaper] outed us. They came by, interviewed me, said, "The two lesbians that run Ruby's Café . . ."

I moved [the café] to Loring Park in 1990, right next to Amazon Books. On Sundays it would be mayhem. We'd have a waiting list for most of the day. I would have people who would come in from Greater Minnesota, just to be in the restaurant and just to feel okay with themselves for a little while. You could not be yourself at the time. I remember we had a letter carrier, on his last day before retiring he wore high-heeled red pumps on his whole route. It was like, *Finally, you can't fire me for being who I've been this whole time.* People always said one thing about Ruby's: You could see who went home with who from the lesbian bars because of who came in for breakfast together. It was the place for lesbians to go on Sunday to see what happened on Saturday.

Miss Richfield 1981

Russ King: When I came of age—1985, '86—they had just closed the bathhouses, there were still public sex raids, and AIDS was everywhere. I volunteered at a place called Grace House, essentially hospice. I'd volunteer every Wednesday night for a five-hour shift. It was an interesting time; people were dying so fast. You'd leave on a Wednesday, come back a week later, they'd be like: Tim died, a new woman came, she died, this is the new guy. People ten years older than me, they lost everybody. They had ten friends; nine died. It really wasn't that long ago. I was just a little younger, and I worked for the Minnesota AIDS Project, and I didn't actually care for drag at the time. It was like, *Oh, it's Pride, there's a guy dressed as a woman. Shocker.*

But we had to recarpet at the AIDS Project, and it was a hassle. To celebrate it being over, we threw a big party. I took the old carpet, cut out stars and circles and made key chains for everyone, and dressed as Carpetina, with the gifts of carpet.

Mark Addicks was having a party for Miss America, and my friend and I thought it would be funny to go as contestants. I was Miss Richfield 1981; he was Miss Little Rock 1986. But the joke was on us: I thought we were going to a party of ten people. It was a hundred. And it wasn't a costume party.

Things really took off. Mark helped me put together a cabaret show at the Bryant-Lake Bowl; he got me connected to the Toyota Comedy Festival. Next thing you know I'm onstage with the Minnesota Orchestra doing Rodgers and Hammerstein. Then Orbitz, Provincetown, Atlantis Cruises, star of stage and sea.

I will gladly be a landmark. Just know I'm more someone who created a character than a drag queen. I don't do impersonations. I sing and use my own voice, and I guess I'll use that voice now to note that AIDS pulled everybody together, even when their families were leaving them and all these terrible, truly terrible deaths were happening. But it pulled us together, and social distancing feels like it's pulling us apart.

Ye Gadz
On Loring Park, Minneapolis; 1982–84

Billy Beson: Ye Gadz had beautiful, beautiful gay-boy waiters. We'd go there for breakfast, lunch—more of a liquid lunch—and the entertainment was the waiters. They had flawless bodies, tight pink shirts. Some taught aerobics next door, and you could peek in and watch—Ye Gadz indeed. You could meet people so much easier then. Everyone wanted to meet someone. It was a lonely existence.

John Veda: I worked there in the mid-eighties, and it was the first openly gay-owned and gay-operated restaurant in Minneapolis. The location was key, right there on Loring Park. On Fridays and Saturdays we were open till two o'clock [in the morning], so all the kids from the Saloon would come. It was a mad dash. The leather boys would shiver in their chaps, and the drag queens would hold court, and they'd all be standing in line. It was quite the scene. Everyone would get a fried chicken sandwich on a croissant with house-made chips and an Oreo malt.

To be able to have a job with two gay bosses and a clientele that was gay, and to have no repercussions? It was special. The walls were Pepto-Bismol pink, and the tables and chairs were black lacquer—that eighties art deco thing. And we wore pink button-down shirts and black shorts, with scrunchy pink or white socks and black penny loafers. Right out of the *Preppy Handbook*. It was prestigious to work there; you had to have a certain look. Occasionally Tommy, the owner, would take a few people out, usually to the Saloon, and there was this air of, *It's the Ye Gadz boys!*

The Tubs, the Locker Room

Stewart Van Cleve: The bathhouses were subject to really violent police raids. The Minneapolis police department was brutal. They would drag men out on the street naked in the cold and line them up and along the street. By the 1980s, with AIDS, the police department and civic leaders wanted to shut [the bathhouses] down right away, and there were all these high-profile examples where they would confiscate pornographic pictures and hangings and display them in city hall to try to humiliate gay men and show how wicked they were.

Sidewalk Sales

Scott Mayer: A sidewalk sale is when you're standing outside a bar after it closes, and you try to pick up a date. It went on outside the Saloon and the 90's every Friday and Saturday night, fifty-two weeks a year. I have a very good friend who's thirty-five, and I said, "Do you know what a sidewalk sale is?" He thought it literally meant nonprofit organizations setting up tables to sell stuff.

Russ King: I feel sorry for the guys who will never experience the sidewalk sale. At one o'clock the bars closed, so you went out on the sidewalk and talked, and sometimes you'd go home with somebody, sometimes you wouldn't, but there would be *hundreds* of people in front of the 90's. It was a really fun heritage. Nobody does that now.

Minneapolis's Gay Beaches
Glitter Beach (the Thirty-Second Street Beach on the east side of Bde Maka Ska), Hidden Beach, Bare Ass Beach

Scott Mayer: For me, that Thirty-Second Street beach was the definitive place to meet people like me. Everybody had a beach towel, a chair; you wanted to get as tan as possible. There were boom boxes playing disco, and people would walk up and back to the refectory to check out the guys in bathing suits. And, oh, that beach volleyball.

Russ King: Cedar Lake's Hidden Beach, it was like a nudist sort of place. You had to park your car and hike in. It was super relaxed, gay and straight, and people would just be naked. Public sex was reasonable at the time. There was lots of brush and foliage to tuck away in; it was a very wooded area. Just really fun. If you wanted to be sexual you could, or you could just sunbathe in the nude and no one cared.

Billy Beson: For two or three blocks, it was all pretty tan boys in little Speedos, with a sidewalk going through the whole thing, and no one blinked or batted an eye. Bare Ass Beach—we used to go skinny-dipping there, after the bar scene; it would always get busted. We'd put our Speedos on and run to the car and get the hell out of there. The city was a little sexier in those days, but a little more innocent.

The Other Gentrification: Driving out Gay People

The Club, the Anchor, the Onyx, and the rest of the Twin Cities' bull-dozed downtowns

Stewart Van Cleve: I began to see this pattern of urban planning, for both cities. The cities got built up, got run down, LGBTQ+ people moved into the nooks and crannies, built something, then the powers that be declared them vice districts or bad and criminal in some way and knocked them down.

Thousands of men would descend on Minneapolis and St. Paul when seasonal labor [in farm fields] was done. They'd drink and fight and have sex. That was the sort of activity that horrified city leaders, and they spent decades trying to get white nuclear families—the quote-unquote normal people—back downtown. Gaviidae Common, Galtier Plaza, they were shopping malls that we tore down something beautiful to get, and if you look beyond and underneath them, you'll discover these rich tapestries of queer experience that got cleared away. Minneapolis and St. Paul both really tried to scrub away parts of city life that are just essential. Both cities realized too late you need parts of cities that are chaotic and unruly, that allow for experimentation in terms of sex and gender, and you need small little affordable buildings to pull that off. If you look at the most exciting parts of Minneapolis and St. Paul today, they are all those places that escaped demolition, while the urban renewal buildings they put up are likely totally empty.

What's amazing is, around 2000, you go from having gay men and lesbians being seen as the symptom of urban decay to a sign of urban vitality, and then you lose a lot of the institutions where LGBTQ+ people gathered in just at that same moment. There hasn't been a lesbian bar in the Twin Cities for going on twenty years now, and there's a real sense of loss. Meanwhile, drag has become explosively popular—the queens back in the clubs in the 1970s would have been dumbfounded. The 1970s were such a weird time; the height of terrible urban planning, and then so much of what they were trying to wipe out with those bad decisions is what we value now.

A Brother's Touch
Gay bookstore, first Nicollet Avenue near Franklin, later Twenty-Fourth and Hennepin, Minneapolis; 1983–2003

Jean Tretter: Harvey Hertz came from the Bronx to get sober and ran our bookstore for twenty years. If you know New Yorkers, he was typical—that temper! By God, you didn't want to cheat him. But he was a good friend, and could be very generous, and occasionally liked to dress in drag. No one had more gay authors. We have so many pictures in the archive. I liked him and got along with him real well.

Russ King: I just remember Harvey as such a nice guy. It was back in the day when a lot of those types of guys and those types of businesses were so supportive of community events—hosting workshops, hosting book signings. They were right there to promote and support everything. That's the piece that's disappointing. We don't have those community touchstones anymore. They weren't just *places*—they were *people*.

Boom
Fourth Street and East Hennepin Avenue, Minneapolis; 2000–2006

Charlie Rounds: Oddfellows and Boom, the gay bar on Hennepin—that was my baby, along with four other guys, including Mark Addicks. We needed a place to take our parents; we needed a place to take our siblings. I remember the opening, January 13, 2000. It was the first gay bar in the state of Minnesota to have windows. That was such a huge deal. We felt so strongly that we would no longer live in the closet. We had twenty-foot-high glass windows facing Hennepin Avenue, and it was vitally important that we would never hide, that we were no longer ashamed.

On that opening night we had the front windows papered. And then I'll never forget taking the paper down ceremonially at five. Outside, it was snowing, it was dark, there was low cloud cover and this beautiful orange streetlight glow with this gentle snow— it was magic.

So many people met their life partners at Boom. It was a very safe, nonsexual space. We had fundraisers, the *Queer Eye* guys came and did a fundraiser. Bea Arthur came to dinner. And of course it was really the gay man's arrival to political power. We had three gay city council members, and nobody had that, not New York or Los Angeles. It was an important place.

RSVP Travel
LGBTQ travel agency, University Avenue near the Witch's Hat, Minneapolis; 1985–2006

Charlie Rounds: I say I was a paid gay. Kevin Mossier, who owned the Travel Company, started RSVP Travel to give 5 percent of the profits back to the gay community. And it grew into the largest gay company in the world, period. Kevin chartered a cruise ship in 1986, filling it with gay customers—it was the first time someone had done that on that scale. That's part of the lost history of the Twin Cities. We printed a million inserts to put into gay newspapers around the country. Less than 5 percent of our customers were local to the Twin Cities, though we did buy a hundred-passenger cruise ship called the *Sea Spirit*. On the back it said: "Port of Minneapolis."

Our biggest business was cruising from New York up to Fire Island, Boston, Provincetown, and dock overnight. We had truly fine dining on board, brilliant food. We'd sail from New Orleans through the Caribbean; when Grand Cayman island heard we were a ship full of gay men, they wouldn't let us dock. We said, "We will not dock at Grand Cayman for the next twenty years," and we didn't; everyone else liked our money. The sad thing is that a lot of people took our cruises because they were dying, and they wanted to have one week of their lives to live in freedom before they died, to not be stared at and not be in fear.

Kevin died in 1996; I helped give away his $13 million through his foundation. He couldn't have been more humble. When Joan Rivers or Debbie Reynolds came to perform on our ships, he was like: "You handle it; I am not a celebrity person." I remember Debbie Reynolds was like: "Is there someone on board who can do my hair?" I said, "Ms. Reynolds, we have a thousand gay men on this ship; we got this."

Betty's Family
General Mills' LGBTQ employee group; 1990s–present

Mark Addicks: The untold side of the marriage win in Minnesota was about internal corporate employee networks. The Human Rights Campaign came up with a genius strategy in the 1990s. The way to equality wouldn't be through the federal government, given where the Republican Party was and the way they used the gay community as a piñata. HRC created an equality index, ranking all the major companies. Anyone recruiting talent wanted to have a good rating. With these ratings, LGBTQ+ employee groups asked for meetings with executives to get the ratings up. Every year HRC lengthened the list, and behind the scenes all those meetings got people to know each other.

When the Minnesota GOP started talking about an anti-gay marriage amendment, behind the scenes, a lot of corporations said to the state GOP and chamber of commerce: "This is against our employees; you don't want to go there." Nevertheless, Michele Bachmann and her little friends, they thought they were going to win.

What ensued was a number of private conversations inside major companies. Around Pride, General Mills hosts LGBTQ+ groups from other companies. And it was at that ceremony, the year of the vote, that our chairman came out to say General Mills would be against. This was major. After that, several corporations came out and said the same: We're the same; we vote no. The joke we made at the time was, everyone just knows employee network groups as the most boring part of the Pride parade. But look at us now.

Patrick's Cabaret

Various south Minneapolis locations, including 506 East Twenty-Fourth Street; 1986–2018

Patrick Scully: I started Patrick's Cabaret because at the time, if I had work to show, first I had to get somebody else's approval to get on their stage. At the time, when people talked of diversity, there was resistance to including gay and lesbian people. And without a place for queer-identified work, it would simply never be seen.

I found I was HIV positive six months before the first Patrick's Cabaret, and it gave me a clarity of purpose that allowed me to take risks.

What I'm proudest of at Patrick's was that even when we did a queer boys' night, I always included a tagline like: *It's all gay boys performing onstage, but everyone is welcome.* I think when we embraced everyone, it made some space for people to embrace us back. There were and are large and powerful forces in this country that don't want gay and lesbian people to exist, and during our performances we were the center, and we created a new vision of how anyone and everyone could be. Artists are the people who make the psychic space for activists to imagine a future and for politicians to follow.

I was up in Detroit Lakes recently, touring my Walt Whitman show, and I met with the Gay Straight Alliance at a local high school. I introduced myself, mentioning something like, "I'm one of the first post-Stonewall HIV-positive gay men out front in the culture in Minnesota."

Excuse me, what's Stonewall? Someone else raised their hand: *What's HIV?*

Driving home I thought: *Okay, Patrick. Translate that into your own experience.* If someone talked to me when I was that age in Roseville in the 1970s about something fifty years earlier, that would have been the end of World War I—which to me then may as well have been ancient Greece. So I've been asking myself, "How do we pass on our experience and information to subsequent generations?"

Thirty-Eighth and Chicago: Holy Ground

Mpls.St.Paul Magazine, July 2020

Like many in Minneapolis, I experienced the murder of George Floyd and the subsequent uprising with profound grief, fear, and despair. I live close to Lake Street, and I watched from my front porch as car after car unloaded white folk with nunchucks sticking out of their backpacks. I went and photographed their license plates, just in case. I filled trash cans with water and sat on my stoop holding a garden hose, as did all my neighbors, guarding against fire. After all our drugstores burned I spent the following year driving my elderly neighbor to the nearest pharmacy in the suburbs.

Coming of age at *City Pages*, where Minneapolis's outrageous police brutality was a regular beat, I was not surprised. Participating in Minneapolis's public schools, reading Minneapolis newspapers, seeing how inequality and poverty in the Twin Cities are braided cruelly with racism, I was not surprised. But I was riven. I remember my sister calling from Japan: "Well, what else is going on in your life?" I looked at the police helicopter above, darted my eyes toward the National Guard trucks on the streets as I scurried home before curfew: Nothing?

At first, I didn't want to write about George Floyd and the memorial space that has been built up by the community at the south Minneapolis intersection now known as George Floyd Square. I thought, *What does a white lady have to say about any of this?* But my editor pushed me to go: "People want to know what you see, through your eyes." So I went.

Visiting the corner of Thirty-Eighth and Chicago in Minneapolis, and the transfiguration of George Floyd.

"Get out of there; you're standing on his body!" the minister yelled at the tourist.

The tourist, who looked like she mainly did Pilates a hundred hours a day, jerked down her selfie-capturing phone and leaped into the air as if electrified, her nylon shorts flapping. She pranced off the painted figure that symbolizes George Floyd's body.

It's blue and spectral, with white angel's wings, and it's painted in the street on Chicago Avenue, right in front of Cup Foods, north of East Thirty-Eighth Street: George Floyd's body. It's right where George Floyd died as three Minneapolis police officers kneeled on his body, killing him, and a fourth Minneapolis police officer stood guard, preventing the crowd from intervening.

All around George Floyd's blue body, thousands and thousands of souls rally, day and night.

The pain and horror from this—what do we call it? a modern-day lynching? an extrajudicial execution?—have now sparked protests against Minneapolis police and solidarity for Black Lives Matter in Sydney; London; Los Angeles; Washington, DC; and too many other places to name. These protests are sometimes peaceful, sometimes raging. And they have been met with often shockingly bloodthirsty responses, as if to prove that no one is safe from police brutality, whether they live in Buffalo, New York; Washington, DC; or here.

But it's different at Thirty-Eighth and Chicago, where a spontaneous space of mourning, reflection, and celebration has taken over the intersection. The road is blocked at Thirty-Seventh and Thirty-Sixth Streets and a block over each way on Thirty-Eighth Street. The shutdown has created a traffic-free plus sign, or a cross, widened at two sides by an empty parking lot and an abandoned gas station.

Volunteers provide security. After the first few days, no one has seen the police here. A big old school bus, now painted white and outfitted with bandages and supplies, blocks one road as a medical tent. Past it, a real ambulance from Hennepin Healthcare waits with a few National Guard soldiers, just in case.

Inside this space, tens of thousands have come: to mourn, to dance, to give speeches, to say prayers, to leave artworks, to take selfies, to buy or sell T-shirts, to hand out religious literature—to do all the human things.

I went because you always go to the funeral. I think I was in my twenties when I picked up those words to live by. At first I thought you always went to the funeral for the family and friends, to show support and bear witness to their grief. Eventually I realized you also go to the funeral for yourself, to focus your own grief and stop being so self-involved and busy all day. You do it for your soul.

The first time I went to this particularly open and open-ended funeral, I did not want to go. I didn't want to feel more pain. But what I found was so moving and healing, I ended up going to the corner of Thirty-Eighth and Chicago four times in a week.

The first time I made my way there, it was early in the day, and as I arrived, so did maybe 150 church folk, including a few dozen Lutheran ministers with hand-embroidered stoles bearing white doves, rainbow crosses, moon-faced choristers, and such.

It was on this visit that the minister yelled at the tourist. Then we were all on our knees in the gravel-filled road, reciting the Lord's Prayer. The idea that we must *forgive those who trespass against us* seemed relevant but uniquely difficult, as gentle George's face loomed down from every vantage point: hundreds of images— poster board and canvas, oil and acrylic, spray paint and marker— taped to and leaned against the outside of Cup Foods. These portraits were interleaved with bunches and bunches of flowers, like a museum and a florist had both decided to flee town in a hurry.

On my feet again, looking at George Floyd's face alongside sayings like *Rest in Power* and *Gentle George*, it felt like a very Powderhorn place, that neighborhood of artists and the working class. Handmade signs about justice wallpapered the bus stop, joined by one lone plush tiger sitting on the bench, as if waiting for that bus to justice. It all felt like a shrine.

People cared. A lot. A lot of people cared a lot.

More art was coming as I stood there that morning. Men and women, singly or in pairs, arrived on foot bearing their tributes. I watched a gaunt man in faded green plaid approach with a black-and-white ink sketch of Floyd's face on thick paper. He tucked it in among the other offerings on the west wall of Cup Foods, took a step back with closed eyes as if in prayer, bowed his head, and walked quickly away.

I came back a few nights later and wished the trespassing tourist could have returned with me. For that night there was no scolding minister, and the tourist could have done what many others did. Namely, lie on George Floyd's blue paint shadow, like a child in a snow angel made by a parent. There, she could have taken a selfie or had friends photograph her from above. She could have lain beside him and wrapped her arms around him, as if the two were in bed, as so many visitors around me did.

That night was ecstatic and charged. Barbecues everywhere. Free food everywhere. A dance party raged in the now inactive and boarded-up gas station, Speedway. Several abandoned couches stood beneath the metal canopy where cars would ordinarily gas up, and upon them people lounged. A punk rock girl in an elaborate 1980s London outfit sat on top of a gas pump, shaking her shoulders to the sounds of Public Enemy, which blared from speakers to the north end of the Speedway. A handful of people danced; others stood in line for free food.

To the south end of the Speedway parking lot, a soul DJ spun classics like the Delfonics' "La-La Means I Love You." It all felt a bit like the Gay 90's, some thirty blocks north, with different adjoining nightclubs for different ages and stages. A dozen men climbed an aluminum ladder to the top of the Speedway roof. Two of them held large dogs on their backs. They had a microphone, and they started a few chants: "When I say George, you say Floyd—George FLOYD, George FLOYD."

Then one bearded man in a black ball cap began to speak. "I have never felt so much love. I have never felt so much pride in saying: *I am from Minnesota.* Everyone you see—you see what we are capable of. Look around. These are your brothers and sisters.

We can change this world. We can take it back. We are all we've got! White people, you are not silent. You are here with us. This is not a Black problem. This is a human problem."

Behind the figures on the roof, the classic summer sunset clouds—tall as mountains, white and vibrant salmon pink—made the scene seem blessed. Everyone raised one fist, including a puffy-haired toddler sitting on the shoulders of a man in front of me. The angle of the sun made her hair look like a golden halo as she swung her chubby little fist in various directions. I felt hopeful for the first time since the murder.

Suddenly, a ruckus. People from the Speedway roof were calling for the crowd to make room for "Madam Congressperson." Ilhan Omar herself appeared. Pale peach headscarf, pearl-gray dress, she stood in an opening made by the crowd. I could see her only because so many phones were tipped in around her, little satellites in the air, all capturing her image and displaying it on their camera screens.

"I can't believe in 2020 we're going through this," Omar began. "But we're doing this for our kids. I don't want to see my children murdered in the streets. And I don't want to see any children murdered in the streets. That's what you guys are here fighting for. We're fighting for the freedom we all deserve.

"I shed a tear the other day, when Lake Street and north Minneapolis were set ablaze. I did not cry because there was property that was being destructed. I cried because that was a symbol of dreams and opportunities that were being faded right before our eyes. What I do know is that every single day when we pour out to the streets, it gets us closer to making sure that we are no longer begging for crumbs, but we are getting proper investment in our communities."

She talked about legislation she's bringing forth with other House members, including Ayanna Pressley, of Massachusetts, to condemn police brutality and demand national reforms. She closed by leading chants of "Say his name—George Floyd!" before a selfie line formed around her.

The dance parties resumed.

I had brought my twelve-year-old daughter. As we headed home before curfew, I asked her what she'd remember from the night. "I thought a lot about what one of them said," she told me. "No one is going to change this for us. We have to change it ourselves."

I'll change my maxim about funerals now: Always take your kids to the funeral.

The last time I saw Thirty-Eighth and Chicago, it was the night of the real family funeral—the one Al Sharpton flew in to lead. And the corner was wildly crowded, state fair crowded.

I assume this followed the day's television coverage. The big, big media was there. CNN had stationed a white satellite truck as big as a south Minneapolis rambler, a Yukon XL as big as a garage, and maybe a million bucks' worth of gear.

"She's the one who was talking to Don Lemon," a passerby said, gesturing toward a reporter in a lavender shirt and rhinestone necklace, who stood on top of a camera case to get a better perspective on the crowd.

"I'd be more impressed if she talked to Lester Holt," replied her companion; apparently the younger news host didn't carry the weight of the old guard.

I managed to get stuck in a crowd between CBS News camerapeople and the documentary unit of Ben Crump, who is George Floyd's lawyer and also the host of A&E's *Who Killed Tupac?* They mainly talked about what there is to eat near the Marriott. (Not much.)

The whole area in front of the Speedway was now a free store, with long tables under tents heaped with food-shelf items like ramen, boxes of cereal, soap, and tampons. Certain fashion trends emerged, like blue surgical masks with pieces of silver duct tape at the mouth and "Can't Breathe" written on the tape. Or double T-shirts, with a new "We Still Can't Breathe" shirt worn over the shirt you came in wearing.

I talked to a Black man who grew up in the neighborhood but now lives in North Branch. He asked me if the neighborhood was any better, and I didn't know what to say, given the circumstances. At the main stage, a Native American organizer played "Amazing Grace" on traditional instruments.

When he concluded, I talked to some beautiful African American teenage girls who'd each matched her cloth face mask to her outfit. They were from Lakeville and asked if I had made my way to see the grand piano, in the middle of Thirty-Eighth Street near the CNN trucks. When I got there, a ponytailed pianist was playing "Somewhere Over the Rainbow" and "Piano Man."

A white man told me that members of the neighborhood would arrive in the night, remove the pavement of the intersection with a jackhammer, and erect a roundabout containing a statue of George Floyd. I didn't bother telling him that this would never happen unless the intersection also got widened to accommodate city buses. Chicago and Thirty-Eighth is an important bus station in a low-income neighborhood.

A chaplain from Billy Graham's "Rapid Response Team," identifiable by his embroidered royal blue polo shirt, told me he came in from Florida. He flew to hot spots all the time. The man who believed in the coming roundabout said he was on the bridge when the gas tanker truck nearly killed everyone but ended up killing no one. One of the greatest acts of love he'd ever seen was the protesters running in to save the truck driver from the crowd that was beating him.

"I thought I was going to see a guy pulled to chunks and thrown over the bridge into the river," roundabout guy said. "But they were real pacifists. Like here. This is the safest place in the world right now."

I was trying to get a handle on what about this space of grief was so profoundly healing. Was it George's face? In the course of my visits it had multiplied in the number of images, and now in size. The back of the bus shelter had become a vast black-and-white image. Or maybe the soothing magic here came from the mutual effort to create a sacred space?

I thought I should try to write down the names of the flowers beneath the south-facing George Floyd mural, the orange-and-blue one. I spotted mums, freesia, lilies, roses. Countless bunches of grocery store bouquets, wrapped in clear plastic. Classic FTD-florist-style arrangements, in pink and yellow vases, with religious cards on sticks. Had floral delivery workers placed them here, on behalf of mourners in other cities and states and countries? I took in the hardware-store hanging petunia baskets and elaborate casket toppers and easel pieces. Garden peonies with their stems wrapped in a wad of wet paper towels and crinkled aluminum foil.

During this reverie, a group of larger, older Black men suddenly paused nearby. One of the men was yelling to his friends—urgently and profanely—that what happened to Floyd could never happen to him. If he were handcuffed with three cops on his neck and back, he would have chewed off the officers' thumbs.

His friends informed him he was crazy; he insisted it was they who were crazy. Didn't they know he was stronger than Mike Tyson, who could bite off ears?

At first I thought: George's body is right there. But then the statement haunted and wound through me—the bluster, the foolishness, the whistling in the graveyard. I started to love that statement more every moment I stood there. This man made a difficult pilgrimage through closed streets and crowds to say: It couldn't happen to me. When the only reason we were all gathered here was because it could and it did.

No one makes the hard climb to the top of the mountain to tell a prophet he doesn't matter. Standing there, as three African American folks burned giant, arm-sized bundles of sage, I finally felt like I understood what Thirty-Eighth and Chicago had become. Like Robben Island, like the National Civil Rights Museum in the Lorraine Motel, where Dr. Martin Luther King Jr. was assassinated, this was a space where change erupted from brutal and intolerable loss. Changes to policing, changes in seeing oppression, changes in resolving to do something about it. It started from this one corner in Minneapolis and from marching, fists raised, all over the globe.

We had all come to the funeral, and so been gifted with a birth.

Good Stalk: Rhubarb
. . . .

Saveur, April 2013

> When I think about the way Minnesota has healed me, the
> rhubarb described here—still going strong next to the roses
> in an unlikely spot it seems to like—is part of that story. If
> you've never had rhubarb and roses and a quiet place with a
> little dog and kids who love you, it may seem like a small thing
> not worth mentioning. But to me, it's everything.

New York City in the 1980s was not safe for children. Some were
disappearing to kidnappers; others were disappearing to crack.
Between that and the garbage strikes and divorce, the best place
for kids was inside, in front of the television. I think that's why
the New York City natives I know from that era all became different sorts of hothouse flowers, strong and strange. As for me, I got
bored with the reruns on TV and turned to my mother's bookcase
of college classics, which caused me to become obsessed with, of all
things, the American Midwest, as seen through the eyes of F. Scott
Fitzgerald and Willa Cather. The Midwest was a fantasyland where
the skyscrapers were built of prairie clouds, and where the biggest
danger seemed to be quiet yearnings for excitement.

I arrived in Minnesota for college in the last months of 1988
and never looked back. Upon graduating I realized you could buy a
house with an attic that smelled like a barn and a covered porch—a
real Victorian-era house that was walking distance to an organic
bakery and a Vietnamese restaurant—for less than a hundred thousand dollars. So I did. Then I headed to the garden center for my
first real purchases as a landholding midwesterner. I wanted a
rosebush and a rhubarb patch. Just like Willa Cather had.

But my friend Mitch told me that you can't buy rhubarb plants just anywhere; usually people just had them. Well, what then? His mother knew of a farm stand. And by the side of the road, there they were: strawberry-hued rhubarb plants growing in plastic gallon milk jugs, the tops scissored off, holes punched in the bottom. A table made of planks had a clear and direct sign: $5. Another plastic jug was nailed to the plank tabletop. You just put your cash in the jug. Cash in a jug at the side of the road, where anyone could take it. But no one ever would.

Now bear with me, because here things get dull. The rhubarb went in the ground and thrived. That's what rhubarb does. Whether you're in Minnesota or Tibet, Missouri or Latvia, England, Alaska, or Iran, rhubarb grows like a weed pretty much anywhere with usable soil and a hard freeze in the winter, which the plant needs to thrive. But now things get interesting again, because at my local farmers' market, and at all of those in the rest of the snowbelt, this weediness makes rhubarb one of the superstars of early spring. That's when bundles of rhubarb stalks appear alongside ramps, fiddlehead ferns, and wild watercress. They mark the true end of winter, the beginning of the edible outdoors, the start of local cooking becoming exciting, even exuberant, again.

There are in fact a wealth of exciting and exuberant ways you can cook rhubarb: braised in syrup until custardy; baked into rustic upside-down cake; whipped into an elegant rhubarb mousse; juiced into lemonade or ruby-tinted granita. Though of course you can do all sorts of things with rhubarb, you probably won't, because here in the United States, rhubarb means pie: rhubarb pie, strawberry-rhubarb pie, rhubarb crumble, strawberry-rhubarb crumble. In English-speaking lands, rhubarb is so closely associated with pie that it's often called pie plant.

That's a homely end to what was once a very interesting life for a globe-trotting political pawn. *Rheum rhabarbarum*, thought to have originated in northwest China, was once the subject of hot dispute between Russian czars and Chinese emperors. Rhubarb was first written about some 2,700 years ago in *The Divine Farmer's Herb-Root Classic*, one of China's earliest known pharmaceutical texts, and was prized for the medicinal value of its roots, for they had a remarkable ability to cure dysentery, diarrhea, and constipation—it was the Pepto-Bismol and Ex-Lax of the preindustrial age and a key export of China. In the book *The Silk Road: Two Thousand Years in the Heart of Asia*, historian Frances Wood quotes the ambassador to Samarkand in 1405, who enumerated the good stuff that came along the Silk Road from China: "silk, satins, musk, rubies, diamonds, pearls, and rhubarb." In seventeenth-century Russia, rhubarb was so valuable that much of the country's treasury was derived from the medicinal sales of the imported rhubarb root. When Chinese emperors and Russian czars had a border dispute, withholding rhubarb was China's biggest weapon.

Rhubarb, in its sour, vegetable, nonmedicinal guise, came into common kitchen and garden use only after plantations made sugar widely available and affordable in the past few centuries—the sweetener is what made rhubarb fit for pie. The part of rhubarb we eat, the stalks—white, pink, crimson, grasshopper green, whitish green, or red, depending on the variety—are actually rhubarb leaf bases called petioles. Other petioles we commonly eat are celery, Swiss chard, napa cabbage, endive, and, arguably, asparagus. Stick to the petioles of rhubarb—the leaves, which contain toxic oxalic acid, can be lethal to those with sensitivities to it or to rhubarb-leaf gluttons (five kilos would be enough to poison most people). In my own Minnesota neighborhood I've seen kids chasing each other with rhubarb leaves as if they're murder weapons that could kill on contact.

Marcus Jernmark, the Swedish-born chef of the vaunted restaurant Aquavit in Manhattan, remembers those types of rhubarb shenanigans, as well as the ritual of peeling stalks of rhubarb and chewing them raw during his childhood in Gothenburg. Now he's one of the high-end chefs leading a charge to get rhubarb out of the pie: "In early spring, peas and rhubarb really set the tone of the menu, sometimes with ramps or morels," says Jernmark, whose offerings last spring included herring in a rhubarb-spiked brine and pickled rhubarb with sturgeon, citrus, cilantro, nasturtium flowers, and sweet Maine shrimp—each touched by rhubarb's tart freshness and bearing its vibrant rosy color.

Across cuisines, rhubarb's defining sourness is often seen as its greatest asset. According to Louisa Shafia, author of *The New Persian Kitchen*, "Rhubarb got to Persia along the Silk Road and stayed because Iranians love sour food—pomegranates, lemon juice, lime juice, sour-orange juice, barberries—all those ingredients are very tart." She likes to use fresh minced rhubarb as the finishing acidic note to a savory stew of barley and lamb. "I add it right at the end and stir it in, so it gets soft but not mushy, because then you lose the great sourness."

I usually like to take farmers' market bundles of spring's first rhubarb, cut them into pieces, and roast them in the oven with honey, orange juice, and warm aromatic spices like cardamom and star anise. The resulting mixture makes a great compote to be strewn over pound cake or ice cream. Sometimes I cook the compote down and strain away the solids. The reduced syrup is perfect for a locavore variation on a lemon drop—a little midwestern vodka, a little rhubarb syrup, well chilled. I like to drink a rhubarb drop sitting in my porch swing, overlooking my own garden rhubarb patch, while considering czars and emperors of yore and a world in which rhubarb was as valuable as diamonds and pearls and made headlines—not pie. For this New York City hothouse flower gone country, it's a tart taste of the peculiar past, and it answers the question: What's dull and interesting and good all over? Rhubarb in the spring.

Panic in Bloom

Mpls.St.Paul Magazine, October 2013

Is outside a place? My journey from understanding "the outside" has been long and piecemeal. When I was in high school, there was a sixty-foot-wide vacant lot on Manhattan's Lower East Side, and I joined a protest to "protect nature" by not replacing the building that had once stood there. Because I thought the stray grass in the abandoned tires was virgin wilderness? It took Minnesota and decades of thinking to get myself out of that New York City lack of understanding. Nothing opened my eyes to where we really are in the poisoned world more than working on this story. I still hear from people who converted their own gardens to native pollinator habitat after reading it. For what it's worth, I think we're in the spot in history where nothing matters more than creating conditions for the various webs of life around us to help us make it to a more enlightened spot in the future. Please don't use your time on this earth to spread poison, knowingly or unknowingly.

Bees are dying. So are moths. And every other kind of pollinator. No pollinators means no flowers, no fruit, no nuts. Is this the end of the world as we know it?

Part 1: Sex and Death

Your local honey bun kicks off with nothing but sex and horror. It all starts when the virgin queen takes some practice flights, trying out her wings, never used before and soon enough never used again. Her pheromones bring all the drones to the yard—drones, of course, being the small number of male bees that any beehive produces, slackers who do no work, gather no pollen or nectar, and eat what their sisters procure while waiting for their one big shot at glory. That shot arises. The virgin queen takes flight, high and fast into the air, her pheromones signaling that now is when. Drones pursue, and the first fast and fleet enough to mate the flying queen deposits his sperm. With that act, he is disemboweled from jewel to juicy bit and plummets to the earth.

As many as forty-some more drones will follow in that first fellow's lustful, successful, and gory steps. When the no-longer-virgin queen returns, she will have all the sperm she will ever need in her life, and she will spend the rest of her time laying as many as two thousand eggs a day over her life span. The success of her colony is dictated by the number of partners she achieves on that memorable day. The more partners, the longer her life. Likely, she will not remember the sexy massacre that launched her million children on their path to serving as the vehicles for completing the sex lives of plants. She will remain in the dark, never again flying, enslaved till the end. Natural selection is a bitch.

But not as much a bitch as unnatural selection.

As you've no doubt heard by now, honeybees, those sexy beasts, are in severe, catastrophic decline. Pollinating bees contribute as much as $15 billion a year in value to the American agricultural system by pollinating the food that turns into one of every three mouthfuls we eat. However, in the early 2000s beekeepers started noticing their bees vanishing. In 2006 colony collapse disorder was named, and despite a name and a flurry of research and publicity, the American honeybee's plight is worsening. This past winter a third of commercial bees died, ten million hives died, and there were barely enough living bees to pollinate important crops such as California almonds, worth $4 billion a year. When *Time* magazine recently considered the dire state of the honeybee, the author concluded that unless robot bees emerge, we may be leaving the era of commonly available fruit. Are Minnesota apples soon to be as rare as Minnesota moose?

What's killing all the bees?

We are.

Part 2: It's All Our Fault

We are killing the bees the way a big dog might knock over knick-knacks in a china shop, a few here, a few there, just by turning and roaming and looking up and generally being us.

The varroa mite didn't help. Called *Varroa destructor*, it's a nasty, microscopically small thing that sucks the blood of bees. It came here from Asia because of our human habit of moving hives hither and yon. Another parasite called *Nosema ceranae* didn't help, either. The parasite itself isn't a big deal, but scientists recently discovered that when honeybees eat a typical diet of generic American pollen contaminated with twenty-one agricultural chemicals, the parasite kills the bees.

The pesticides, they don't help. Neonicotinoids, the newest class of pesticides, are "systemic," which means they are absorbed by a plant, move through its tissues, and stay there forever, ending up in every bit of pollen and nectar produced over the plant's whole life. When the bees take the pollen and nectar home and concentrate it, as they do in honey making, they transform what was thought to be a dilute and safe pesticide into a concentrated and lethal one. Neonicotinoids are currently the most popular pesticide in the United States, and virtually all non–organic certified corn planted in Minnesota is treated with a neonicotinoid.

The genetic modifications to corn—altering it so that it expresses the Bt toxin—aren't helping. Minnesota has one of the highest uses of Bt corn in the country—more than two-thirds of the corn in the southwest corner of the state is Bt.

Roundup Ready, or glyphosate-resistant, corn and soybeans don't help either, not because of anything about the corn or soybeans, particularly, but because by their very definition the crops, currently thought to be 90-plus percent of American soybeans and more than 70 percent of American corn, are designed to be drenched with herbicides. These herbicides have eliminated the wildflowers honeybees need for food between commercial agriculture crop blooms. In 2011, the latest year data is available, the Minnesota Department of Agriculture reported more than 25 million pounds of glyphosate being poured on the ground to kill everything that wasn't corn or soybeans, like wildflowers.

For bees, life is now a thing in which periodic all-you-can-eat buffets of low-dose poison are interleaved with stretches of starvation.

We also kill a few more by converting marginal lands to subsidized commodity crop production, especially corn, and guaranteeing that marginal land will earn the farmer the same price as prime farmland would. Minnesota is number four in the nation in collecting farm subsidies.

We kill a few more by buying cheap counterfeit Chinese honey at chain stores. In 2011 *Food Safety News* tested chain store honey and found three-quarters of what's out there and cheap is fake honey from China. Fake, cheap honey puts downward price pressure on North American beekeepers, leading them to do stupid things like take too much healthy honey out of their hives and try to feed the bees corn syrup or sugar water.

And we probably kill a few more building housing on former wildland and spraying pesticides in our gardens and around our churches. And someone's dog probably ate a few. A few million dead bees here, a few hundred thousand there—pretty soon it all adds up, and you're talking real bee death.

But that's not all. Honeybees, of course, are notable to many of us because they are responsible for maybe $15 billion a year in agricultural value and bring us apples, muskmelons, and pumpkins, locally, and honeybees are the bees from which we gather honey. But there are other bees, bumblebees, mason bees, digger bees, leafcutter bees, sweat bees, wild bees of every stripe—the bees that inhabited North America before Europeans brought honeybees here—and those wild bees are facing the same collapse that honeybees are, except they have no lobbyists or magazine covers. Neither do the moths.

Part 3: But Who's Counting?

How are our Minnesota moths doing? "We actually don't know a lot about our moths," says Susan J. Weller, a professor at the

University of Minnesota and executive director of the Bell Museum of Natural History, a woman with large, friendly eyes and an exceptionally calm demeanor. "Estimates for all the insect species in the world range from 10 to 12 million—we don't actually know. There are about 130,000 butterflies and moth species known today and probably another 20,000 out there yet to be discovered. We have undiscovered species in drawers right here," she says, gesturing to the University of Minnesota's insect collection, on the St. Paul campus, a few buildings away. "We identify species and sometimes find they're extinct."

If we had been watching and counting those moths, in drawers, now extinct, would we have diagnosed them with colony collapse disorder too?

The great difference between pollinators in general and honeybees in particular seems to be that honeybees have various multibillion-dollar industries documenting their particular fall off a cliff. But the catastrophic collapse of pollinators is happening all over the place. And it's not merely a story of interest to bug huggers.

Look out a window. Any window. "Seventy percent of the world's flowering plants are dependent on pollinators," explains Marla Spivak, MacArthur fellow and distinguished McKnight professor in entomology, who runs the Bee Lab at the University of Minnesota and has the exasperated air of someone who has been trying, for many, many years, to convey that the house is on fire to a bunch of people absorbed with their televisions. "But people don't care. Most people don't like bees. Most people clump them in with all insects, all creepy-crawly insects, and all creepy-crawly insects need to be destroyed."

And destroyed they are being. Which might put 75 to 80 percent of everything you see out the window in current mortal peril. Pollinators are what's known as a keystone species. Lose the keystone, and the arch holding up the church comes crashing down. No pollinator, no plant; no plant, no bug; no bug, no bird, no fox, no wolf, no raptor. We'll probably be fine, eating corn and drinking vitamin water, but everything else will be gone. Welcome to the Anthropocene.

Part 4: It's a New Era!

"First of all, I'm not crazy about that word," says Jonathan Foley, director of the Institute on the Environment (IonE) at the University of Minnesota, where he is a professor and McKnight presidential chair in global sustainability. He also leads the IonE's Global Landscapes Initiative and cofounded Ensia, the University of Minnesota's digital initiative to showcase environmental thought.

"There's no real agreement about the best way to even say it." You could say *an-THROW-pa-seen* or *an-THROP-a-seen*. "The notion is that the geologic era that the earth is in has been the Holocene, and it's been the Holocene for about the last ten thousand years, since the last ice age. We've had a nice, stable, pleasant weather forecast for ten thousand years.

"But people are now saying: 'Gosh, sometime recently we've taken the earth out of that ten-thousand-year normal into a new normal which is fundamentally different. And this new normal is a new climate, a new biosphere, a new land, new waterways, and new chemicals everywhere. Most of these changes are due to growing food the way we do."

These food-growing changes are no small potatoes. The International Union of Geological Sciences, the folks who decide the earth's timescale, have convened a group of scholars to officially decide whether the Holocene is over and the Anthropocene has begun, meaning human influence is so great we are the single entity most impacting the earth's crust. Us and our corn and our cows, explains Foley. "We've converted about 40 percent of the earth's land surface to growing food," he notes. An area the size of South America is used for farming, and an area the size of Africa is used for pasture. Just about the rest of the earth can be accounted for in city, lawn, desert, a little rain forest, and ice. "Almost everybody would accept the notion that we're now living in a human-dominated planet. That's simply the most observable fact about earth today.

"Imagine the aliens come to visit the earth every one hundred years. I'm not a UFO guy, of course, but metaphorically, ET comes by every one hundred years, looking down with his digital camera, taking a picture of the earth. 'Hey, Mom, look where I've been,' and he posts it on ET Facebook or something. And they come back today after the last visit a hundred years ago: 'Wow, these people, these humans, have gotten really busy. They've cleared most of the planet. They built all these cities. All of a sudden you can see their cities at night. They're getting rid of the rain forests. They're over-reaching, don't you think, Mom?'"

Foley's eyes narrow when he confronts a problem. He seems concerned I might think his UFO metaphor is a tacit endorsement of *X-Files* extraterrestrial believers and miss the point that we've made a new planet, emptied of many plants, full of new chemicals, which is killing all the pollinators and possibly 70 to 80 percent of all the plants, which includes a good chunk, maybe 30 percent, of the stuff we eat. Goodbye, nuts.

Farewell, fruit. Bid thee well, flowers.

Hello, panic.

Part 5: Don't Panic

Is it time to freak out? What with our terraformed planet of novel chemicals and toxins leading to mass extinctions? No, say the scientists. "Freaking out is just not a very good strategy," Foley says. "I've never seen anybody solve a problem by freaking out. If something bad were happening to me and my health, I want the doctor who doesn't freak out—'Oh, shit, you're sick!' I want the doctor who comes in and says, 'Okay, this is deadly serious. I'm going to calmly think about what we do. Now I have a plan.'"

Karen Oberhauser has thought calmly about these things. She's a professor at the University of Minnesota's Department of Fisheries, Wildlife and Conservation Biology and director of the Monarch Larva Monitoring Project.

"At its base I think this is the tragedy of any problem with many causes," she says. "Humans are good at solving problems that have one cause: the CFCs [chlorofluorocarbons], which caused the hole in the ozone layer. Now we don't use CFCs, problem solved. [The insecticide] DDT was one thing. What's happening to butterflies and bees is many things." So the first thing we need to do is to stop looking for "a Colonel Mustard in the library with the candlestick"-type answer.

"The biggest problem facing monarchs is the loss of breeding habitat," Oberhauser explains. But there's more: "Milkweed, their food, used to be in cornfields, and now it's not. The insecticides used to kill adult mosquitoes kill monarchs too. Neonicotinoids are in so much of the nectar that insects encounter." So the way forward for monarchs is simple, but it's not one thing; it's several: Start planting milkweed, start putting back some of the food that was taken away, and make sure it isn't poisoned.

Oberhauser recently oversaw the establishment of a native plant butterfly garden outside of her lab on the St. Paul campus of the University of Minnesota, and she found it remarkably difficult to guarantee that the plants weren't grown from seeds treated with a neonicotinoid, which would make them generate toxins for their entire lives. But she did it, and today that bee- and butterfly-friendly garden is a riot of life, with bright-purple asters, thick stalks of fleshy milkweeds, and dragonflies zipping along the seed heads.

"Inch by inch, we need to do this," she says. "Inch by inch we need to think about our domination of nature and start shifting it in a deliberate way, or we'll just be counting things while they go extinct. A yard doesn't have to look the way it does, low grass to mow, patches of exotic flowers here and there. If lawns were replaced with plants which benefit wildlife, it would add up. It's been five years since I took out the grass at my house. Most of my neighbors love the way it looks now, the native flowers. One didn't. She put up a fence."

Part 6: The Way Forward

Biodiversity is not an aesthetic most people are in tune to these days. "We feel like we should sit on our decks and not be bothered by a spider," Oberhauser says. "We feel like it should be 70 degrees all the time. But we need to understand that we really are part of nature, and if we destroy everything, it's not going to be good for us. Our well-being is not the same thing as our being 100 percent comfortable all of the time. I'm not saying we should not have lawns, but I am saying we should not only have lawns. Just that little change in our mindset could change so much."

Elaine Evans is a graduate student who works with Marla Spivak and spends much of her time trying to count rusty patched bumble bees. Her Midway neighborhood garden in St. Paul is full of mints such as bee balm and wildflowers such as Joe-Pye weed. She has seen rusty patched bumble bees only a few times in her life—and one of those times was in her plain old house garden in the heart of the city. Another time was near the rose garden at Lake Harriet. Why is this imperiled fuzzy bear in those two places? Because bumblebees go where there is bee food.

If you yourself live within a mile or two of St. Paul's Como Lake or Minneapolis's Lake Harriet rose garden and you dropped everything and planted bee food, you personally could be responsible for saving the rusty patched bumble bee. And then if someone within a mile of you did the same, well, you can see how it goes; we could witness the same resurgence in rusty patched bumble bees that we've seen with bald eagles. But it requires doing something, planting something, right away.

"There are three hundred native species of bees in Minnesota and eighteen different species of bumblebees," explains Evans. "All the bumblebees are generalists and will travel two miles from their nests for food. If you plant food bees like, without pesticides, that can make a big difference." Once they have food, they also need shelter. Bumblebees breed and overwinter in nests; the fuzzy fat little critters require bare ground they can burrow into for winter. That black plastic lining so many gardeners put down as a weed barrier indirectly kills bees too, by limiting their nesting sites. Trees are bee food also, especially native Minnesota maples, lindens (also called basswoods), and willows. For Evans, the way forward is to plant bee food, short and tall, free of black plastic.

Foley has a way forward too, and while a lot of it involves marshaling science and presenting it in such a way that big actors, such as corporations and governments, can see things such as how bad use of water can lead to unstable commodity prices or populations, he also takes steps at home. He has what he calls a "nano-orchard" on his standard tiny Crocus Hill house lot, with cherries, apples, pears, gooseberries, and currants. His neighbors all have fruit trees now too: apricots, peaches, even Russian quince providing pollen and nectar for the local pollinators, who in turn make the trees bear fruit. "We have a bunch of birdhouses and bat houses and stuff, just for fun," Foley says. For Foley the way forward includes hard science, a refusal to panic, and nano-orchards with neighbors.

Part 7: It's Quite Simple, Really

For Marcie O'Connor, there's nothing nano about it. She and her husband bought a 450-acre farm in western Wisconsin, not too far from Pepin, and when the kids went off to college began "unfarming" it, restoring it to its native blend of prairie and savanna. Before that, when O'Connor was raising her children in St. Paul, the former botany major converted her front yard into prairie and her backyard into woods. They had a cabin on the St. Croix, and she restored its shoreline to native wetland.

"My idea of what's beautiful correlates to what's alive," she says. "A lawn to me is a dead thing. You don't see any bugs. You don't see any dragonflies. You don't see anything. When you have a prairie it's constantly moving. There are moths, butterflies, flies, dragonflies, and all the birds who eat the bugs. People don't understand that birds are utterly dependent on native bugs and native seeds."

O'Connor documents her unfarming at aprairiehaven.com. One day in July she counted 465 Baltimore checkerspot butterflies. She has put her "unfarm" in a land trust, so that it will always be a haven for native species. "It's really rewarding, really fun," says O'Connor. "I think we've reached a point in thinking about the environment where we need to realize saving the eagles is great, but what about everything that's not the eagles? If you save the habitat, you save everything."

O'Connor also has a condo in Falcon Heights, and she worked with the board to return some of the condo's farther-flung grounds to native prairie and wetland. Now everywhere O'Connor goes there are butterflies on blooms, and sometimes foxes, luna moths, and scarlet tanagers.

Can it be that simple? Yes and no. To get a few hundred million people to recognize a crisis and act together to reverse it doesn't often happen. But it could.

"There's a lot of fatalism out there," notes Spivak, who has been watching the issue of colony collapse disorder unspool over the last decade, while the wild bees and other unsexy pollinators collapse publicity-free. "But if everybody would just plant flowers, as many as you can, just grow organic bee food, every bit would help. A little pot of flowers on your doorstep is not enough to support a whole colony of bees, but a whole neighborhood filled with pots might be. If everybody does a little, collectively it would be a big help. We need to stop thinking of ourselves at every turn."

We think of ourselves even when we're not thinking of ourselves, with our culturally passed-down, unconscious values of how a yard should look and which flowers express love. "We breed flowers to be pretty to us," says Spivak. "But a bee can't get into a Valentine's Day rose. Bees need native flowers. We've decided we need monocultures of corn, of soybeans, of lawn. For some reason anything we grow we want edge-to-edge only that thing. Why can't we go back to diversified agriculture? Why can't there be some places for flowers? It's time for a correction. The bees are indicating that with their death."

Look out the window. This is the Anthropocene, and you're living in it. Some 75 percent of everything is in grave danger, and you could fix it, by a little understanding and appreciation of the less cuddly parts of the environment and planting or encouraging the planting of some poison-free native flowers.

The moths and butterflies and bees can't tweet. They can only flap and buzz. And to really get a point across they fall over dead. Can you ever look at your local honey bun the same again?

Between the Sheets at FantaSuites
· · · · · · · · · · · · ·

City Pages, August 28, 1996

> This sort of story was an absolute staple of alt-weekly jour-
> nalism: a little prurient, a little literary, good to have in your
> pocket during a slow news week. I picked it for this collection
> because in it I see all my skills: lively, illuminating dialogue,
> revealing details, a zippy structure. When this one ran, I was so
> very proud of it, one of my first bigger published stories. Turns
> out I still am!

Our tour guide, Susie, is clearly not of the age of consent

She wears suntan hose, navy flats, a corduroy jumper, and the
unflappable air of a girl for whom the commerce of kinkiness represents little more than gas money. About thirty of us are taking
Susie's tour of romantic fantasy, as offered by Burnsville's Quality
Inn & Suites Hotels. The "FantaSuites" are large, theme-decorated
rooms with theme-related whirlpools, a sort of creamy, Disney
theme park of latent and blatant sexuality, a postmodern temple
of love, or, as the narrator of the "Suite Suite Magic Video Tour"
puts it, the suites are "unique, out of the ordinary, novel and sin-
gular works of imagination."

Susie describes our first stop, Suite Romance, as "the most like
a regular hotel room." This fantasy features an oval coffee table,
a four-poster bed, two wingback armchairs, and two televisions.
"Yeah right," snorts one of the three young beauties on the tour.
"If I wanted to have sex in my parents' bedroom, I would," she says,
turning heel and exiting. At the Castle, she seems more apprecia-
tive. "This is more like it," she says, admiring the long, arched tunnels, stenciled on charcoal gray walls. Peering from the tunnels are
a few leering creatures: an erect-nippled, Elvira-like vampire and a

yellow-eyed Frankenstein's monster. The windows are draped with crinkled red velvet, the chairs appear hewn from half barrels with protruding screws, and the bed is medieval-seeming, despite the water mattress. Contemplating the carnal possibilities, the beauty announces, "I could get into this," and peers into the yellow-tiled, cement-stalactite-bordered whirlpool.

Down the industrial carpeted hall lies Wild, Wild West, billed as a room for families, since it features two beds, the first of which—a ten-sided waterbed inside a tipi—has an unbreakable mirror over it, giving a fun house effect due to its flexibility. The other bed is in a covered wagon and features Nintendo. We ask if a lot of families rented the Wild, Wild West. Susie, narrowing her eyes, snaps, "We're not allowed to give out that information." (This becomes her standard response to all our queries. She is expert in her denials. In fact, no information for this article is gotten from tour guides. It is simply not possible.)

Mildly more communicative than Susie is the Suite Suite Magic Video Tour. One "of our most popular suites is Le Cave, or 'the Cave,'" advises the video. "This prehistoric fantasy also features the custom-made ten-sided waterbed and many other exclusive amenities found only in the FantaSuite hotel." There are the painted pterodactyls on the ceiling; giant yellow-leaved plastic plants; and molded cement rocks. (Incidentally, the ten-sided waterbed is now a ten-sided ordinary bed. This was made clear by the many women who walked in and slapped a palm on the bed, like a wily car buyer kicking a tire.)

Concealed behind another ordinary door lies the Grecian. Fluted columns trail vinyl ivy, plush green carpet tufts from bed to bath, and the overpowering smell of sweat unites it all. In the Grecian our talkative beauty loudly announces, "This is the best one. What is that horrible smell?" Whereupon she whispered in her companion's ear and left, mysteriously.

"If your fantasy is a drive-in movie or a secluded lover's leap," advises the video, you had best rent Lover's Leap—a room with a bed inside a maroon 1973 Oldsmobile Delta '88 Royale convertible. A cement wall rings the room; painted above is a crude cityscape, a vain attempt to create the effect of being at the local hilltop make-out spot. (Asked if a Lover's Leap connoted suicide, and wouldn't Lover's Lane be more apt, our tour guide feigned deafness.) An actual picnic table with actual carvings of love—"JS & LN 4EVR"—served as the table, and the entryway boasts photoprint wallpaper of yellow birches, to create the sense of woods. A television lounge is papered in the same print and offers, for viewing comfort, oddly, a 1970s colonial lounge chair and love seat set to one side, incongruous to all but satyr couch potatoes. A woman with red curly hair and the bluish skin of an office job has been clinically evaluating each love nest. She stands in Lover's Leap, arms akimbo, and says, "This does it for me." Her mustachioed companion nods.

Exhaustion is already setting in, and the FantaSuites are too numerous to see on one tour. Rooms we miss include the Log Cabin, which the brochure says includes a screen door; Moby Dick, which has a "whaling boat queen-sized waterbed, TV built into a captain's treasure chest, and tilted whirlpool inside a whale's mouth"; Pharaoh's Chambers with a "sarcophagus waterbed"; Space Odyssey with "Re-creation of a Gemini space capsule . . . [and] moon crater whirlpool"; and, crowning them all, Cinderella, wherein, the Suite Suite Magic Video Tour assures us, "Fairy tales do come true, in a FantaSuite." We finish the tour and leave through the generic, fantasy-free lobby assured of this fact: Fairy tales *do* come true. It could happen to you!

The Ghost in Room 308

Mpls.St.Paul Magazine, July 2019

I've always been a little psychic, in the way a lot of people are. I couldn't sleep the night my grandma Kaye died; I was thinking of her all night; I didn't even know she was sick. Sometimes if I think about someone a lot, they call. Meet ten people in a bar and a handful will admit that's their experience of life too. Spooky action at a distance? Intelligence at work in deep ways that are screened from the conscious mind? You tell me.

I wrote this story about the haunting of Pipestone's Calumet Inn in July of 2019. Less than a year later, it was declared a fire hazard and closed by the city. As of press time for this book, it has yet to reopen. Are the ghosts still there?

Spend a night at the Historic Calumet Inn, a spectacular hotel in Pipestone with a cursed history. You'll also find a sacred Native quarry, the Stonehenge of North America, and the largest smokable pipe in the world in the ghost-filled town.

Ghosts. Are they real?

Nervous laughter is the conventional response to this question. We're not superstitious, are we?

I'm not superstitious, but I do believe in ghosts. Just not the banging-doors and glowing-in-the-night kind.

Let me explain. A few weeks ago, I drove down to Pipestone from Minneapolis, arrowing two hundred miles southwest toward the South Dakota border and climbing a thousand feet in an imperceptible but consistent rise. I spent nearly the whole drive on the phone with my mother as she kept deathbed vigil beside one of history's kindest and most intellectually inquisitive Uncle Jacks. As I write this, I'm preparing for the funeral.

I was pilot to a carful of ghosts. Most were Ukrainians, my mother's uncle and aunts: John, Stella, and Irene (the latter two of whom I've never met). And, of course, Katie, my grandmother, whom I loved fiercely, and who died when I was little, having survived cataclysms on two continents, and who spent her final years mainly in the company of her own troubled ghosts.

Outside the car, ghosts innumerable. All of south and central Minnesota is Dakota country. In the southwest, the ghost of Alexander Ramsey shapes everything you see. He was the former superintendent of Indian Affairs and the state governor who prosecuted the US–Dakota wars of the 1860s. This was the period when he declared, "The Sioux Indians of Minnesota must be exterminated or driven forever beyond the borders of the state." Largely, that's what the government did.

As a fourth-generation New Yorker, I'm shocked by all the parts of this story. I lived for a decade in my south Minneapolis Victorian home before I realized it sat on Dakota land. That is, land appropriated (stolen) in an 1805 treaty, written in English and unreadable by its Native American signatories.

And where was my family back then—the mother of the mother of the mother of Jack on his deathbed? Family legend holds that my grandma Kaye's parents came from a sect of the Russian Orthodox church called the Old Believers: puritans of the Russian Orthodox Church. What were they doing in 1805? Suffering from state persecution, suffering from starvation? Beats me.

As I passed through rolling cornfield after rolling cornfield, I tried to picture the prairie that would have once been here. A landscape that should have been booming this time of year with the mating calls of prairie chickens. In Minnesota's Public Land Survey, from 1847 to 1908, surveyors counted 18 million acres of prairie. A little over 1 percent of that ecosystem remains here today.

Do prairie chickens have ghosts? Is it ever worth arguing with anyone about ghosts?

Most people will tell you there's no such thing as ghosts. But

I think America is actually ghosts on top of ghosts, ghosts all the way down.

And I thought that before I saw Charlie the surveyor, ghost of room 308 in the Calumet Inn, in Pipestone, a few doors down from where I would spend the night.

The Binderful of Ghosts

Charlie, Charlie, Charlie. Died on Valentine's Day night, 1944, in a fire in room 308. Guests have been arguing about his ghost ever since.

A white plastic binder sits by the registration desk at the Calumet Inn, right beside a creepy doll in a white dress. Guests who have ghost encounters write down what they've experienced. The hotel dates back to 1888, and the binder is three inches thick.

Most of the stories involve Charlie. He leans in doorways, he makes phones ring, he claps the toilet lid up and down in the night, he playfully nudges people, he appears in mirrors, he writes in dust.

Other stories in the binder concern other ghosts, possibly the Reverend Orcutt, who also died in the Calumet. Inexplicable music; rocking chairs that rock all on their own. That sort of business.

Sometimes the binder describes the side effects of contemplating ghosts. A girl named Cassie—later-grade-school age, to judge by her handwriting—was retrieving a bottle while babysitting her little brother, Tanner. When a door in the room slammed, she peed her pants and called the police.

YouTube bubbles with videos by amateur ghost hunters stalking the specters of the Calumet Inn. This grand red-rock hotel is, economically speaking, kept from ghosthood itself by this paranormal interest. There's the ParaFriends weekend spring event, the every-Saturday-night summertime Pipestone Ghost Walks (which include the Calumet), and the annual October Pipestone Paranormal Weekend, with its candlelight Calumet Inn walkabout and cemetery tour.

In 2014 something legitimately scary and extensively documented happened at the Calumet. It was briefly infested by the celebrity chef Gordon Ramsay—no relation to Alexander Ramsey—who came to tape an episode of the Fox series *Hotel Hell*. Ramsay is chiefly remembered by staff for promises unkept, but on camera he appeared in his customary fits, as if possessed, yelling and sputtering. He ultimately painted a room green before returning to his celestial celebrity firmament. Still, reruns of the episode bring a certain number of guests.

The Calumet's new owner, Tammy Grubbs, sees all this excitement as dollars in the ledger toward fiscal survival. Grubbs took possession last August as the four-story Victorian property stumbled toward abandonment.

The circumstances were, in fact, more dire than that. The building's signature red stones were falling off a rear wall and threatening to create more ghosts from local townspeople. In turn, the city of Pipestone had given the hotel six days to either begin repairs or evacuate the premises.

Grubbs, a talented painter with long brown hair and a patient, persistent manner, had been brought on by the previous owners because of her lengthy career turning around failed restaurants.

"I think I've saved the Calumet from shutting down four times since I got here," Grubbs told me when we sat for a few hours one afternoon in low chairs not too far from a cradle filled with dolls, one in a hideous state of decay. (Grubbs is not above giving the paranormal fans what they want.)

"I was always drawn to the Calumet because of its history, because of what it meant to the town," Grubbs continued. "I couldn't imagine Pipestone without the Calumet."

The Calumet rose at a time when four different railroad lines all happened to pass through the town. This great number of passers-through inspired the building of a great and grand hotel, the Calumet, as well as a number of other local attractions surprising for a prairie town, like an eight-hundred-seat opera house. Contemplate the Calumet today and it looks like a pink fortress, a castle painted in blood—something more fitting to Milan or Transylvania. The stone itself represented the main business of the town: quarrying it, selling it, putting it on the many railroads, and also sleeping and seeing opera in it.

Grubbs's first act at the Calumet was to hire stonemasons to fix the exterior stonework. To pay for it, local fans established a "Save the Cal" fund.

As part of act two, she turned the breakfast area into an all-day coffee shop and café. She decoupaged the tables with fascinating pieces of Pipestone and Calumet ephemera, from early menus to archival news bits. Her broader personal vision involves turning the whole of the architectural gem into her own art project of murals and hallway galleries, full of her own art and pieces from other artists. One Calumet room, for example, features a Grubbs mural of a prairie farm, with a red barn and ethereal clouds overhead. Another room displays her take on Viking ships cresting the waves.

And then we come to Charlie's room, 308, where Grubbs has painted a mural of a surveyor (like Charlie) with his equipment. That's where I witnessed him—right on the wall, just as Grubbs has seen him in repeated encounters.

"He's one hard worker, and he likes us, so that helps," Grubbs told me patiently, in the way of someone asked to tell the same story ten times a day, month after month, year after year.

He particularly likes to compel Grubbs to chase him all over the hotel to stop the playing of phantom music.

"My dream is to have each room in this hotel interpret a story about Pipestone," Grubbs said. "Starving artists always have to have a side thing. And when I got here and the Calumet was on the verge of shutting down, I thought, *This gorgeous, wonderful artist building needs someone to come in and turn it around.*"

In my day and a half in Pipestone, I observed Grubbs's own supernatural powers. She doesn't look too unearthly, with her frank, dark eyes and her taste for the kind of practical clothing that allows you to both get up on a ladder and seat guests for dinner in the same hour. But if living without sleep is a supernatural power, Grubbs has it. I saw her registering guests, making coffee, and helping employees around the clock.

She told me, then, how she came to take ownership of the hotel. She had been working on the turnaround and saw the property heading toward financial trouble. Every time a utility—like the gas or electricity—was about to be shut off, she transferred it into her own name.

"I felt kind of like a pirate," she said. "I had climbed aboard this ship that was abandoned at sea"—a ghost ship, as it were—"and then was just trying to keep it going."

The Ghosts of the Three Maidens

The Calumet Inn takes its name from the calumet, a ceremonial pipe traditionally made from pipestone. The rock has likely been quarried for some seven thousand years by tribes who traveled here from all over North America.

The town is called Pipestone, as is the county. The historic water tower in the northeast corner of town was fashioned in the shape of a traditional calumet. Everything in this small corner of the state is a pipe or a pipestone or at least pipestone-colored because it's made from Sioux quartzite, the harder rock that's kith and kin to the sacred rock.

"It's a small-town treasure," says Larry Millett, the state's preeminent architectural historian. "I remember the first time I went to Pipestone, I knew there were going to be a lot of local stone buildings. But to actually see them is another thing. It's a very expensive granite. You only see it in buildings like the Van Dusen mansion in Minneapolis. And if you look closely, you see it wasn't carved much. It's too hard. It's tombstone-quality granite. But obviously the quarries were right there, and they had masons who knew how to work it."

Millett got on a roll about Pipestone. "I always tell anyone who goes down there, go to Sioux City, Iowa, to the Woodbury County courthouse, where Purcell & Elmslie"—the same architectural firm that designed the Purcell-Cutts house, by Lake of the Isles—"did all of this over-the-top terra-cotta ornament. It's magnificent. And go to Blue Mounds State Park. Oh, and stop and see the Jeffers Petroglyphs."

Blue Mounds State Park holds a 1,250-foot-long arrangement of rocks that lines up with the sunset and sunrise on the vernal and autumnal equinoxes. It's the Stonehenge of North America. And it lies within thirty minutes of Pipestone.

The Jeffers Petroglyphs historic site, a seven-thousand-year-old collection of some five thousand rock carvings sacred to Native Americans, is older than Stonehenge. It lies within an hour and a half of Pipestone.

The Pipestone quarries—now the Pipestone National Monument—once held their own petroglyphs, carved into the red cliff wall behind a set of boulders thought to symbolize three sacred maidens. George Catlin, the famed portraitist of the West, arrived in 1836 and wrote these notes on the Dakota territory:

> It is evident that these people set an extraordinary value on the red stone, independently of the fact that it is more easily carved and makes a better pipe than any other stone. For whenever an Indian presents a pipe made of it, he gives it as something from the Great Spirit. And some of the tribes have a tradition that the red men were all created from the red stone, and that it thereby is "a part of their flesh." Such was the superstition of the Sioux on this subject, that we had great difficulty in approaching it, being stopped by several hundred of them, who ordered us back and threatened us very hard, saying "that no white man had ever been to it, and that none should ever go."

Nonetheless, Catlin pushed past. He eventually came to the boulders known today as the Three Maidens. Native visitors would leave tobacco and other tributes before touching the rock.

"The veneration of them is such that not a spear of grass is broken or bent by his feet within four or five rods of the group," Catlin observed. "The surface of these bowlders I found in every part entire and unscratched by any thing, and even the moss was every where unbroken, which undoubtedly remains so at this time, except where I applied the hammer."

For this bravura act of cultural vandalism, pipestone gained the geological name "catlinite."

The Three Maidens petroglyphs were chiseled out by a man named Charles H. Bennett in 1888 or 1889, either because he was trying to protect them or because he wanted them to decorate his lawn. There they remained until his death in 1926.

A number were lost. But today the remaining Three Maidens petroglyphs live inside the visitor center of the Pipestone National Monument, in front of a beautiful mural of both the monument and the vivid and nearly extinct prairie, made by none other than Tammy Grubbs.

The Ghosts in the Pipe Keepers' Headquarters

Bud Johnston was born in 1942 and grew up traveling to the Bad River Reservation in northern Wisconsin with parents who survived the Indian boarding school years. This was the period when the federal government forcibly removed children from their tribal homes and forbade the learning of Native American languages and the practice of Native religions.

"It was hard for me," Johnston said when I talked to him, first on-site and later over the phone. He has the mellow vibe of a true child of the sixties, and a way of standing a bit more solidly than most people do, legs wide and loose, as if he's about to catch something very big from the sky. "My mother, all my aunts and uncles, denied being tribal. I really hungered for my tribal stuff, though. 'Buddy,' they said, 'why don't you ditch that Indian stuff and pass for white?' But I wouldn't do that. I would get in a lot of fights. It was not cool to be Indian in those days."

He first spotted a pipestone pipe as a child. "I was digging in my grandpa's stuff," Johnston recalled. "He said, 'Oh, my son, you shouldn't monkey with that. We use that for saying our prayers.' I said, 'Where'd it come from?' He said, 'Somewhere in Minnesota.'"

For a time, Johnston saw Native culture only distantly. A hobby fixing up thirty-dollar cars led to a career fixing airplanes for airlines across the country. Some forty years later, after connecting with urban Indians in San Francisco and transferring to Sioux Falls on a new United route, Johnston saw another pipe. A passenger was carrying it through the airport, and they started talking. That's how Johnston heard of the ancient and sacred quarry in Pipestone.

"'Holy shit,' I said. 'I gotta get a quarry permit.' I got some tools; I got my tribal ID badge. You have to show your tribal ID before you can even talk about the pit."

That discovery set Johnston on the road to founding his "multi-lineage" organization for the preservation of pipe culture, the Keepers of the Sacred Tradition of Pipemakers. Any member of any tribe can join. So can Lutherans, Catholics, atheists, or anyone else who wants to support the pipe traditions.

Johnston says visitors often describe seeing spirits above the falls at Pipestone National Monument, site of an ancient quarry.

The Pipe Keepers headquarters sits halfway between the Calumet Inn and the Pipestone National Monument. It occupies the old Rock Island railroad depot—you'll know it by the thirty-foot-long steel calumet that Johnston built out front. *Reader's Digest* called it the largest smokable pipe in the world.

The building may not be much of a secret. But most people don't know that the headquarters was paid for by Stanley Crooks, the powerful and longtime leader of the Shakopee Mdewakanton Sioux Community, until his death in 2012.

"He said, 'I was going down I-90, and I didn't plan to come up here,'" Johnston recalled. "'But I went to the Pipestone Indian school, and before I got rich, I was a pipemaker. What are you doing here?' I told him I was going to protect the quarries for all tribal people and educate people about the pipe."

Crooks wrote a check the very day Johnston first opened a Pipe Keepers checking account. "Pipes have been used by over five hundred tribes for ceremonies for over three thousand years," Johnston told me from his Pipe Keepers headquarters. Here, he sells pipes and Native art and teaches others how to make these religious items.

"They're used for everything. If you want to ask for guidance in your life for any kind of decision—you want to move, you want to go to war, you want to buy a car, you want to sign an agreement—you'd do a pipe and ask for help. They're labeled peace pipes by some people, because they were used in treaty signings. But they're much more than that."

When Johnston started the Pipe Keepers, he said, the nearby Pipestone monument included a wall plaque that claimed Native Americans had quarried pipestone there for just a few centuries.

"I call it propaganda," Johnston said. "And I did the research and showed them the scientific papers to get them to change it to thousands of years."

Pipestone pipes from Minnesota have been found in Ohio's Tremper Mound, dating to around the year zero. And polished stone beads, between 4,600 and 5,600 years old, have been found in Florida's Thornhill Lake mounds.

Spend enough hours in Pipestone and you begin to perceive a kind of equation: Time plus ancestors equals ghosts. The Pipe Keepers headquarters is full of them, Johnston said. They play with his wife's hair when she's working the cash register. They turn guest book pages when visitors are milling about. One even slapped his mother-in-law's ex-husband, who kept digging in the fridge.

"Spirits don't normally do that; for them it takes a lot of energy," he said. "But this guy was very irritating."

Johnston told me that tourists—the Pipestone Chamber of Commerce estimates around 50,000–80,000 pass through town a year—see the ghost-hunting apps on their iPhones light up when they visit the Pipe Keepers building.

Then there's the sacred quarry grounds of the monument. "Many people who visit us go and walk the trail, and they'll see a spirit sitting up by the falls. I've had lots of feelings out there myself. We put tobacco down and say a prayer."

Johnston knows a guy who has formed a scientific explanation for the spiritual goings-on. "He monitors satellites, and he says every time the satellite goes by Pipestone, it glows red. He feels that's because of the pipestone, which has a lot of iron oxide in it. It causes a thinning of veils between the different dimensions."

Johnston said I should be sure to invite all you readers to bring a group and make your own pipes. "Take a few minutes; feel the energy that's here," he said. "I think it's a life-changing event."

The Ghost in Room 308

Charlie did not wake me up. The creepy dolls in the cradle by my room remained unmoved, as near as I could tell. I did have a feeling of profound reverence walking the circle trail through the pipestone quarry. But I get like that, especially when there are soaring red-rock cliffs with the mist from a waterfall clouding toward them, feeding green lichens.

I did, however, have a real-life encounter with the world beyond the grave.

It happened when my mind was full of my uncle Jack and all the ghosts I left behind in New York, which I now found had been packed along with me in the portable chamber of my very own head.

The circle trail of the monument was partly closed for flooding, and after walking the longer segment that remained open, I went to see another small trail. I took three steps in, peering past the silvery heaps of leadplant to the cliffs beyond, when a prairie chicken leapt up practically under my feet, like a hot-air balloon. Its orange neck sack puffed up to the size of a tennis ball; its tail fanned out. It was like fireworks.

A prairie chicken, here? I wouldn't have expected that. Most of the prairie chickens have disappeared in this corner of the state, along with the prairie itself. Was I confused by a rogue pheasant? Was I seeing things?

I ran my sighting by Bud Johnston, who confirmed this kind of thing happens. "Lots of people who come here see spirits, all different, all over town."

Maybe Pipestone gives us only the ghosts we can handle?

Superior Days

· · · · · · · · · · · · ·

Mpls.St.Paul Magazine, March 2021

Lake Superior is unspeakably beautiful, in all seasons. During the pandemic we wrote about it a lot in *Mpls.St.Paul Magazine* because everyone was stuck at home going crazy. Repeated visits made me realize a few things. One, the light up there is unique; when the lake is frozen and there's feet of snow on everything, light bounces and jounces around so much you feel like a tiny grain of sand on a big white platter. Two, the antidote to being stuck at home going crazy is to breathe in the clean air you find above a pine-needle trail, right by a white birch tree trunk.

The North Shore restores wild life to a tame era.

"Just up this path is the most beautiful thing I've ever seen," I told my kids, holding the puppy leash in one hand and helping them up the snow-covered trail that leads from the highway pullover beside the Temperance River with the other.

We found our way up the white trail, using boulders for handholds. The pines were spooned all over with new snow, like every Christmas card you've ever seen. "What if we fall?" my daughter asked.

"Try to land on your bottom. It's worth it."

The children had been skeptically extracted from a suite at Bluefin Bay, one with a full kitchen, an up-close water view of Lake Superior as big as a movie screen, and a real-wood fireplace. We've never lived with a real-wood fireplace before. "Does it always sound like that?" my daughter asked at first, warily listening to the steam created by the bits of snow on the birch logs before concluding,

"All fires should make noise like a bonfire. It's way better." We even roasted marshmallows inside.

The dog slept on the braided rug in front of the fire, and my daughter circled around with her phone, taking pictures: "She looks just like a dog in a photograph!" I knew what she meant. This past year, especially, we've lived in a world with our noses pressed against the glass of a screen where everyone does things while we type alone in our house. Now we were *doing*.

Our little family made it up to the North Shore twice during COVID times. In summer, we climbed the steep staircases and picked our way over the stepping stones at the base of Gooseberry Falls. We carefully scanned the ground with our eyes, looking for favorite rocks where the Temperance River feeds into Lake Superior. Pines, wind, red rocks—life! Tennyson, and, yes, I am going to haul poor old Alfred, Lord Tennyson in here, talked of "Nature, red in tooth and claw" as the bad thing that wrests humans away from our noble pursuits.

After a year inside, all I want is nature red in tooth and claw— and cliff and pine needle too.

The call for wildness echoes nationally. Walking the dog, I chatted with a guest who had driven from *New Jersey*. "Vermont is too crowded," he explained. "The whole East Coast is too crowded." He had come to ski up in the Sawtooth Mountains at Lutsen and to hike and to stare out the window at the crashing surf. "I can't believe no one's ever heard of this." He gestured at Lake Superior. No one? Still, I imagine the awareness of Tofte and Grand Marais is pretty low in New Jersey. The North Shore is obviously worth the drive: the sheer blood-colored cliffs, the dozens of waterfalls bouncing through crevasses and leaping over stone, the miles and miles of hiking, the clean silver lake—all so noble, all so brisk.

But back to the most beautiful thing I've ever seen. Once the puppy bounded up the snow-covered trail and the kids followed, we hit a peaceful plateau with a few trees and a red-rock outcrop. "Right around this corner," I said, guiding them open-armed like a traffic cop, and I waited for the gasps.

The Temperance River was frozen solid at its upper falls and also at its lower falls, but just here in the middle it bounced and crashed furiously through a narrow crevasse and spun through a brief whirlpool, sending mist into the air. The mist caught on every pine, every blade of grass, every twig and trunk above the crevasse, covering them with hoarfrost, rendering everything white and sparkling, creating a lace of diamonds, a metropolis of glitter, a chapel, a heaven.

"This is real?" my teenage son said, and he started to laugh at the improbability of it all. "I didn't know this could be real." We oohed and aahed over the scene, which looked like the place snow fairies hold royal snow fairy weddings when no expense is spared. We photographed, and picked up the dog and took selfies, and videoed, and kept repeating to each other that we couldn't believe it, and did all the things you do when you encounter a miracle.

Finally, the sun was sinking, for you always find a sunset if you hike long enough, and we headed out. "I'm so glad you came and got us," my daughter said as we climbed in the car. "It was the most beautiful thing I've ever seen." And so it was that we learned, once again, that life is as real and miraculous as you will go out and let it be, in difficult years and easy ones too.

Wandering the Edge of Big Blue

· · · · · · · · · · · ·

Mpls.St.Paul Magazine, March 2022

> If I could, I'd live like an eagle, taking in all the sun and air of
> this beautiful world—and I'd do it on Lake Superior. In my
> mind, the lake lives as silver light and a changing wind that
> brings pine and clean mist and the smell of stone. If you've
> never been, please drop everything and go. If you're a lifer,
> here's what I see when I see the miracles you see!

*The miracles and magic of the North Shore experience will surprise you
at every turn.*

Bopping up the sunny trail at Split Rock Lighthouse State Park this
past summer, I was positively abuzz with the pure joy of feeling air
and light on my skin. Goodbye, gloom city; hello, beautiful world.

Lake Superior sparkled to one side, blinding white coins of
early sun on an infinite pewter dish, while mountain ash trees
caught the wind on the other and picked-clean raspberry brambles crowded in around my feet. Ahead of me: a bounding pom-
pom, Clio, my tiny black terrier mutt on her bright purple leash,
scrambling, scrambling, as she followed a trail rich with scent. We
reached a rock plateau of generic gray anorthosite, which makes
up much of the cliffs around Split Rock. Anorthosite is probably of
little interest to many who visit here, except for me. That's because
I know it's also found on the moon. *The moon!* Current moon science proposes that the moon formed when a planet the size of
Mars smashed into us, and the debris from the impact became the
moon. If you're not going to get to stand on the moon anytime
soon, standing on some boring-looking anorthosite is as close as
you can get.

I scooped up my bounding little pom-pom for a selfie with the biggest freshwater lake in the whole wide world as our backdrop. Behold: We are on a cliff of moon high above 10 percent of the world's fresh water! All glory and thanks to the visionaries who protected all this for us, the eight state parks along the 145 running miles between Duluth and Grand Portage, the Canadian border. How fantastic that Minnesota has such a commitment to our land, our wildlife, our citizens, our collective inheritance that wilderness enthusiasts, environmentalists, and legislators have worked to protect for us since the late 1880s. In these desperate last few years, it has been too easy to see only the bad in our screens and take our past victories for granted. There's another version of our world where this cliff may have lived only on the land of a private mansion, with no access for a city slicker to bliss out on the trails. Thankfully, that's not the case.

Happy, heart full, I set down my pom-pom and returned to the trail, which dipped into a stand of small, scrubby, twisty cedars, hollowed into a sort of tunnel showing—what?—more pom-poms? One, then two raccoon-sized black bodies shadowed swiftly across the trail, silhouetted against the light of the lake. I stopped, yanked the leash, and started drawing it in like a yo-yo string. That's when I saw a very large peak-nosed pom-pom lean into the shadow box of this trail-tunnel and then withdraw, evidently having called home her black bear cubs.

Imagine how fast one writer can get down a mountain, singing an improvised song that has as its main lyric: "Clio, we've got to go home!" Home was our campsite, and I looked at the steel bear box protecting my human food differently from that point on. Of course, in my thinking mind, I'm more afraid of causing bears harm than I am of being harmed by bears. Humans have decimated their habitat, and the summer fires and drought only added more pressure in their world, driving them into people areas. But given that this was the first bear I had ever seen in my life, I ran. Maybe, in hindsight, because of a noble impulse to give them space? Let's say it was that. But this unexpected and sometimes startling beauty is why we go to the North Shore! For the miracles.

The miracle of a veiny fuchsia pouch of a lady's slipper northern orchid, the brightest thing on a dark pine-needle forest floor. The miracle of a million agate-bright stones, fused together by clear winter ice into a sort of candy brittle for enchanted unicorns. A place so wild with mountains of ice and thundering waves one season and lupine-filled, berry-strewn byways another. *Miracle*, like all words, came to us through time. I particularly like one Latin root, *mirari*, "to wonder at, marvel, be astonished." Last year I spent about a month exploring the North Shore and found marvels and wonders too numerous to count that rendered me astonished. Here are just a few on a list that continues to grow each time I journey north.

Lava, Lava Everywhere

As you crest the big hill to Duluth, your stomach yanks and lurches like you're on a roller coaster, and instantly you know it: You're in a different world. Our continent tried to split once upon a time, and if it had worked, Duluth would be oceanfront and so would Superior, Wisconsin. Instead, magma rushed up from the earth's molten iron core, creating all the red rocks you see from Duluth to Canada and also all the iron in the Iron Range. This magma made some bits of land so heavy they sank down; made other bits of land jostle up to get out of the way; and in all the earth shuffling we got a giant rift, the "Superior trough," that filled up with the water we now call Lake Superior. Next time you're at Gooseberry Falls, play the old kids' game The Floor is Lava. What do you see that used to be lava? Everything? Except the water? Isn't it amazing to notice that the North Shore is, in a way, a whole lot like Hawaii or Iceland, a new world of drama built by water meeting lava?

Three Bears and Beeping Squirrels

How often do you chance upon a bear family eating berries on a moon cliff? This is a wonder I'll never forget (see above), but it's not the only surprise sighting I had along the shore. For instance: What looks like a gigantic regular gray squirrel with a skinny tail, stands around like a prairie dog, and chirps like a 1980s beeper?

A Franklin's ground squirrel! Native to the north-central United States and parts of Canada, these adorable squirrels have recently taken up residence in various sites along the North Shore. The DNR definitely has recorded them at Gooseberry Falls State Park, and the three nights I stayed at a campsite in Split Rock, I had a Franklin's ground squirrel as a campsite trickster, running in to try to get the dog's food, then, when repelled, standing in the nearby brambles to alert its friends by beeping, beeping, beeping. Seriously, it sounds like a beeper! The first time you hear a Franklin's ground squirrel, don't be surprised if everyone suddenly accuses everyone else of getting a phone call.

Stairways of Stone

Explore the eight state parks strung from Duluth to Canada, and you'll go up and down absolute miles of staircases built right onto cliff faces: Bob's Staircase at Split Rock is around six stories; some two hundred steps lead to Devil's Kettle at Judge C. R. Magney; towers of staircases also are found elsewhere, including at Tettegouche. If you're paying attention, you feel the hands, the labor, the intention of so many individuals working so we can safely see these rocks, these cliffs, these mists. We all stand on the shoulders of those who came before, and never more so than when we find it challenging to even walk the steps that someone before us had to build *without stairs*.

Broiling River, Mythical Trees

The Brule River, in Judge C. R. Magney State Park, just north of Grand Marais, got its name from French voyageurs who noticed how its waters seemed to "broil" over the rapids—think crème brûlée and you have the right idea—before jumping over some superhard lava called rhyolite and then disappearing into a hole. A hole at the bottom of the waterfall! How is life so cool? Continue on your way in the park, and you'll enter a bit of forest with moss thick as sheep's wool. You'll also wander past various trees that appear to be joined—say, a birch and a pine—in that rare natural marvel called inosculation. *Inosculation*, which derives from the Latin "little mouth," is a fancy way of saying that the trees are really kissing, as in the myth of Philemon and Baucis, a married pious Greek couple whom Zeus rewarded by letting them spend eternity together, entwined as trees. Where else on earth do you find a broiling river leaping into a devil's soup pot and mythical kissing trees in such close proximity? Magical miracles!

A Giant Rock Tumbler

Whether you're scouring the agate beach at the mouth of the Baptism River in Tettegouche State Park, walking the oval-stone beach at Split Rock, or sifting through bright-colored stones at the covered bridge that adorns the mouth of the Poplar River below Lutsen Lodge, every pretty, polished rock that defines the North Shore comes from this one weird phenomenon: Lake Superior is a giant rock tumbler. The waves crash, crash, crash night and day, and below the surface, that roiling action is lifting and tumbling rocks with every wave. At the myriad river mouths, a third direction of waves comes in, bringing inland stones to polish. That's why river mouth stones will typically be both smaller and more various. And what are agates? When all that lava turned into rock (see above), it was full of bubbles. The bubbles filled up with minerals, and those are agates. Agates are harder than lava, so when the water wears away the lava, agates remain. Parenting tip: Set a rock limit in the car on the ride up, because if you try to take home every pretty rock you see, you'll break an axle.

Subarctic Falls

Up beyond Mount Josephine, some forty-odd minutes north of Grand Marais on Highway 61 just before the border to Canada, you forsake the pine-and-old-lava North Shore you thought you knew and enter a whole new world. Welcome to the southern edge of the low, pale world of the subarctic boreal forest! This jack pine and aspen forest covers most of Canada and Alaska but only touches northern Minnesota. Pull into the Susie Islands Overlook near the top of Mount Josephine, and peer over the edge to see the dark emeralds of the thirteen protected Susie Islands, sacred to the Grand Portage Band of Lake Superior Chippewa, stretching to a watery horizon. It's all so spare, so pristine, so artistic, it looks like . . . a place a noble archer elf would contemplate from his steed before going to battle evil in *The Lord of the Rings*? Head onward to the 120-foot High Falls—the highest in the state, and not so terribly much shorter than Niagara's 167 feet, right? Iron-red, crashing with frothy light brown water, it's like most every other North Shore old-lava-and-fresh-water fantasia, except this waterfall is higher, and the people watching from the other side are in *Canada*. You could throw a Frisbee to Canada! Have they ever seen such a thing? Discuss.

An Artist's Vantage Point

Narrow wee-boardwalk-planked paths sheltered by pines trailing lichen like mermaid hair, broad stretches of lichen-spotted rock reaching right into the water, hidey-holes, a lighthouse, and rock chasms galore: Welcome to the Grand Marais island called Artist's Point. A favorite North Shore destination for many, it's also home to one of the state's most diverse lichen populations. (A lichen is three organisms creating a symbiotic community together: an alga, a fungus, and a yeast. This was discovered in only 2015!) From Artist's Point you can see my favorite waterside restaurant, Angry Trout Cafe, which offers a daily fresh fish and vegetable special so good that people line up for hours awaiting it. You can also see the whole art and craft scene that makes Grand Marais a big art-crawl draw, from Joy and Co. for knitting, woodworking, and other crafts to Sivertson for the big-name northern painters. Down past Angry Trout is the North House Folk School, which teaches everything from boat making to the bread arts. This artsy bit of rock with a view of both lake and shore is named Artist's Point because you could bring a sketchbook to capture the view, but it actually answers the bigger question of what the point of being an artist is—to see, to make, to celebrate, and to share with others who get the point too.

A Moose Before Breakfast

As a city slicker, I've always found the Gunflint Trail mysterious—is it for dogsledding, or is it mainly historical like the Pony Express, or what? Now I do understand it, and it's so obvious I feel foolish: The Gunflint Trail is simply the name for the main road that goes nearly sixty miles northwest out of Grand Marais into the Boundary Waters Canoe Area, our precious million-acre dark-sky wilderness. It ends at the Chik-Wauk Museum and areas where you can leave a car and launch a boat if you want to go farther out. Along the Gunflint, little spurs take you to dozens of hiking trails, one with a naturally magnetic rock, another that allows you to climb a spire of a trail to a lookout—a spot that locals also climb to in the dark, using headlamps, to watch meteor showers. Off the Gunflint, various short roads also lead to resorts and lodges and lakes, and smack-dab at the midway point of the Gunflint Trail is the appropriately named Trail Center, a restaurant and lodge with phenomenal pancakes attached to a general store selling bug spray, rain ponchos, and racks and racks of homemade dehydrated food kits under the brand Camp Chow.

· · · · · · ·

You learn a lot about the North Shore by exploring, but one of the blessings of this beautiful place is the knowledgeable, helpful people—the insiders and the experts—the residents, the outfitters, the people who work at the restaurants and the hotels and resorts who help you discover even more of the local magic. When I stayed at the Poplar Haus, just up from Trail Center, I excitedly shared with owner Bryan Gerrard how a luna moth had clung to our cabin wall, as if it were painted, big as my hand and bright green. Unsurprised, he told me I should take it up a notch and try to see a moose. Was this possible? "Just get up before sunrise and drive to the end of the trail," he explained.

It seemed improbable, but I left my dot of a dark cabin as the sky was getting light and drove slowly and anxiously, peering into every roadside bit of water, where moose can be found swimming or wading and munching. I saw a truck behind me coming fast, so I pulled over to let it by. A few minutes later, I caught up to where its driver had pulled over to see: a moose! A gargantuan moose in the green sunrise brush. A moose, in real life, is a giant so big it makes your heart race. Being a city slicker, I had a sense that a deer and a moose were roughly similar. No. A typical big white-tailed deer is 150 to 300 pounds. A typical big moose is 1,500 pounds. With antlers, a bull moose can be ten feet tall. Ignoring my stammering heart and the instinct to flee, I sat tight, taking phone pictures because who would believe me otherwise? Eventually, the moose got tired of everyone sitting in cars looking at it and crashed away. The next day, I dragged the kids out before dawn, and believe it or not, we saw another moose! Or maybe it was the same moose. Amazing, no matter what. So now I deeply understand what the Gunflint Trail is: Head away from the lake out of Grand Marais, and before you know it, you're in an enchanted forest with magnetic rocks, a tall spire to the Milky Way, and dawn moose.

One Total Bummer Paragraph About the Time I Saw the Miracle of a Luna Moth

I read books my whole life in which the luna moth, that big green miracle, featured. I've unfortunately also lived my whole life in a human-made great extinction crisis. I was born, I have read, in a world with twice as many birds and fish. I was born into a world with luna moths but now just read about them. That's what makes the Boundary Waters so special; it's one of the few places where wildlife is saved, like Jews beneath the floorboards in Europe in 1940. Sorry, I know that's dark and jarring, but we all know it's true. One morning I discovered a luna moth, bigger than my hand, clinging to the cabin wall outside, near the porch light. I couldn't believe how beautiful it was, and then I burst into tears. God bless and keep all these moths. May the next generation have the wisdom of the people who protected this beautiful space, and not the lack of wisdom of generations who can't seem to do anything to stop this march of bad history. Is being clear-eyed about what's happening worth anything? Luna moths: I have seen one; they're real; we live among magic; please, God, let other people have their eyes opened the way mine have been. Miracles, do we get them so we can change? Thank you for miracles, world.

Your Miracles?

What miracles will you yourself find if you head to the North Shore? Like everything, it probably depends on your receptivity to and eagerness for miracles. I saw a moose at dawn because I set an alarm and headed out in the dark to look. I saw a black bear because I explored a distant trail. I'd never have seen either if I'd stayed home in Minneapolis. The best way to encounter miracles is to go where they are abundant, and from what I've seen with my own eyes, miracles on the North Shore are common as sunlight sparkling on an everlasting, ultraclean freshwater rock tumbler.

The Secret Grand Canyon of the North

Gourmet, 2008

When I first started talking to the Minnesota Historical Society Press about an anthology of my writings, including this story was one of my top priorities. Magazine writing is an effort of collaboration and compromise—most of the time to great benefit. I love working with magazine editors. Sometimes, though, page counts plummet, and something you wrote at an assigned four thousand words runs in print at fifteen hundred. Such was the vexed life of this story about that wonderful canyon separating Minnesota and Wisconsin. Here, for the first time, it lives entire. Revenge!

I'm not sure upon whom I'm wreaking revenge, exactly; my *Gourmet* editors were certainly on my side. So: Revenge upon time? Revenge upon things going wrong? Anyway, I feel gleefully vengeful at being able to share this full article, so join me: Revenge is sweet—and sometimes surprisingly full of ancient hydrology.

As I hold my toddler tight in my arms the way you do a big baby getting so chunky you often want to set them down, we both raise our chins, higher, higher, trying to see the eagles above, screaming. We're at the bottom of a far northern red and gray bluff canyon, where little pines creak out from the rock seams, angling toward the sun, all sixteen hours of it in summer and as dim as a high candle glimpsed in a distant church window in winter. Nothing makes you aware of the varying lengths of days like a baby. You never get the same day to do over with them; they change that fast—now they have a fever from a tooth, now a fever from a cold;

now two weeks have vanished, everything's different, they know twenty new words, their former favorite toy is dead to them.

As my baby and I walk on the pine needles where river meets cliff, the two of us are absolutely disconsolate and absolutely blissful. It's always like this. Those awkward days in the life of a year-and-a-half-year-old; he loathes his stroller, because it's for babies and it stops him from careening where he wants to go; but also he needs his stroller right away the second he needs it, because his fat, wobbly legs tucker out and abandon him, and he has to go into his impenetrable cocoon of sleep. We forget the eagle; now he wants down, to throw stones in the water. Can we hear the splashes? Not really. It's roaring down here.

I want to tell you about this, one of my favorite places in the world, which I call the Grand Canyon of the North, and will continue to do so until the Arizona Grand Canyon sends me a cease and desist. Basically, it's the zigzag on the map separating Wisconsin and Minnesota.

I come here all the time, with the baby. On this riverside day, not far from Taylors Falls, Minnesota, where the eagles were squabbling, the waterside roar is deafening. The river noise ricochets in layered echoes, the sound ripping from one side of the red rock canyon to the other, bouncing back, bouncing again. In deep winter, however, locked in with ice and snow, it's absolute quiet—yet more heart racing because the noise of mating and disputing coyotes and foxes fills the air with ever-echoing ghost yips.

I think we, the people who live around this canyon, I think we've done everything wrong, name- and branding-wise. We call this canyon by its hydrological names: It's the upper St. Croix, the lower St. Croix, the lower Mississippi; we talk about the Minnesota River as part of it—no, no, no. A failure of communication. In talking to *Gourmet* editors, I have discovered that just about no one who calls New York's concrete canyons home has even heard of our northern breathtaking, jaw-dropping, heart-quivering river valley. We need a better story, a more *real* story. The real story is this: The Grand Canyon of the North, splitting Wisconsin and Minnesota, it feels like one great thing because it is, or rather, it *was*.

For eons and eons, the Great Lakes were even greater, if you can imagine. Glacial Lake Agassiz was not too much smaller than Germany; it was one of the biggest lakes in the history of the world. It took up much of central Canada, and drained into the thing we are now talking about. Glacial Lake Duluth, meanwhile, simultaneously sat on the site of Lake Superior, but was undoubtedly its superior, as its water level was four or five hundred feet higher than what we've got today. Imagine Lake Superior, but stretching up and submerging everything, the water levels so high that it drained not east but south.

For eons and eons these glacial lakes flowed straight south into the Mississippi we know today, through this Grand Canyon of the North of which I speak, rushing straight through the parts we now know as the St. Croix valley. These canyon bits of St. Croix, they're the old path of the Mississippi, when it drained those ancient lakes. It wasn't the sleepy, slow river Huck Finn would recognize. No, it was a raging, turbulent, grit- and ice-filled glacial Mississippi, one that ground the soft sedimentary rock around it into eight-hundred-foot-deep canyons. Eight hundred feet deep! It was the Grand Canyon of the North. It later changed, silting in, raising up, but, in the same way you can look at part of a fossil and sense the whole, look at an elder and sense the child who birthed them, I insist you can feel this ancient roaring glacial river when you stand on these banks today.

It was here just yesterday! Well, yesterday in geologic time, anyway. Scientists estimate that our ancient, gouging river was around as recently as 9,200 years ago.

Then, as life is change and life went on, things changed. Personally, some years after the river got slow, I had a baby. That's a big time marker. I thought I never would, but then my life suddenly turned into a cosmic relay race: There's a new person around, to carry on the baton I didn't know I had been holding this whole time. I look into his deep brown eyes and know if I handed him anything, cosmic baton or no, he'd take it in his gummy fist and chew on it.

The baby and I come down to this river canyon a lot, and par-

ticularly would when he was teething and we needed the tranquil-
izer of speed.

Speeding, I'd push play for the ten thousandth time on the
Smithsonian recordings of Lead Belly my little boy loves the way
a fish loves water. We listened to the tale of a goose who outlives
and outsmarts everyone; after being shot and then boiled for six
weeks, the goose flies off, "With a long string of goslings, Lord,
Lord, Lord. And they all went quack quack, Lord, Lord, Lord."
Geese have been using this northern canyon, this flyway and nesting ground for their goslings since the time of the ancient, bigger
Mississippi. What is time? Babies make you wonder, because you
never sleep and your mind starts cosmically wobbling; because
they're babies, a leap into the time after you.

You see how it's really a Grand Canyon most clearly in midwin-
ter, when the softening veil of green leaves is stripped away, and
the place bristles in all its primordial, primeval, spooky glory. Gold
sheer cliffs ooze with frozen waterfalls or moss. Steeples of fragile
sedimentary rocks poke up from bluff tops like witches' fingers,
like castle spires. Hawks, bald eagles, and turkey vultures catch the
updrafts from the bluff faces and circle so high in the sky they're
inconspicuous as stars.

What makes a person with a baby gravitate to a canyon? It's
because you get wrenched out of clock time, I think. Meetings and
typing are one thing the day before you have a baby, something
else the day you have one. They don't matter as much; they never
will. Now everything is life and death. Sometimes I think about
how old he'll be before I tell him: *Never, never underestimate that
river*. It kills about half a dozen people in the Twin Cities every
year, often those who look at the placid, iridescent gleam of the
top layer of water and don't suspect the roaring, murderous currents below.

You can see the river at its most deceptively peaceful at a wide
place in the Mississippi called Lake Pepin. Here, a thousand miles
north of the Gulf, the Mississippi appears to hold its skirts back
and tiptoe, and in its reluctance spreads itself into glassy, pano-
ramic flats that catch the light like shallow pans of silver. At

sunrise, at twilight the humps of mountains, the towers of bluff are doubled in this silver, and when a bald eagle pours through the gleaming one's heart leaps into one's throat. When the water here isn't spreading itself into mirrors it's breaking itself to bits, streaming around low islands, as if the cloth the river was weaving had been pulled into pieces and threads at its edges, for trimming or possible expansion. In the fringes of these edges twenty-pound catfish nose around like somber, swimming pigs and blue herons stand as kings, stately, indifferent, poised to plunder the population of frogs.

From the Twin Cities we typically get to Pepin, on the Wisconsin side, by car, and go there for the one famous restaurant: the Harbor View Café. They're famous for their soups (don't miss the beautifully cheese-gooey, dark caramelized onion soup); they're famous for scratch comfort foods, such as beef cheeks braised with bacon, which produces something very much like the best pot roast you ever ate. They're also famous for pie: chocolate buttercream, Georgia walnut. I keep saying they're famous because, like Radio City Music Hall, after enough years the place has become famous for being famous. I always like going there, but I'd say they're as popular as they are because the drive is so delightful, through that Grand Canyon of the North. Humans, we're called to our own migrations, in this case through grandeur to pie.

To birds, that nine-thousand-year-gone river means everything: They are following it even today, to their summer homes in Canada and along the Great Lakes. In late winter and spring bird-watchers cluster on the banks of the St. Croix and Mississippi hoping to see ospreys, American kestrels, belted kingfishers, and, once in a great while, if they look very carefully, tundra swans or sandhill cranes. But even a four-eyed city kid can see the bald eagles standing on the ice just below the dam at the river town of Alma in late winter, when the nationally significant birds gather in groups of five, twenty, or more. Silent, oblivious to both their talons and their symbolism, they look like bored commuters waiting for the bus. Probably they're just waiting for spring, for the excitement of mating, nesting, and difficult hunting, because the open water just below the dam offers them all the fishing challenge of an ice sculpture holding all-you-can-eat shrimp on a cruise ship buffet. Occasionally one of them leans over the open ice pool and bobs a head down, snatching up a silver fish in an instant. The other eagles don't even look over, as if to convey their silent disdain: Would they turn their heads to see Barry Bonds play T-ball, to watch George Balanchine sort his socks? They would not. Flocks of wild turkeys are equally easy to spot. They cluster in the trees at the side of the road like gangly pumpkins, pumpkins with the craggy, unknowing heads of lizards. "Look, turkeys!" I call to my baby, as he clutches with great interest for his toes. "Look, eagles!" I insist to my toddler, as he politely looks where I look.

Bald eagles, wild turkeys, ospreys, and such are particularly easy to spot in the bluff lands surrounding the little towns of Fountain City and Alma, Wisconsin, and Wabasha, Minnesota, all of which are on the 240,000-acre Upper Mississippi River National Wildlife and Fish Refuge. When life is very, very good I take my baby on a two- or four-hour road trip to those little towns built on the banks of a river that used to be really big and is now still big.

Fountain City is all Victorian brick churches and wood Old West clapboard houses fit for a Wyatt Earp gunfight, but the two sorts of architecture are stacked so precipitously against the bluff walls that they look like children's blocks, about to spill down into the river. The main bar in town, the Monarch Public House, has the same pressed-tin ceilings and intricately carved oak bar it had when it opened in 1894: That spindly, delicate, even fussy bar speaks volumes about how much of Old West hooliganism was reaction to buttoned-up Victorian priss. The house beer at the Monarch, Fountain Brew, is based on a recipe that has been brewed in this old steamboat port since 1862. They call it one of America's original pre-Prohibition ales, and it's crisp, clean, and good—though probably a modern drinker could never enjoy it as much as someone who'd been stoking a steamboat engine all day.

Alma is another favorite town of mine, not least because you can sit at one of the polished wood tables in the front window of Kate and Gracie's restaurant with a glass of wine and a good Wisconsin cheese plate and watch the eagles dive. In summer you can often spot our national bird up on the crane that loads barges right below the Alma dam. Wabasha has bald eagles year-round too, as the river narrows significantly there, resulting in open water for easy fishing in all seasons. The fishing on these rivers is famous among more terrestrial types as well: Between the dozens of trout streams that feed the big rivers and the catfish, bass, muskies, panfish, and such that live in the big rivers, it's not uncommon on a sunny Saturday to find the river towns empty as the ice and all the cars parked out on the roads between the towns. Each parked pickup truck or car is linked to a fisherperson happily off in some water.

For those whose idea of big fish worth stalking is limited to Roseville Pottery, Stickley chairs, and Tiffany lamps, the valley holds countless antique shops, which are often stocked with surprising finds due to the region's late nineteenth-century prosperity. This prosperity came from lumber, from a pine rush not unlike California's gold rush.

The pineries of northern Minnesota and Wisconsin in previous centuries were nothing like the low, scrubby pine forests people know today. They were old-growth white pines, trees a hundred feet tall and sometimes five feet across. This pine rush began before Minnesota was even a state, in the 1840s, with packs of lumberjacks venturing illegally into the territory to poach trees and make rogue land claims. Lumber speculators, sawmill operators, drunken lumberjacks, and "river pigs" followed—the latter being men who stood on rafts of logs and guided them down the river from former forest to mill. Pictures of the river from the time look like a surrealist photo collage, with every drop of water in the rivers replaced with logs. There was a time when the lumbering trade made this valley one of the most prosperous places in America— in fact, the state capitals for both Wisconsin and Minnesota were nearly placed here. However, the lumbering practices of the nineteenth century were not well considered. As the lumberjacks clearcut the pineries they left all the valueless small timber and brush behind. In October 1871 the Peshtigo Fire took care of this tinder, killing at least 1,200 in northeastern Wisconsin. In 1894 this replayed in Minnesota, with the Great Hinckley Fire killing at least 418. The pine rush was done.

One legacy of those lumbering days are the many, many, many state parks lining both sides of both rivers here—Interstate, Afton, Kinnickinnic, Willow River, Merrick, Frontenac, and more. Once they were logged, the "useless" lands were essentially turned over to the state for hunting. But time did its thing, and the trees returned. Today there are hundreds of miles of trails to hike or bike, and a local population that really, truly appreciates the importance of conserving nature. It's where their money comes from, carried in by tourists.

In some towns B&Bs seem to outnumber residences. One of the prettiest is the Asa Parker House in Marine on St. Croix, where the palatial Greek Revival home of one of the valley's most successful sawmill operators now boasts tennis courts out back, whirlpool tubs, and romantic couples canoodling beneath the eaves. Then again, the old jailhouse also sees its fair share of romantic couples, as it's now the Old Jail Bed and Breakfast in Taylors Falls. The Octagon House B&B, in Red Wing, was an early mayor's house. The Round Barn Farm Bed & Breakfast, not too far from Red Wing, has, you guessed it, a beautiful round barn on the property. Potters rent out a spot near Lake Pepin called Pepin Farm Pottery and Guesthouse.

All these B&Bs thrive because of a number of highways that hug the river. It's hard to explain, but the Great River Road goes from the Gulf of Mexico to the headwaters of the Mississippi in the middle of the state, and in Minnesota and Wisconsin that route tends to hopscotch between Highway 61 (of the Bob Dylan song) on the Minnesota side and Highway 35 on the Wisconsin side. There are plenty of bridges connecting the two, and more roads too, all of which seasoned travelers use to zip back and forth, up and down, meaning the gargantuan river here is no more problem for locals than the Seine is for Parisians.

What's special about the Grand Canyon in Arizona? That it never got wrecked, mainly. Surely you've heard about the plans to dam it, to fill it up like a swimming pool. What's so special about the Grand Canyon of the North? Same thing. It's a natural miracle that survived all the mess of the past, but it retains some of the cuter bits of that past, mainly as inns and restaurants. Awe and grandeur, but with restaurant tables and hiking trails! Awe matters. There used to be a giant natural whirlpool at the top of Manhattan; people dynamited it to make shipping safer. Before the skyscrapers the waters around the island of Manhattan were one of the world's more important bird nesting grounds. I think about that a lot—how our wonder and awe is rooted in what we can see, what survives. Would we have less awe if the Grand Canyon were a bathtub for motorboats? I think so.

I mean: What is eternity?

One definition is standing in a canyon, counting the layers of rock with your baby.

Time, time, time: Count it with your fingers; here's where the dinosaurs are; touch it; now here we are; hit it with a stick.

"Wow" was one of my little guy's first words. "Wow" he'd say, following my pointing finger to the eagles eating fish on the ice. "Wow" at the rocks I threw into the edge of the rapids. "Wow" at the good olives at the Harbor View. "Wow" at the mirror of Lake Pepin. "Wow" at the layers of rock he hit with a stick.

Parenting: It's a chance to redo the errors of your own childhood and to fail in ways you never expected. (Let's not discuss the time my son upended an entire restaurant salt shaker into his mouth and screamed at the pain of a mouth full of salt.) Wonderfully, it's years of chances to get up the next day and fail better.

As I reflect on his *wows*, I am suddenly stabbed with a writer's jealousy: Did it just take me towering castles of words to convey the essence of northern America's most underappreciated canyon, when he did it with just that little one? *Wow*. Wow. It's how a modern kid conveys praise and hallelujah, and it's why you bring a baby to a canyon and try to tell the whole wide world about it too. In the grandest canyon of the north, eternity is a thing you can go right into—and bang rock walls with a gummy stick while you listen to the river roar.

Afterword

· · · · · · · · · · · · ·

This will probably be the closest thing to a memoir I ever write. I find dwelling in the trauma of my childhood too powerfully upsetting. I also loathe the pressure on memoir writers to provide real life lessons, a happily ever after, a neat bow. My life actually got a happily ever after: a big house with a climbing rosebush, reaching for the sky; a little fenced backyard with a tiny, funny dog running at any squirrels who dare touch the grass; two wonderful, smart kids who talk with me and trust me. We laugh and laugh. My greatest accomplishment is these bright, kind, confident kids. Another is breaking the cycle of abuse. They've never had a hand raised against them; they've never regarded the doorknob as a grenade that might blow. My third greatest accomplishment? Putting in the many years to heal myself. The fourth: All the writings tucked in here, for you.

My whole life, I have treated books like dolls. When I was little, I used to sleep with a copy of *The Wind in the Willows* so I could have Ratty and Badger and everyone with me all the dark night. I remember waking up one morning to find the book splayed face-down on the floor. I jumped out of bed, heart in my throat: *Are you okay? Did any bones break?*

As a younger teenager, *Bright Lights, Big City* was my forever companion. It seemed like a message from the future: *Look, you can live in absolute chaos and emerge with art!* I used to keep it in the pocket of my raggedy vintage suit coat, the style for smallish teenage girls at the time, worn over bike shorts. I can still remember it banging against my thigh as I scrambled up a catwalk ladder at Limelight, a New York City club made from a Gothic church, where everyone encouraged older children on drugs to go up onto the catwalks high above the dance floor. *Bright Lights, Big City* makes a character of the writer Joseph Mitchell, and that novel was how I found Mitchell, who more or less pointed out the path for my life.

I think of all the writers who influenced and inspired me— Dorothy Parker, Katherine Mansfield, Oscar Wilde—as something like Superman's parents. They took their hopes and dreams, bundled them into a capsule, and threw them forward into the unknown future, where maybe the world would be better?

My greatest hope for this book is that it does those two things: that it lands like a capsule in the future, and that it finds exactly the person who needs it, to give them comfort in the dark night. If that's you: Hello, goodbye, and thank you. If a smart mess like me could have a wonderful life like this, you can too.

It's been a life of conversation, empathy, discovery, and self-discovery, and for my openness I've been rewarded by the embrace of an entire state's worth of readers, a gift no one in their right mind could ever expect, and which has filled my whole heart with gratitude.

We have reached the end of the book. To those who made it I say: Congratulations! You've had the full Dara experience. Hopefully you'll never forget it. I know I never will.